QBASIC
PROGRAMMING
FOR
DUMMIES™

QBASIC PROGRAMMING FOR DUMMIES™

by Douglas Hergert

IDG BOOKS

IDG Books Worldwide, Inc.
An International Data Group Company

San Mateo, California ♦ Indianapolis, Indiana ♦ Boston, Massachusetts

QBasic Programming For Dummies

Published by
IDG Books Worldwide, Inc.
An International Data Group Company
155 Bovet Road, Suite 310
San Mateo, CA 94402

Library of Congress Catalog Card No.: 94-75722

ISBN: 1-56884-093-4

Printed in the United States of America

10 9 8 7 6 5 4 3 2

1B/QU/SW/ZU

First printing, April, 1994

Distributed in the United States by IDG Books Worldwide, Inc.

Distributed in Canada by Macmillan of Canada, a Division of Canada Publishing Corporation; by Computer and Technical Books in Miami, Florida, for South America and the Caribbean; by Longman Singapore in Singapore, Malaysia, Thailand, and Korea; by Toppan Co. Ltd. in Japan; by Asia Computerworld in Hong Kong; by Woodslane Pty. Ltd. in Australia and New Zealand; and by Transword Publishers Ltd. in the U.K. and Europe.

For general information on IDG Books in the U.S., including information on discounts and premiums, contact IDG Books at 800-762-2974 or 415-312-0650.

For information on where to purchase IDG Books outside the U.S., contact Christina Turner at 415-312-0633.

For information on translations, contact Marc Jeffrey Mikulich, Foreign Rights Manager, at IDG Books Worldwide; FAX number 415-358-1260.

For sales inquiries and special prices for bulk quantities, write to the address above or call Tony Real at 415-312-0644.

 is a registered trademark of
IDG IDG Books Worldwide, Inc.
BOOKS

Acknowledgments

Several people worked hard to produce this book. Chris Williams suggested the idea and got it all started. Trudy Neuhaus was the book's first reader, and expertly directed the editorial and production processes. Susan Pink edited the manuscript with poise and skill. Don Hergert searched carefully for errors. And Claudette Moore provided guidance, advice, and encouragement. My sincere thanks to all.

(The publisher would like to give special thanks to Patrick McGovern, without whom this book would not have been possible.)

About IDG Books Worldwide

Welcome to the world of IDG Books Worldwide.

IDG Books Worldwide, Inc., is a subsidiary of International Data Group, the world's largest publisher of computer-related information and the leading global provider of information services on information technology. International Data Group publishes over 195 computer publications in 62 countries. Forty million people read one or more International Data Group publications each month.

If you use personal computers, IDG Books is committed to publishing quality books that meet your needs. We rely on our extensive network of publications, including such leading periodicals as *Macworld*, *InfoWorld*, *PC World*, *Computerworld*, *Publish*, *Network World*, and *SunWorld*, to help us make informed and timely decisions in creating useful computer books that meet your needs.

Every IDG book strives to bring extra value and skill-building instructions to the reader. Our books are written by experts, with the backing of IDG periodicals, and with careful thought devoted to issues such as audience, interior design, use of icons, and illustrations. Our editorial staff is a careful mix of high-tech journalists and experienced book people. Our close contact with the makers of computer products helps ensure accuracy and thorough coverage. Our heavy use of personal computers at every step in production means we can deliver books in the most timely manner.

We are delivering books of high quality at competitive prices on topics customers want. At IDG, we believe in quality, and we have been delivering quality for over 25 years. You'll find no better book on a subject than an IDG book.

John Kilcullen
President and CEO
IDG Books Worldwide, Inc.

IDG Books Worldwide, Inc. is a subsidiary of International Data Group. The officers are Patrick J. McGovern, Founder and Board Chairman; Walter Boyd, President. International Data Group's publications include: **ARGENTINA'S** Computerworld Argentina, Infoworld Argentina; **ASIA'S** Computerworld Hong Kong, PC World Hong Kong, Computerworld Southeast Asia, PC World Singapore, Computerworld Malaysia, PC World Malaysia; **AUSTRALIA'S** Computerworld Australia, Australian PC World, Australian Macworld, Network World, Mobile Business Australia, Reseller, IDG Sources; **AUSTRIA'S** Computerwelt Oesterreich, PC Test; **BRAZIL'S** Computerworld, Gamepro, Game Power, Mundo IBM, Mundo Unix, PC World, Super Game; **BELGIUM'S** Data News (CW) **BULGARIA'S** Computerworld Bulgaria, Ediworld, PC & Mac World Bulgaria, Network World Bulgaria; **CANADA'S** CIO Canada, Computerworld Canada, Graduate Computerworld, InfoCanada, Network World Canada; **CHILE'S** Computerworld Chile, Informatica; **COLOMBIA'S** Computerworld Colombia; **CZECH REPUBLIC'S** Computerworld, Elektronika, PC World; **DENMARK'S** CAD/CAM WORLD, Communications World, Computerworld Danmark, LOTUS World, Macintosh Produktkatalog, Macworld Danmark, PC World Danmark, PC World Produktguide, Windows World; **ECUADOR'S** PC World Ecuador; **EGYPT'S** Computerworld (CW) Middle East, PC World Middle East; **FINLAND'S** MikroPC, Tietoviikko, Tietoverkko; **FRANCE'S** Distributique, GOLDEN MAC, InfoPC, Languages & Systems, Le Guide du Monde Informatique, Le Monde Informatique, Telecoms & Reseaux; **GERMANY'S** Computerwoche, Computerwoche Focus, Computerwoche Extra, Computerwoche Karriere, Information Management, Macwelt, Netzwelt, PC Welt, PC Woche, Publish, Unit; **GREECE'S** Infoworld, PC Games; **HUNGARY'S** Computerworld SZT, PC World; **INDIA'S** Computers & Communications; **IRELAND'S** Computerscope; **ISRAEL'S** Computerworld Israel, PC World Israel; **ITALY'S** Computerworld Italia, Lotus Magazine, Macworld Italia, Networking Italia, PC Shopping Italy, PC World Italia; **JAPAN'S** Computerworld Today, Information Systems World, Macworld Japan, Nikkei Personal Computing, SunWorld Japan, Windows World; **KENYA'S** East African Computer News; **KOREA'S** Computerworld Korea, Macworld Korea, PC World Korea; **MEXICO'S** Compu Edicion, Compu Manufactura, Computacion/ Punto de Venta, Computerworld Mexico, MacWorld, Mundo Unix, PC World, Windows; **THE NETHERLANDS'** Computer! Totaal, Computable (CW), LAN Magazine, MacWorld, Totaal "Windows"; **NEW ZEALAND'S** Computer Listings, Computerworld New Zealand, New Zealand PC World; **NIGERIA'S** PC World Africa; **NORWAY'S** Computerworld Norge, C/World, Lotusworld Norge, Macworld Norge, Networld, PC World Ekspress, PC World Norge, PC World's Produktguide, Publish& Multimedia World, Student Data, Unix World, Windowsworld; IDG Direct Response; **PANAMA'S** PC World Panama; **PERU'S** Computerworld Peru, PC World; **PEOPLE'S REPUBLIC OF CHINA'S** China Computerworld, China Infoworld, PC World China, Electronics International, Electronic Product World, China Network World; IDG HIGH TECH BEIJING'S New Product World; IDG SHENZHEN'S Computer News Digest; **PHILIPPINES'** Computerworld Philippines, PC Digest (PCW); **POLAND'S** Computerworld Poland, PC World/Komputer; **PORTUGAL'S** Cerebro/PC World, Correio Informatico/ Computerworld, MacIn; **ROMANIA'S** Computerworld, PC World; **RUSSIA'S** Computerworld-Moscow, Mir - PC, Sety; **SLOVENIA'S** Monitor Magazine; **SOUTH AFRICA'S** Computer Mail (CIO), Computing S.A., Network World S.A.; **SPAIN'S** Amiga World, Computerworld Espana, Communicaciones World, Macworld Espana, NeXTWORLD, Super Juegos Magazine (GamePro), PC World Espana, Publish, Sunworld; **SWEDEN'S** Attack, ComputerSweden, Corporate Computing, Lokala Natverk/LAN, Lotus World, MAC&PC, Macworld, Mikrodatorn, PC World, Publishing & Design (CAP), Dataingenjoren, Maxi Data, Windows World; **SWITZERLAND'S** Computerworld Schweiz, Macworld Schweiz, PC Katalog, PC & Workstation; **TAIWAN'S** Computerworld Taiwan, Global Computer Express, PC World Taiwan; **THAILAND'S** Thai Computerworld; **TURKEY'S** Computerworld Monitor, Macworld Turkiye, PC World Turkiye; **UKRAINE'S** Computerworld; **UNITED KINGDOM'S** Computing /Computerworld, Connexion/Network World, Lotus Magazine, Macworld, Open Computing/Sunworld; **UNITED STATES'** AmigaWorld, Cable in the Classroom, CD Review, CIO, Computerworld, Desktop Video World, DOS Resource Guide, Electronic Entertainment Magazine, Federal Computer Week, Federal Integrator, GamePro, IDG Books, Infoworld, Infoworld Direct, Laser Event, Macworld, Multimedia World, Network World, NeXTWORLD, PC Letter, PC World, PlayRight, Power PC World, Publish, SunWorld, SWATPro, Video Event; **VENEZUELA'S** Computerworld Venezuela, MicroComputerworld Venezuela; **VIETNAM'S** PC World Vietnam.

About the Author

Douglas Hergert has been writing successful computer books since 1981. He's written many books about applications, especially spreadsheets and database management, but his favorite writing projects over the years have been on programming languages. His books on QuickBasic and Visual Basic have been top sellers.

Credits

Vice President and Publisher
Chris Williams

Senior Editor
Trudy Neuhaus

Imprint Manager
Amorette Pedersen

Project Editor
Susan Pink

Technical Reviewer
Don Hergert

Production Director
Beth Jenkins

Production Coordinator
Cindy L. Phipps

Production Staff
Tony Augsburger
Valery Bourke
Mary Breidenbach
Chris Collins
Sherry Gomoll
Drew R. Moore
Kathie Schnorr
Gina Scott

Proofreader
Nancy Kruse Hannigan

Indexer
Liz Cunningham

Book Design
University Graphics

Book Cover
Kavish + Kavish

Contents at a Glance

Cartoons at a Glance

By Rich Tennant

page 187

page 357

page 69

page 1

page 117

page 155

page 213

page 311

page 253

page 7

Table of Contents

Introduction

Welcome to *QBasic Programming for Dummies,* your tour guide to a new adventure in computing. If you've been thinking you'd like to try your hand at programming, now is the time to do something about it. In the era of personal computers, programming is no longer the clannish terrain of high-tech specialists. Anyone who has a PC to use and some time to invest — *anyone who's ever imagined that there might be some fun and profit in learning how to program a computer* — should give it a try.

Where do you go to get started? What do you have to buy? Maybe you've stopped by the local computer store recently to gaze wistfully at those huge, expensive, and daunting boxes of software in the Programming Languages section. Not exactly what you had in mind. There should be a simpler way to learn programming!

Here's the big secret of this book: There *is* a simpler way, and it's free. If you use a computer that runs on DOS — version 5 or beyond — you *already* have a programming language, hidden away on your hard disk, waiting for you to discover it. The language is called QBasic, and this book shows you where to find it, how to use it, and what you can do with it. QBasic is an ideal place to begin developing your own computer programs. It's a refined and practical tool that gives you ready access to your computer's resources. It's simple, speedy, and versatile — and it's already yours.

The 5th Wave   By Rich Tennant

" NO, THE SOLUTION TO OUR SYSTEM BEING DOWN IS _NOT_ FOR US TO WORK ON OUR KNEES."

About This Book

As you thumb though this book, the first thing you notice is that it's packed with examples of QBasic programs. Throughout the book, programs are printed in a distinctive typeface, like this:

```
' Welcome program (WELCOME.BAS)
' Displays a welcome message
' on the screen.

DECLARE SUB ShowMessage (inName$)
DECLARE FUNCTION GetName$ ()

CLS
ShowMessage GetName$

END  ' WELCOME.BAS

FUNCTION GetName$

   ' Asks you to enter your name.

   INPUT "Hi there. What's your name"; yourName$
   GetName$ = yourName$

END FUNCTION  ' GetName$

SUB ShowMessage (inName$)

   ' Shows the welcome message.

   PRINT
   PRINT "Welcome to QBasic, ";
   PRINT inName$; "!"
   PRINT "Roll up your sleeves"
   PRINT "and get ready for some fun."

END SUB  ' ShowMessage
```

The reason for all these examples is simple. One of the best, most time-honored ways to learn programming is to start tinkering with *existing* programs. Accordingly, this book offers you an abundance of sample programs you can run, explore, and even revise. As you do so, you absorb the techniques you need to begin writing programs on your own.

How to Use This Book

QBasic is a complete and self-contained *programming environment* — a collection of tools designed to help you write, test, and fine-tune your programming creations. The first task ahead of you, in Part I, is to master these tools.

After that, you turn your attention to the details of the *language*. This book introduces QBasic by major programming topics. You can take up each topic in the order it's presented or you can jump around from one topic to another. Almost every chapter presents a sample program designed to help you master a particular part of the language. Here's how to use each example:

1. Type the program into your computer and save it on disk. Chapter 2 shows you how to do this.

2. Correct any mistakes you may have made in typing the program. Chapter 3 introduces QBasic's debugging tools, which you use to find errors in a program you've created.

3. Run the program. Follow the instructions provided in each chapter. Use the input data in the chapter, or try your own data.

4. Read the rest of the chapter. Focus on individual statements and techniques that the program illustrates.

If steps 1 and 2 begin to seem like too much work — or if you're really keyboard averse — you can order a disk containing all the major programs from each chapter. The disk offer is in the back of the book.

About You

Your enthusiasm, curiosity, and creativity are the main qualifications for this adventure in programming. *QBasic Programming for Dummies* makes few assumptions about your technical background or computer experience.

Maybe you use your PC primarily for one particular kind of job — spreadsheet calculations, for example, or word processing. You might have a private wish list of other jobs you'd like to see your computer do, but you've never figured out how to do them. Get that list out, open up your mind to new possibilities, and consider creating your own programs for these jobs.

How This Book Is Organized

This book is divided into nine parts. Part I introduces you to the programming environment, and the remaining parts cover the QBasic language, topic by topic. Here's a preview of what you'll find in each part.

Part I   A Tour of QBasic: The Programming Environment

Here you learn what a program is, and why QBasic is a good environment for creating one. You try your hand at typing a program, and you make a first attempt to run it. You learn what to do when something goes wrong — and where to go for help.

Part II   Using a New Language: Input and Output

In Part II you begin focusing on the QBasic language. You start by learning two of the most common tasks that programs perform — getting information from the user at the keyboard, and supplying the user with information on the screen. You also learn a lot about variables (the names you create to represent the specific data items a program works with) and about types of expressions you can use to calculate data.

Part III   Organizing the Tour: Structured Programming

Next comes the important topic of structured programming. In Part III you learn how to organize a program into small sections called procedures, and you learn to work with the two kinds of procedures available in QBasic, identified by the keywords SUB and FUNCTION. You also examine techniques for sending information to a procedure. Finally, the last chapter in Part III is a survey of QBasic's built-in functions, which are special tools you can use to perform calculations or accomplish other data-related tasks.

Part IV Where to Go Next: Decisions in QBasic

The ability to plan decisions for the computer to carry out is one of the most powerful features of programming. QBasic gives you two ways to incorporate decisions into a program: the IF statement and the SELECT CASE structure. You learn how to use both of these in Part IV, and you focus on using each appropriately.

Part V   Destinations Revisited: Loops in QBasic

Repetition is one of the computer's major skills. To control repetition in a program, you use one of the two loop structures that QBasic provides: the FOR loop or the DO loop. Part V introduces loops and provides examples.

Part VI   Memories: Arrays and Records

Arrays and records are two important and powerful structures for working with large quantities of data in a QBasic program. In Part VI you learn how to create these structures, how to assign data to them, and how to gain access to the data they represent.

Part VII   Keeping Track: Data File Programming

Part VII is a fearless guide to data file programming in QBasic. You learn to write programs that store data in files on disk and then read information from the files. You work with text files and random-access files.

Part VIII   Photo Opportunities: Graphics in QBasic

In Part VIII you look at programming techniques for displaying graphics on the screen. You see examples of both text graphics and high-resolution graphics.

Part IX The Part of Tens

Part IX presents two lists of ten: menu commands and the major precepts of structured programming.

Icons Used in This Book

 This symbol points to an advanced QBasic feature you can postpone reading about until you've mastered the basics. You can skip these sections your first time through the book.

 Here's a useful piece of information, an important word of advice, or a shining gem of wisdom that you just can't do without. Don't skip the tips.

 This symbol is a reminder of a salient fact that you may have already learned elsewhere; the text often refers you to another chapter for more information.

 This symbol warns you of a danger you should watch out for in the design of your program or in the usage of a particular QBasic statement or function.

What to Do Next

Roll up your sleeves and begin at the beginning. Keep in mind that you have to learn how the QBasic programming environment works before you get too involved in the details of the language. Go through the exercises in Part I carefully; they provide a solid introduction to QBasic's menu commands and other important features.

Part I

A Tour of QBasic: The Programming Environment

The 5th Wave   By Rich Tennant

After spending hours trying to get the system up and running, Carl discovers that everything had been plugged into a "Clapper" light socket when he tries to kill a mosquito.

In This Part . . .

*Q*Basic is both a computer language and a slick environment for developing programs. Before you get too involved in the nitty-gritty details of programming, you need to examine the tools QBasic gives you for the development process.

Part I is your introduction to the programming environment. Here you learn what a program is and why QBasic is a good place to create one. You start exploring the steps and pitfalls of entering programs into the QBasic editor, and you make your first attempt to run a program. You also find out how to use debugging tools when a program is not behaving the way you want it to.

Finally, you learn where to get instant answers to all your most pressing, personal, and persistent questions . . . about programming, that is.

Chapter 1
Starting Out

· ·

In This Chapter

▶ What is programming?

▶ What is QBasic and *where* is it?

▶ Starting QBasic

▶ A short history of BASIC — and why you should be interested

▶ What does a program look like?

· ·

A computer, left to its own devices, doesn't do much more than sit on a desk. To get anything accomplished, it needs instructions; it needs to be told what to do. You use a programming language to write and record instructions for the computer.

Under the guidance of a program you create, the computer can perform a great variety of activities. It can accept information from the keyboard, organize data in the computer's memory, perform calculations, display messages and graphics on the screen, send text to your printer, store and retrieve data on disk, make decisions, and carry out repetitive tasks. Your job as a programmer is to plan a sequence of activities and write the instructions that guide the computer through these activities.

These days, programming languages are popping up in unexpected places. Many major applications (such as spreadsheets, word processors, and database management programs) now have built-in programming languages that you can use to customize and automate the operations of the applications themselves. These are often called *macro languages*. Macros are application specific; you can't run a macro outside the application it was designed for.

But QBasic is a language of its own. It's not attached to other software, and it doesn't rely on the presence of other applications on your computer. All it relies on is *you:* your ideas, imagination, ingenuity, and cunning.

Of course, there are many other programming languages besides QBasic. Some you may have heard of include C, Pascal, FORTRAN, and COBOL. *A language is itself a program,* or more often a set of programs, designed to simplify the process of creating software and getting it to work on your computer.

Language packages typically include some combination of the following features:

▶ A convenient on-screen environment in which you can type and revise the statements of your program.

▶ Simple ways to check the syntax of the statements you write to ensure that they conform to the rules of the language.

▶ Techniques to help you locate and correct possible flaws in the logic of your program.

▶ A process for converting the statements you write into a form that the computer can use. (In some high-level languages, including QBasic, this process takes place automatically, and is practically invisible to you as you prepare to run your programs.)

QBasic has all of these features, which together are known as the *programming environment.* The more you can learn about this environment at the outset, the better time you'll have with the language itself.

This first chapter is an overview of QBasic: its history, purpose, and special features. You start up QBasic and see how it looks on the screen. Then you take a first brief look at a real program and preview the learning path ahead of you.

QBasic Basics

When you start QBasic (which you'll do in a minute), your screen displays a View window in which you can begin typing the lines of a QBasic program. Alternatively, you can open a program you have written (or someone has given you) from disk; when you do, the lines of the program appear in the View window.

Here are some QBasic highlights that you learn more about in the first several chapters:

▶ QBasic has a menu-driven environment. To use QBasic, you pull down one of the menus identified by name at the top of the screen and choose a command from the menu. You can use the keyboard or the mouse to choose menu commands.

▶ The QBasic editor is like a programming expert watching over your shoulder as you enter statements in the View window. If you write something that doesn't match the rules of the language, the editor instantly alerts you to the problem by displaying an error box on the screen. You then have the opportunity to correct your statement or ask for more help before you go on.

✔ Speaking of help, QBasic has a built-in help system that is always just a keystroke or a mouse click away. You can use it to find out how a menu command works or how to use a statement in the language. The help system is complete, convenient, simple, and reliable. You'll like it.

✔ QBasic also has an Immediate window in which you can test the result of a statement you're writing. The Immediate window, as its name implies, performs a QBasic statement as soon as you enter it, so you can see exactly how the statement behaves before you add it to your program.

✔ When you run a program, QBasic switches to a special output screen, where all the program's action takes place. On this screen, you see any information and questions that the program displays and your responses as you enter information from the keyboard. When a program finishes, you can return to the View window to examine the lines of the program.

All these features work together in QBasic to make programming as easy as it can be. The environment is surprisingly responsive to your activities and catches errors almost before you make them. Don't you wish the rest of your life worked this way?

Where Is QBasic?

Whenever MS-DOS (version 5 and beyond) is installed on a computer, the setup program automatically stores QBasic in the \DOS directory of the hard disk. QBasic consists of two main files in the directory: QBASIC.EXE is the program itself, and QBASIC.HLP is the on-line help system. (There may be an optional third file named QBASIC.INI that records changes you make to customize the programming environment.) If you can find these files in your DOS directory, you have everything you need to get going.

Get current

QBasic has been available since MS-DOS 5. Before that, DOS included a much less amusing version of the language named BASICA. If you happen to be running an older version of DOS, it's time to upgrade. DOS accumulates new features with each release, and you are missing out on a lot by staying with an outdated version. A DOS upgrade is inexpensive and can make your computing life easier and more agreeable.

Besides, you don't want to use BASICA as your introduction to programming. It's no fun at all. (If you still have some good old BASICA programs — there were lots of them in the BASICA heydays — you can run them in the QBasic environment.)

A Peek at QBasic

Depending on how your system is set up, starting QBasic may be as simple as this:

1. Turn on your computer.
2. Type QBASIC at the DOS prompt.
3. Press Enter.

Try it now. If it doesn't work (DOS gives you an inscrutable error message such as `Bad command or file name`), you may have to take the extra step of moving to the DOS directory. You do that by typing CD \DOS at the prompt and pressing Enter. Then type QBASIC and press Enter again.

When you first start QBasic, your screen looks like Figure 1-1. A Welcome box gives you two options: press Enter to see the QBasic Survival Guide, or press Esc to go right to work. Because this is your first time in the programming environment, press Enter now. The Survival Guide won't tell you what to do in a flood. It will provide notes about using the QBasic menus and getting help. Read the notes now if you want; you learn much more about these techniques later. Then press Esc to close the Survival Guide.

Now take a look at the programming environment, as it waits for you to start creating your first program. The QBasic menu bar is at the top of the screen. Beneath it is the View window, where you type the statements of a program. Figure 1-2 shows QBasic with part of a program displayed in the View window. The Immediate window is at the next position down the screen. The reference bar is the bottom line of the screen; it displays helpful messages at various points in your work. These areas will be the focus of your attention as you learn how to program in QBasic.

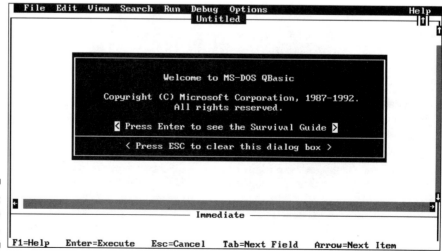

Figure 1-1: Welcome to QBasic.

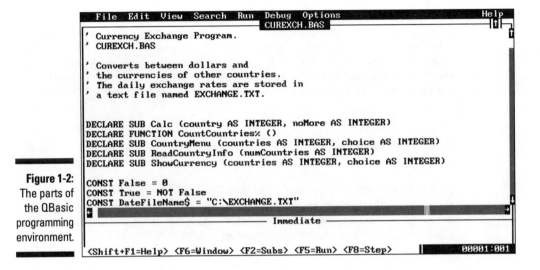

```
   File  Edit  View  Search  Run  Debug  Options                    Help
                           CUREXCH.BAS
 ' Currency Exchange Program.
 ' CUREXCH.BAS

 ' Converts between dollars and
 ' the currencies of other countries.
 ' The daily exchange rates are stored in
 ' a text file named EXCHANGE.TXT.


 DECLARE SUB Calc (country AS INTEGER, noMore AS INTEGER)
 DECLARE FUNCTION CountCountries% ()
 DECLARE SUB CountryMenu (countries AS INTEGER, choice AS INTEGER)
 DECLARE SUB ReadCountryInfo (numCountries AS INTEGER)
 DECLARE SUB ShowCurrency (countries AS INTEGER, choice AS INTEGER)

 CONST False = 0
 CONST True = NOT False
 CONST DateFileName$ = "C:\EXCHANGE.TXT"

                           ─── Immediate ───

 <Shift+F1=Help> <F6=Window> <F2=Subs> <F5=Run> <F8=Step>        00001:001
```

Figure 1-2:
The parts of
the QBasic
programming
environment.

That was a nice, quick visit. Now how do you get back to the DOS prompt? It's easy:

1. Press Alt to activate the menu bar.

2. Press F to pull down the File menu.

3. Press X to choose the Exit command.

And voilà, there's the DOS prompt again. You'll start and exit QBasic many times as you work through this book. When you begin typing lines of a program into the View window, QBasic always keeps track of whether or not you've saved your work to disk. If you try to exit without saving, a message box appears on the screen asking whether you want to save the current program before leaving QBasic. You see how this works in Chapter 2.

A Short History of BASIC

In the early days of small computers — even before the arrival of the IBM PC — each popular new machine had its own version of BASIC. Some came with almost no other software; from the user's point of view, BASIC and the operating system were one and the same. If you wanted to do anything with your computer, you had little choice but to write your own programs in BASIC.

All the versions of BASIC in those days had common characteristics: they were austere, awkward, and esoteric. But nobody knew any better. Programmers by the thousands spent hours and hours hacking away at their computers — sometimes achieving truly ingenious results. Meanwhile, they took every opportunity to tell each other how writing programs in BASIC was so much fun. It wasn't.

The logic behind BASIC programs often was mysterious to almost everyone, except maybe the original programmers. Programs even *looked* intimidating. Each line in a program had to be numbered. A statement could refer backward or forward to another statement by line number. For example, to repeat a task until a condition was met, the program had to loop back to the statement where the task began. You did this by putting GOTO statements in your program, like this:

```
200 GOTO 150
```

In this example, the program would loop back to line 150 whenever it reached line 200.

People quickly discovered that GOTOs created a kind of spaghetti logic in a program. Studying some programs, you could never be certain where one action ended and another began. The more GOTOs a program had, the harder it was to figure out how the program worked or why it *didn't* work.

Incompatible BASICs and grumpy programmers

There was another problem with BASIC programming in those days. Each version of the language was different; there was no widely accepted standard BASIC. You couldn't write a program that would work on all the computers available at the time. The versions were different enough to cause headaches and unpleasantness if you had to move a program from one brand of computer to another. Many people became adept at the dubious skill of translating programs between versions of BASIC. Fortunately, this skill turned out to have no future in the job market.

IBM, DOS, and BASICA

The IBM PC arrived in the early 1980s, followed quickly by its many clones. At the same time, Microsoft's operating system, DOS, became a new unifying factor in the confusing market for personal computer software.

The early versions of DOS included the language called BASICA, which had a few advantages over most previous versions of BASIC. For example, you no longer needed to use GOTOs because the language included a variety of *control structures*. These control structures were statements for carrying out repetitions and decisions in a well-organized and logical way. Now one BASIC program would work on any IBM PC or clone — any computer that used DOS as its operating system. For this reason alone, BASICA became a standard version of the language for some years.

But BASICA inherited fundamental weaknesses from previous versions. There still was no convenient environment in which to develop programs. More importantly, BASICA provided no well-structured way to organize a long program into small, self-contained tasks. Superficially, you could separate blocks of statements into parts called *subroutines*, but structurally these weren't much better than the GOTOs everyone had given up long before.

QuickBASIC and QBasic

In the mid-1980s, Microsoft finally came out with a good new version of the language called QuickBASIC. With this version, BASIC started looking like a professional programming tool. You could create, revise, test, and fine-tune your programs in one setting. Line numbers were finally gone, forever. No one missed them.

QuickBASIC introduced BASIC buffs to the joys of procedural programming. In a *procedural language,* you divide a program into individual tasks, or *procedures,* each with its own name and distinct place in your program. To perform a procedure from some point in a program, you simply *call* it by its name. You can develop a library of your own general-purpose procedures to use in any number of programming projects.

In addition, QuickBASIC was a *compiler*, a product designed to create stand-alone programs. After you fully developed and tested a QuickBASIC program, you could efficiently transform it into an independent program file on disk. This enabled you to run your programs directly from DOS, without starting the QuickBASIC environment. You could also distribute your compiled programs to other people, who could run them without having to buy QuickBASIC.

Finally, QuickBASIC led to QBasic, a streamlined, economical version of the same language and programming environment, with almost all the same features. True, QBasic lacks the facility for creating stand-alone program files. To run a program, you start QBasic, open your program into the environment, and choose QBasic's Start command. But you may never give a thought to this missing feature, for three reasons:

- ✔ QBasic is fast. Performance from the QBasic environment is just fine for most programs.

- ✔ You can issue a single command from the DOS prompt to start QBasic and immediately run a program. (See the sidebar for details.)

- ✔ Every DOS user has QBasic, so you can easily share programs with other people.

This is not the end of the BASIC story, of course. Microsoft's latest version of the language, Visual Basic, is a remarkable new product you can buy for DOS or Windows. It streamlines the process of creating professional looking programs with windows, menus, dialog boxes, icons, buttons, and so on.

Visual Basic is more intricate, and considerably more demanding, than QBasic. In general, QBasic is a better place to begin, especially for a new programmer on a budget. The good news is this: If you later decide to switch to Visual Basic, you can transfer all your new programming skills — and most of your QBasic programs — directly to the Visual Basic environment.

Summing up the lessons of history

It's hard to think of any other software product that has as long a history in the world of personal computers as the BASIC language. What conclusions can you draw from this history? First, you're exceedingly lucky to be starting your programming career now with QBasic than with the versions that came before it. Although those previous versions were widely used and resulted in huge libraries of creative and imaginative programs, working with them was tedious, clumsy, and difficult. QBasic is a lot more fun.

Second, keep in mind that QBasic is a language with a past. It inherits a mixed bag of characteristics — good and bad, elegant and blundering, smart and downright stupid — from its many predecessors. You can enjoy programming in QBasic without pretending that you cherish every moment of the process. Like any other piece of software, QBasic has some features you'll love to use and others you'll do almost anything to avoid.

The one-step startup

You've seen how easy it is to start QBasic; you just type QBASIC from the DOS prompt and press Enter. You can start QBasic and run a program almost as easily — in one step. Suppose that you have a QBasic program named Cards that helps you keep track of your credit-card balances. To start QBasic and run the program, you can enter the following command from the DOS prompt:

```
QBASIC /RUN CARDS
```

The /RUN part of this command instructs QBasic to open your program and run it immediately.

You can simplify this process even more by putting the QBASIC /RUN CARDS command in a batch file. A *batch file* contains a list of one or more commands that DOS performs in sequence. You create a batch file in any text editor, and assign the file an extension of BAT. For example, you could create a file named CARDS.BAT that contains the command to start QBasic and run the Cards program. Then you simply type CARDS from the DOS prompt and press Enter to start your credit-card program.

All the same, QBasic remains an eminently accessible tool for creating all types of programs; it's a fine place to get started in programming. You can expect to enjoy QBasic and to use it profitably.

Looks Can Be Deceiving

Now it's time for a quick, casual look at a sample program. Relax, it isn't as complicated as it looks. In fact, you'll probably be surprised about how much you can learn simply by looking at an example. And don't worry, you won't be typing this program into your computer or trying to make it work — well, not yet anyway.

The text of a program is called a *listing*. A listing contains all of a program's statements, along with any *comments* a programmer supplies to describe what's supposed to be happening. The listing can be printed on paper or displayed on your computer screen. (By the way, QBasic programs are always stored on disk as text files, so it's easy to load a listing into a different editing program.) The statements of a QBasic program are known as *source code*. One of QBasic's main jobs is to convert your source code into *machine code,* which is what the computer can work with.

Your comments, please

Writing comments to describe your code is an important part of programming. Good comments provide descriptions, clarifications, elucidations, and interpretations of the code, written in plain nontechnical English. Comments are recorded as a permanent part of the listing. When you run a program, QBasic ignores the comments. The purpose of comments is to help *people* read and understand a program's code. In particular, comments often prove invaluable to the original author of a program. As time goes by, you can easily forget what you had in mind when you designed a piece of code in a certain way; comments help remind you.

Comments are a great opportunity for you, the programmer, to have your say. You can use them to identify the purpose of a statement, to defend the rationale behind your program's organization, and to provide explanations of particularly difficult passages in the code. ■

Unfortunately, the typical programmer hates to write comments. Programming can be an intense and extremely focused activity, and programmers often think of writing comments as an unwelcome distraction from their real work. If they get around to writing comments at all, it's often as an afterthought at the very end of a project.

You'll be a different sort of programmer, of course. You will carefully comment each program you write, in clear, crisp, grammatical, and properly punctuated English. (If you don't, this book is ingeniously designed to self-destruct after your very first programming project, and there will be no refund.)

Comments are marked by an initial apostrophe ('). Wherever this character is found in your code, QBasic ignores the remainder of the line. Here is an example:

```
' Read the file and store information
' in the three arrays.
```

You can place a comment also at the end of a line, after a QBasic statement:

```
PRINT result    ' Display the result of the calculation.
```

Try to get into the habit of writing comments while you develop your code. It takes a few minutes more, but in the long run you'll be doing yourself a favor. As you look through the upcoming program listing, you'll see lots of examples of comments.

An example: the Currency Exchange program

The sample program you'll examine is created for the business traveler who regularly goes to exciting international destinations on work trips. Imagine that you're scheduled to take one of these trips yourself. You need to reserve hotel rooms and rental cars, and make appointments for conferences and business lunches. To plan your budget for the trip, you're faced with the problem of converting between dollars and the currencies of several other countries. The Currency Exchange program helps you solve this problem.

To prepare for using the program, you begin by creating a text file containing a list of the countries you're planning to visit, the names of their currencies, and today's value of each currency in dollars. For example, here is the currency file for an upcoming trip to Europe:

```
Austria, Shilling, .0866
Belgium, Franc, .0284
Denmark, Krone, .1493
England, Pound, 1.5075
Finland, Mark, .1724
France, Franc, .1748
Germany, Mark, .6089
Greece, Drachma, .004250
Holland, Guilder, .5386
Italy, Lira, .000629
Norway, Krone, .1388
Portugal, Escudo, .005928
Spain, Peseta, .007602
Sweden, Krona, .1243
Switzerland, Franc, .6983
```

You can develop this file — or update it with the latest exchange rate information — in any text editor (the DOS editor is fine). Save it under the name EXCHANGE.TXT.

The Currency Exchange program reads this file and uses the information stored in it to provide a convenient tool for calculating exchange rates. The program displays a menu on the screen, from which you can select any country represented in the file:

```
Currency Exchange
-------- --------

Which country?
         1 > Austria
         2 > Belgium
         3 > Denmark
         4 > England
         5 > Finland
         6 > France
         7 > Germany
         8 > Greece
         9 > Holland
        10 > Italy
        11 > Norway
        12 > Portugal
        13 > Spain
        14 > Sweden
        15 > Switzerland
        16 > Quit

Enter a number: _
```

You respond to this menu by typing the number of a country in the list. (The last menu item is for quitting the program.) When you press Enter, the program clears the screen and conducts a short dialog in which you specify the type of conversion and the amount of money to convert.

Suppose you're thinking of staying at a chic business hotel near the Champs Élysées, and the hotel has quoted you a price of 1750 francs a night. You choose option 6 — France — from the program's country list, and then you continue as follows:

```
France:         One Franc    ->    $0.1748
-------         One Dollar   ->    5.72 Francs


1 > Dollars to Francs
2 > Francs to Dollars

Which conversion (1, 2, or none)? 2
How many Francs? 1750

 1750 Francs equals     $305.90.

 ...
```

After choosing a conversion from Francs to Dollars, you enter 1750 as the number of francs. The program displays the dollar equivalent as $305.90.

You can perform as many currency conversions as you want. When you're ready to choose a different country, you enter none (or just press Enter) in response to the question Which conversion? The country menu returns to the screen, and you can select another country as you continue to plan the budget for your trip.

This kind of dialog is typical of the QBasic programs in this book. The program displays information on the screen, followed by a question, and waits for an answer from the person at the keyboard. In response to the input it receives, the program decides what to do next. The question-and-answer pattern can repeat itself many times while the program is running. In an *interactive* program like this one, the course of the action depends on the selections you make and the information you supply during a program run.

The listing

How is the program organized to conduct this dialog? Take a look at the listing:

```
' Currency Exchange Program.
' CUREXCH.BAS

' Converts between dollars and
' the currencies of other countries.
' The daily exchange rates are stored in
' a text file named EXCHANGE.TXT.


DECLARE SUB Calc (country AS INTEGER, noMore AS INTEGER)
DECLARE FUNCTION CountCountries% ()
DECLARE SUB CountryMenu (countries AS INTEGER, choice AS INTEGER)
DECLARE SUB ReadCountryInfo (numCountries AS INTEGER)
DECLARE SUB ShowCurrency (countries AS INTEGER, choice AS INTEGER)

CONST False = 0
CONST True = NOT False
CONST DateFileName$ = "C:\EXCHANGE.TXT"

DIM num  AS INTEGER

' Count the number of countries in the file.

num = CountCountries%

' ... and dimension the program's three data
' arrays accordingly.

DIM SHARED country(num) AS STRING     ' Names of countries.
DIM SHARED currency(num) AS STRING    ' Names of currencies.
DIM SHARED inDollars(num) AS SINGLE   ' Exchange rates.
```

```
' Read the file and store information
' in the three arrays.

ReadCountryInfo num

DIM choice AS INTEGER

' List the countries on the screen, and
' elicit the user's destinations.

DO

   CountryMenu num, choice

' Display the exchange rates for the
' selected country.

   ShowCurrency num, choice

LOOP UNTIL choice = 0 OR choice = num + 1

END   ' CUREXCH.BAS


' Error routine for missing file.

NoDateFile:
   CLS
   PRINT "Can't find "; DateFileName$; "."
   END



SUB Calc (country AS INTEGER, noMore AS INTEGER)

   ' Calculates a conversion from dollars to
   ' the selected currency or from the currency
   ' to dollars.

   DIM choice AS STRING
   DIM dollars AS SINGLE, curAmount AS SINGLE
   DIM go AS STRING

   noMore = False

   ' List the options, and get the user's choice.

   PRINT
   PRINT "1 > Dollars to "; currency(country); "s"
   PRINT "2 > "; currency(country); "s to Dollars"
   PRINT
   INPUT "Which conversion (1, 2, or none)"; choice

   ' Calculate the appropriate conversion.

   IF choice = "1" THEN
     INPUT "How many Dollars"; dollars
     PRINT
```

(continued)

```
      PRINT USING "$$##,###.##"; dollars;
      PRINT USING " equals ###,###.## "; dollars / inDollars(country);
      PRINT currency(country); "s."
      PRINT : INPUT "...", go
    ELSEIF choice = "2" THEN
      PRINT "How many "; currency(country); "s";
      INPUT curAmount
      PRINT
      PRINT curAmount; currency(country); "s ";
      PRINT USING "equals $$##,###.##."; curAmount * inDollars(country)
      PRINT : INPUT "...", go
    ELSE
      noMore = True
    END IF

END SUB   ' Calc



FUNCTION CountCountries%

' Counts the number of lines in
' the rate exchange file.

  DIM c AS INTEGER   ' Counter.

  ' Set up an error trap to display
  ' a message if the file cannot
  ' be found. Attempt to open the file.

  ON ERROR GOTO NoDateFile
    OPEN DateFileName$ FOR INPUT AS #1
  ON ERROR GOTO 0

    ' If the file is found, read each
    ' line from beginning to end, and
    ' use c to count the lines.

    c = 0
    DO WHILE NOT EOF(1)
      LINE INPUT #1, temp$
      c = c + 1
    LOOP
  CLOSE #1

  ' Return c as the function's value.

  CountCountries% = c

END FUNCTION   ' CountCountries%



SUB CountryMenu (countries AS INTEGER, choice AS INTEGER)

  ' Displays the list of countries
  ' read from the rate exchange file.
  ' Then elicits the user's country choice.
```

```
      CLS
      PRINT "Currency Exchange"
      PRINT "-------- --------"
      PRINT
      PRINT "Which country?"

      ' First list the countries.

      FOR i = 1 TO countries
        PRINT USING "      ##"; i;
        PRINT " > "; country(i)
      NEXT i

      ' The final choice is Quit,
      ' for exiting from the program.

      PRINT USING "      ##"; countries + 1;
      PRINT " > "; "Quit"
      PRINT

      ' Get the user's choice, by number.

      INPUT "Enter a number: ", choice
   END SUB   ' CountryMenu



   SUB ReadCountryInfo (numCountries AS INTEGER)

      ' Reads the information from the rate exchange
      ' file: the country names, the currency
      ' names, and the exchange rates.

      DIM i AS INTEGER

      ' The program has already tested for the
      ' existence of the file, so the OPEN command
      ' can be issued without an error trap here.

      OPEN DateFileName$ FOR INPUT AS #1

        ' Read data into the country, currency, and
        ' inDollars arrays.

        FOR i = 1 TO numCountries
          INPUT #1, country(i), currency(i), inDollars(i)
        NEXT i

      CLOSE #1

   END SUB   ' ReadCountryInfo



   SUB ShowCurrency (countries AS INTEGER, choice AS INTEGER)

      ' Displays the currency exchange rates for
      ' the selected country.
```

(continued)

```
DIM yesno AS STRING
DIM done AS INTEGER

IF choice > 0 AND choice <= countries THEN
  DO
    CLS
    PRINT
    PRINT country(choice); ":";

    ' Currency to Dollar.

    PRINT TAB(20); "One "; currency(choice); TAB(35); "-> ";
    PRINT USING "  $$##.####"; inDollars(choice)
    PRINT STRING$(LEN(country(choice)) + 1, "-");

    ' Dollar to Currency.

    PRINT TAB(20); "One Dollar"; TAB(35); "->";
    PRINT USING " #####.##"; 1 / inDollars(choice);
    PRINT " "; currency(choice); "s"
    PRINT TAB(60);

    PRINT

    Calc choice, done
  LOOP UNTIL done
END IF

END SUB   ' ShowCurrency
```

The first thing you might notice about this program is its length — several pages of apparently very detailed code. True, this much code can take some time to develop, especially when you're starting out in programming. But because QBasic is a procedural language, you can concentrate on one part of the task at a time and build the program piece by piece.

The program is divided into several procedures, each containing less than a page of code. There are two kinds of procedures in QBasic. One kind begins with the word SUB, which stands for *subroutine,* a term inherited from old versions of BASIC. The other kind begins with the word FUNCTION.

For each procedure you write, you devise a name that suggests the main purpose or nature of the job to be accomplished. This name appears just after the word SUB or FUNCTION on the first line of the procedure. For example, the names of the procedures in the Currency Exchange program are Calc, CountCountries, CountryMenu, ReadCountryInfo, and ShowCurrency. As you add procedures to a program you are creating, QBasic automatically arranges them in alphabetical order in the program listing. ■

Because spaces are not allowed in procedure names, programmers often use capital letters to clarify the meaning of names. When you look at the name ReadCountryInfo, you're likely to think, "This procedure reads information about the countries." If the procedure were written as readcountryinfo, you might be less certain. Keep in mind, however, that capitalization within names is a convention some programmers follow to make their programs easier to read; it is not a format that QBasic requires. ▥

The code at the beginning of the program controls the action by making calls to the procedures below it. This top section is known as the program's *main module*. In the listing of the Currency Exchange program, the main module consists of the code located before the program's first procedure, named Calc. In other words, the main module includes everything above this line in the program:

```
SUB Calc (country AS INTEGER, noMore AS INTEGER)
```

Where the action is

Here's an outline of the action that takes place in the program — and a preview of the programming topics covered in this book:

1. The main module calls the CountCountries procedure to find out how many countries are in the exchange rate file.

   CountCountries opens the file, counts the number of lines it contains, and returns this number to the main module. CountCountries is a FUNCTION procedure that calculates and returns a single value. Other parts of the program are SUB procedures, which perform tasks but are not defined to return values. You examine the differences between these two kinds of procedures in Part III.

2. The main module defines some variables and arrays to represent the rate exchange information and the user's input.

   In QBasic, a *variable* is a name that represents a single data item, and an *array* is a name that conveniently represents a list or a table of informa-tion. You learn to work with variables in Part II, and you study arrays in Part VI.

3. The main module calls ReadCountryInfo to store the exchange rate information in the arrays.

   The program reopens the data file and reads its information line-by-line into the computer's memory. Data file programming is an important part of QBasic. You'll often want to read information from disk or create a file to save information your program generates. You learn how to do these things in Part VII.

4. The program makes a call to CountryMenu to display the list of countries on the screen and get the user's country choice.

   To display the menu and conduct this and other dialogs, the program uses QBasic's input and output statements, INPUT and PRINT, respectively. Lots of examples of these two statements are scattered throughout the program. INPUT displays a question on the screen and waits for an answer from the keyboard. PRINT only displays a line of information on the screen. You'll use these two statements in almost every program you write, so it's important to learn how they work as early as possible. Part II covers input and output.

5. After the user has chosen a country, the program calls ShowCurrency to display the currency-to-dollar and dollar-to-currency exchange rates on the screen and to conduct the ensuing dialog.

   The ShowCurrency procedure uses a loop to keep performing conversions until you indicate that you're through. You study loops in Part V.

6. ShowCurrency in turn calls the Calc procedure to perform a currency conversion.

   Remember the franc-to-dollar conversion for the rates at the Champs Élysées hotel? The Calc procedure uses a decision structure to react appropriately to the type of currency conversion you select. You learn how to plan decisions in Part IV.

7. The main module repeats steps 4 through 6 for any number of country selections.

   This is another example of a loop. For each new country selection, the main module once again makes calls to all the program's procedures—to display the menu list, accept a country choice, and conduct a dialog.

8. When the user selects the Quit option in the country menu, the program stops.

   You return to the QBasic environment, where the program listing is again displayed in the View window.

Each procedure has its role in the program's action. The main module directs the show by making calls to the procedures, which do the work. After looking even briefly at this example, you can begin to see how procedures simplify the process of programming. As you create a program, you always concentrate on developing one part of the action at a time.

However, before you work with a lengthy project like this one, you need to learn more about the QBasic programming environment: the editor, the View window, the menus, and all the other features designed to help you develop a program. This is the job ahead of you in the next few chapters.

To save wear and tear on your typing fingers, many of the program exercises you work with in the rest of the book are shorter than the Currency Exchange program. But remember that this program is listed back here in Chapter 1. Later on, when you gain some experience with QBasic, you might want to try entering the program and running it — especially if you're planning a luxury séjour on the Champs Élysées. On the other hand, maybe you'd rather not know how much you're spending.

Chapter 2
Get Ready ... Get Set ... Code!

● ●

In This Chapter

▶ Working with the QBasic smart editor

▶ Developing a main module

▶ Adding procedures to your program

▶ Using the Immediate window to test a statement

▶ Saving your program

▶ Doing a test run

● ●

*P*rogramming is fun, satisfying, and tedious. The fun part is the logical mind-game you play every time you must figure out how to do something. The satisfying part is your sense of accomplishment when you finish a program and regard your creation. The tedious part is the requirement for perfect typing as you enter your code.

Programming languages impose only one simple requirement: perfection. (You are perfect, aren't you?) Like other programming environments, QBasic is exceptionally picky. A single typo can make the difference between a program that works and one that doesn't. A misspelled word, a misplaced punctuation character, or a space that doesn't belong can spell doom for your program. ■

In this chapter, you go through the exercise of typing the text of a program and then running it. You'll see that you're not alone. The QBasic editor watches over your work as you write lines of code. Along the way, you practice the steps for organizing your program into a main module followed by a sequence of short procedures, and you begin to see the wisdom of this arrangement.

To get ready for the exercise ahead, find an ergonomically correct postion, take a deep breath, and start QBasic by typing QBASIC at the DOS prompt and pressing Enter. When QBasic appears, press Esc to clear the Welcome box.

Editors Think They're So Smart

The QBasic editor — sometimes known as the smart editor — is a benevolent nag. It goes to great lengths to help you meet the requirement of perfection. As you type the code of a program, the editor lets you know right away if something is wrong. When you try to run the program, QBasic has additional ways of alerting you to problems.

QBasic has a stock of error messages that show up in little boxes on the screen whenever you try to enter a statement it doesn't like.

When you type a statement and press Enter, the smart editor first checks the syntax. (*Syntax* refers to the grammatical rules of QBasic statements.) If the syntax is not okay, an error message appears.

If the syntax is okay, the following happens:

1. The editor adjusts the statement's format in two small but important ways. It capitalizes the QBasic command words (known as *keywords*) and inserts spaces to make the statement easier to read.

2. The editor translates the statement into machine code that the computer can later perform. This final step is invisible to you. But it means that QBasic is nearly ready to run your program.

In short, two visual cues — one obvious and the other more subtle — help you determine whether the editor has accepted a line of code in the way you intended. First, if an error message appears, you know that you have a problem. But even if you don't get an error message, watch how QBasic changes the format of an acceptable statement. These changes can help you check the validity of your statement, as you see in the next section.

Try it, you'll like it

Before you plunge into this chapter's exercise, try a few experiments with the editor. First, type the following line, just as you see it here:

```
print a,b,c
```

When you press Enter, QBasic reformats your statement as follows:

```
PRINT a, b, c
```

The editor capitalizes the keyword, PRINT, and inserts a space after each comma. As you might recall from Chapter 1, PRINT is the command that sends information to the screen. When you see the reformatted line of code, you know that QBasic has accepted your statement as a correct PRINT command.

But suppose you misspell the keyword in a command. If the resulting statement is syntactically unusable, an error message appears. But you need to be careful; sometimes QBasic misinterprets a misspelled keyword. For example, try entering this statement:

```
prnt a,b,c
```

When you press Enter, the editor adds spaces to your statement, but does not capitalize the initial word. You look back at your statement and realize that you've left the i out of the keyword PRINT. Yet no error message appears. Why? Because QBasic sees this as a plausible statement. It assumes that you've written — or are planning to write — a procedure named prnt and that this statement is a call to the procedure.

If you observe the way QBasic reformats your code as you enter each statement, you can catch errors before they cause problems in your program. ■

Now try a few more experimental lines of code. The program you create later in this chapter contains a loop that sends several lines of information to the screen. One way to write a loop in QBasic is with the keyword FOR. The FOR statement controls the number of repetitions that take place during the looping.

The following line is from the program. Type it into the editor now:

```
for i=1 to num
```

When you press Enter, the editor reformats your statement as follows:

```
FOR i = 1 TO num
```

The statement contains two keywords, FOR and TO. The editor capitalizes both of these, and inserts a space on each side of the equal sign. When this happens, you know you've typed the statement correctly. Now try typing the statement with some deliberate omissions, just to see QBasic's response. Try it this way:

```
for i 1 to num
```

Press Enter, and an error box appears with the following message:

```
Expected: =
```

QBasic examined the line, determined that you were attempting to write a FOR loop, and found that you've omitted the equal sign. In the lower half of the error box are two buttons, OK and Help. Click OK or press Enter to close the error box.

Back in the View window, QBasic places the flashing cursor at just the position where the equal sign belongs in your FOR statement. To correct your statement, type the equal sign, and then press End to move the cursor to the end of the line. Press Enter to complete the entry. This time, QBasic accepts your statement and reformats it as before.

Continue experimenting a little more, with two more variations of the FOR statement. First, enter the statement as follows:

```
for i = 1 num
```

This results in another error message:

```
Expected: TO
```

You can correct the statement by inserting the keyword to between 1 and num. Finally, try this faulty statement:

```
fori = 1 to num
```

This time you've omitted the space between for and i. QBasic displays the following error message:

```
Expected: end-of-statement
```

and highlights the word to in the statement. This message is not as clear as the others. It is trying to tell you that it could accept the statement if you deleted everything after fori = 1. But it accomplishes its goal: to make you examine your statement and figure out what's wrong.

You can't always rely on the QBasic editor to figure out exactly what is wrong in a statement. But if you read the error messages and keep your eye on the automatic reformatting, you can usually determine whether QBasic has accepted a line of code the way you intended. ■

A clear view

Next, you turn to the task of entering this chapter's program into the editor. But before you start, you need to clear the View window to get rid of the code you entered in the preceding section. To do this, follow these steps:

1. Press the Alt key to activate the menu bar.

2. Press F to pull down the File menu.

3. Press N to choose the New command. QBasic displays the following message: `Loaded file is not saved. Save it now?` This means you've typed some code into the editor without saving it to disk.

4. Press N to respond to the message. (You don't want to save the statements you've entered.) QBasic clears the View window so that you can start again.

If you have a mouse, you can use it instead of the keyboard to choose menu commands. Click the File menu, and then click the New command. Click No in the message box to clear the screen without saving your work.

An Exchange Program

This chapter's program is a short variation on the Currency Exchange program you examined in Chapter 1. This new program displays an exchange rate table on the screen. For example, here's a table it creates for the currencies of five European countries:

```
-------------------------------------------------------
Country       Currency     In Dollars    $ In Currency
-------------------------------------------------------
England       Pound        1.5075           $0.66
France        Franc        0.1748           $5.72
Germany       Mark         0.6089           $1.64
Holland       Guilder      0.5386           $1.86
Switzerland   Franc        0.6983           $1.43
-------------------------------------------------------
```

This four-column table displays the name of each country, its currency, the value of one unit of currency in dollars, and the value of one dollar in the currency. All this information is based on the exchange rates for a particular date.

The entire program consists of about a page of code. But you have to type only about two dozen lines, plus a few comments. QBasic supplies some of the code for you as you develop procedures and save your program to disk. Here's what the program listing will look like when you're finished:

```
' Exchange Rate Program (EXCHRATE.BAS)
' Displays a table of currency exchange rates.

DECLARE SUB ShowHeadings ()
DECLARE SUB ShowCountry ()
DECLARE SUB ShowLine ()
DECLARE SUB ShowTable ()

ShowTable
END   ' EXCHRATE.BAS

' The exchange rate information.
DATA 5
DATA England, Pound, 1.5075
DATA France, Franc, .1748
DATA Germany, Mark, .6089
DATA Holland, Guilder, .5386
DATA Switzerland, Franc, .6983



SUB ShowCountry
  ' Read and show one country's exchange rates.

  READ place$, money$, exRate
  PRINT place$, money$,
  PRINT USING "##.####"; exRate;
  PRINT , USING "$$####.##"; 1 / exRate

END SUB   ' ShowCountry



SUB ShowHeadings
  ' Display the column headings.

  CLS
  ShowLine
  PRINT "Country", "Currency", "In Dollars", "$ In Currency"
  ShowLine

END SUB   ' ShowHeadings



SUB ShowLine
  ' Display a line of hyphens.

  PRINT STRING$(55, "-")

END SUB   ' ShowLine
```

```
SUB ShowTable
  ' Display the exchange rate table.

  ShowHeadings
  READ num

  ' Display information about each country.
  FOR i = 1 TO num
    ShowCountry
  NEXT i
  ShowLine

END SUB   ' ShowTable
```

Near the top of the program, you can see a group of lines that begins with the keyword DATA. These lines contain the currency exchange information that the program uses to create the table. Instead of reading currency information from a file stored on disk, this program has the data available as part of the listing. To update the table with the latest currency exchange rates, you can simply revise the rates directly in the program's DATA lines.

In addition to the DATA lines, the program consists of a short main module and four procedures. Here is an outline of the program's action:

1. The main module calls the ShowTable procedure. This is the only action in the main module.

2. The ShowTable procedure coordinates calls to the procedures that display information on the screen.

3. The ShowHeadings procedure displays the column headings, enclosed in dividing lines.

4. The ShowCountry procedure reads one country's exchange rate data from a DATA line and organizes the data on the screen.

   The DATA lines contain the exchange rate for converting the currency of the current country into dollars. The ShowCountry procedure calculates the opposite rate (for exchanging from dollars to the currency of the current country). Note that the ShowTable procedure calls ShowCountry once for each country in the DATA lines.

5. The ShowLine procedure displays a horizontal line of hyphens to divide sections of the table.

You can begin developing this program by creating the short main module and entering the DATA lines.

Take It from the Top

The main module is like a business manager whose style is to relegate tasks to employees. The manager calls on employees to accomplish broadly described jobs in a particular sequence, but lets the employees figure out the details. In this top-down management scheme, the boss's only concern is that the jobs get done; it's up to the employees to decide how to do them.

When you organize a program in procedures, you should keep the main module short and simple. Its job is to make calls to one or more procedures, which do the real work. In this top-down style of programming, the main module at the top of the listing becomes a kind of program summary, a broad outline of the action. The algorithmic details, or steps for performing individual tasks, are in the procedures.

QBasic doesn't impose a top-down programming style on you. You're free to organize your program in any way you like. You can even write all the code in the main module, without creating any procedures. Occasionally, you may decide to do this for "quick and dirty" programs that have simple jobs and need only a few lines of code.

But for longer and more complicated programs, it's always better to use the top-down procedural approach. There are at least three advantages to procedural programming. You can

- Concentrate on one task at a time as you develop your program
- Revise the program easily because you'll know where to find the code that relates to a particular task
- Modify a procedure without disturbing the rest of the program

Ready to code?

The main module of the Exchange Rate program contains only one call, to a procedure named ShowTable. So you don't have to do much typing to get started. The two lines of comments at the top of the listing identify the program by name and by file, and offer a short description of what the program does. The procedure call comes next, and then the END keyword marks the end of the program.

Enter the following lines into the View window:

```
' Exchange Rate Program (EXCHRATE.BAS)
' Displays a table of currency exchange rates.

ShowTable
END   ' EXCHRATE.BAS
```

Notice the blank line between the comments and the call to the ShowTable procedure. You can place as many blank lines in a listing as you like. They make a program easier to read by visually separating different parts of the code. Notice also the brief comment after the END keyword. This comment makes it clear that this line marks the end of the main module and concludes the action of the program.

When to store data in a program

DATA statements must always appear along with the main module — not inside a procedure — so you type them next. Generally, programmers use DATA statements for permanent information that doesn't change, such as the names of the months, the days of the week, or the names of the fifty states. Periodic information is usually stored in data files on disk, independent from the program itself.

But like many other programming rules, this one is fine to break when there's a good reason to do so. In the Exchange Rate program, the DATA lines simplify your work and make it easy to see — and to revise — the information that the program is working with.

The lines contain exchange rate information for a particular date. Enter them into the main module now, starting with a brief comment line:

```
' The exchange rate information.
DATA 5
DATA England, Pound, 1.5075
DATA France, Franc, .1748
DATA Germany, Mark, .6089
DATA Holland, Guilder, .5386
DATA Switzerland, Franc, .6983
```

Each data item in a line is separated from the next by a comma. You can also include spaces between data items to make the lines easier to read. QBasic doesn't make any automatic format changes in the data that you enter in these lines.

Notice that the first DATA line contains only the number 5. This line tells the program how many countries are in the subsequent DATA lines. If you want to add more countries to the program later, you'll need to revise the number in this line.

Saving your program

That's all there is to the program's main module. As you begin adding procedures to your program, QBasic inserts some additional lines, but you don't have to worry about that yet.

For now, go ahead and save your work for the first time. Press Alt to activate the menu bar, F to pull down the File menu, and A to choose the Save As command. The Save As dialog box appears on the screen. In the File Name box, type EXCHRATE and then press Enter. QBasic saves your program in the current directory under the name EXCHRATE.BAS. This name will appear at the top of the View window whenever you view the program's main module.

The Save As dialog box enables you to save programs on any disk or in any directory you choose. Press the Tab key to activate the Dirs/Drives box. Then press the arrow keys on your keyboard to highlight the name of the directory or drive where you want to save the file, and press Enter. (Highlight the .. notation and press Enter to move up one level in the directory tree.) Repeat these steps if necessary to move to your target directory location. ■

Creating Procedures

As you get ready to create your first procedure, you may be surprised to find out that QBasic displays one procedure at a time in the View window. This makes it easy for you to focus on the individual tasks in a particular procedure. You can quickly switch from one procedure to another with just a few key-strokes or mouse clicks.

In Chapter 1, you saw examples of the two types of QBasic procedures, identi-fied by the SUB and FUNCTION keywords. To create a new procedure in your current program, you choose one of two commands from the Edit menu:

✔ New SUB creates a SUB procedure

✔ New FUNCTION creates a function

These commands automatically create the first and last lines of code for your new procedure.

Using the New SUB command

Try creating a SUB procedure now. With the main module still displayed in the View window, use the arrow keys or your mouse to move the cursor to the line containing the call to the ShowTable procedure. (This step is optional, but it is a good shortcut for defining the name of the procedure you want to create.) Now press Alt to activate the menu bar, E to pull down the Edit menu, and S to choose the New Sub command.

The New Sub dialog box appears on the screen, as shown in Figure 2-1. The dialog box contains a Name text box in which you can enter the name for the new procedure you're creating. Because you took the time to move the cursor to the ShowTable call in the View window, QBasic has copied this name in the Name box.

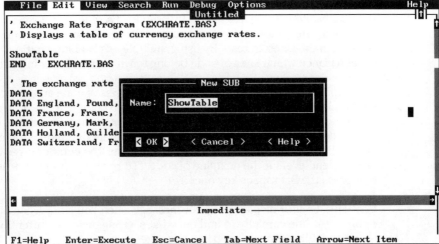

Figure 2-1:
Adding a
procedure
to your
program.

Press Enter to complete the New Sub command. When you do so, QBasic
isolates the new procedure in the View window. At the top of the window are
the following lines of code:

```
SUB ShowTable
END SUB
```

SUB ShowTable is the beginning of the procedure, and END SUB is the final
statement. The cursor appears just after the name of the procedure. Press
Enter to move the cursor to the next line. You're now ready to begin entering
the code of the procedure.

Just follow procedure

Here's the procedure you need to create:

```
SUB ShowTable
  ' Display the exchange rate table.

  ShowHeadings
  READ num

  ' Display information about each country.
  FOR i = 1 TO num
    ShowCountry
  NEXT i
  ShowLine

END SUB   ' ShowTable
```

Notice that the lines between the SUB and END SUB statements are indented by two spaces. You create this indent by pressing the Spacebar twice. You can see additional indentation in the procedure's FOR-NEXT loop. Indentation makes your program easier to read. By using multiple levels of indentation, you can tell at a glance which lines of code belong to which structures in your program.

Start typing the procedure now. There are six lines of code and two comments on lines by themselves. Don't forget to start each comment line with an apostrophe. After you establish the two-space indent for the first line of the procedure, QBasic correctly assumes that you want to maintain that indent for subsequent lines. When you press Enter at the end of one line, the cursor moves to the same indent level for the next line of code. (To remove the indent from a new line, press the Backspace key once.)

If the smart editor displays an error message when you enter a line of code, examine the line carefully to find out what's wrong. Also, pay attention to the way the editor reformats each line you enter. ■

When you finish typing the code, move the cursor down to the END SUB line, press the End key, and then press the Spacebar twice. Type an apostrophe, a space, and then the name of the procedure. Your line should look like the following:

```
END SUB  ' ShowTable
```

This final comment identifies the end of the procedure. Used consistently, comments like this one help you review and recognize the various parts of your program.

Save, save, save

Now pull down the File menu and choose the Save command (press Alt, F, S). QBasic saves the new version of your program to EXCHRATE.BAS, overwriting the previous version.

Get into the habit of saving your program often — at least as often as you save documents in your word processing program. Any time you write some code that you would be sorry to lose, save your work to disk again. ■

More procedures, but fewer than the government

The ShowTable procedure makes calls to three other procedures you still need to create. Start now by moving the cursor up to the ShowHeadings call in the View window. (Make sure the cursor is positioned on the name of the procedure.)

Then pull down the Edit menu and choose the New Sub command. In the New Sub dialog box, ShowHeadings appears as the name of the new procedure you're creating.

Press Enter. Once again, QBasic creates the first and last lines of the procedure and displays them in the View window. Your job is to complete the procedure as follows:

```
SUB ShowHeadings
  ' Display the column headings.

  CLS
  ShowLine
  PRINT "Country", "Currency", "In Dollars", "$ In Currency"
  ShowLine

END SUB   ' ShowHeadings
```

This procedure contains four executable commands: a CLS command, which clears the output screen; two calls to the as yet unwritten ShowLine procedure; and a PRINT statement, which displays the column headings on the screen.

The PRINT statement is the most detailed line in this procedure. It sends four text strings to the screen. Each string is enclosed in quotation marks. The commas between strings instruct QBasic to arrange the output in tabbed columns. Be careful to place these commas *outside* the quotation marks. (A comma inside the quotation marks would simply become part of the output text.) You learn a little more about PRINT later in this chapter and a lot more about it in Part II.

Save your work again by pulling down the File menu and choosing Save.

To prepare for the next procedure, move the cursor up to one of the calls to the ShowLine procedure. Then pull down the Edit menu and choose New Sub. In the New Sub dialog box, ShowLine appears as the proposed name of the new procedure. Press Enter or click OK to continue. QBasic opens a new View window containing the first and last lines of the ShowLine procedure.

This procedure has only one executable line, another PRINT statement:

```
SUB ShowLine
  ' Display a line of hyphens.

  PRINT STRING$(55, "-")

END SUB   ' ShowLine
```

This statement uses STRING$, which is a QBasic *built-in function* designed to produce specific values from information you supply. ShowLine uses the STRING$ function to produce a string of 55 hyphen characters to separate parts of the output table.

Enter this statement carefully. First, notice that the name of the function ends with a dollar sign. This symbol indicates that the function returns a text string rather than a numeric value. Immediately after the function name is a pair of values, separated by a comma and enclosed in parentheses. These values are the *arguments* of the function, that is, the values you send to the function to specify the value you want to receive back. The first argument instructs the STRING$ function to return a text string that is 55 characters long; the second specifies that the return text should consist of hyphens. The resulting output is a line like this:

As before, update your program file on disk by choosing the Save command from the File menu.

Admiring your work

You've typed three of the four procedures in the program. Before you begin working on the final one, take a moment to review your work. The SUBs command in the View menu shows you a list of the procedures included in the program, and lets you select any procedure for display in the View window.

Instant gratification

The Immediate window, which is located below the View window, is useful for testing individual lines of code before you run the entire program. You might want to try using the Immediate window with the PRINT statement that you've just written.

To begin, you must copy the statement from the View window to the Immediate window. Move the cursor to the beginning of the PRINT statement in the ShowLine procedure. Hold down the Shift key and press End to highlight the entire statement. (Alternatively, you can drag the mouse over the statement to highlight it.) Then pull down the Edit menu and choose the Copy command. This action copies the selected text to the QBasic *Clipboard,* a memory area for copy-and-paste and cut-and-paste operations.

Next, press F6 to activate the Immediate window. Pull down the Edit menu again, but this time choose the Paste command. A copy of the PRINT statement appears in the Immediate window.

Now simply press Enter to "run" the statement. QBasic switches to the output window, where you see the string of hyphens that this PRINT statement is designed to display on the screen. At the bottom of the screen you see the message Press any key to continue. When you finish examining the statement's output, press a key to return to the QBasic programming environment.

Take this opportunity to test other statements you're curious about. When you're ready to return to your work in the program, press F6 to activate the View window again.

To open the SUBs dialog box, press F2 or pull down the View menu and choose the SUBs command. The resulting dialog box, shown in Figure 2-2, contains the contents of your program. To view any part of the program, you simply highlight the name of the procedure (or highlight EXCHRATE.BAS for the main module) and press Enter. Your selection appears in the View window.

For now, highlight the ShowTable procedure and press Enter. The procedure appears in the View window. The fourth procedure you need to create, ShowCountry, is called from ShowTable. Move the cursor to the ShowCountry call. Then pull down the Edit menu and choose the New SUB command. Press Enter to create the new procedure.

Here are the final lines of code you need to complete the program:

```
SUB ShowCountry
    ' Read and show one country's exchange rates.

    READ place$, money$, exRate
    PRINT place$, money$,
    PRINT USING "##.####"; exRate;
    PRINT , USING "$$####.##"; 1 / exRate

END SUB   ' ShowCountry
```

The READ command reads a line of information from the program's DATA lines.

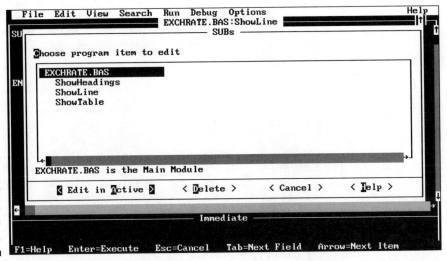

Figure 2-2: The list of procedures in the SUBs dialog box.

```
 File   Edit   View   Search   Run   Debug   Options                Help
                        EXCHRATE.BAS:ShowLine
SU ───────────────────────────── SUBs ─────────────────────────────
   Choose program item to edit

      ┌─────────────────────────────────────────────────────────┐
      │ EXCHRATE.BAS                                              │
   EN │    ShowHeadings                                           │
      │    ShowLine                                               │
      │    ShowTable                                              │
      │                                                           │
      │                                                           │
      │                                                           │
      │                                                           │
      └─────────────────────────────────────────────────────────┘
      EXCHRATE.BAS is the Main Module

        ◄ Edit in Active ►    < Delete >    < Cancel >    < Help >
  ───────────────────────────── Immediate ─────────────────────────
 F1=Help   Enter=Execute   Esc=Cancel   Tab=Next Field   Arrow=Next Item
```

The three PRINT commands are in charge of sending a country's exchange rates to the screen. Once again, the PRINT statements are elaborately punctuated and contain odd combinations of symbols and characters. Two of the PRINT statements have USING clauses that format numeric output values. With all its variations, the PRINT statement is almost like a sublanguage; master it and you'll gain intricate control over the output your programs produce. See Chapter 5 for details.

 Type the READ and PRINT statements carefully, because they are responsible for creating and formatting the information in the exchange rate table. Letter-perfect coding is essential. A missing or misplaced punctuation character in any of these PRINT statements can produce output that is very different from what you intended. ▦

The Finishing Touches

Now that you've finished typing the program's code, save your work again. Then press F2 to view the list of procedures you've created: ShowCountry, ShowHeadings, ShowLine, and ShowTable. Highlight the main module — identified as EXCHRATE.BAS at the top of the list — and press Enter. You may be surprised to discover that the main module contains some new statements supplied by QBasic.

To call the procedures you've included in the program, QBasic needs these procedures to be *declared* in advance, at the top of the main module. QBasic creates the appropriate declaration statements automatically, as soon as you save the program with its new procedures. Here is what the declaration statements look like:

```
DECLARE SUB ShowHeadings ()
DECLARE SUB ShowCountry ()
DECLARE SUB ShowLine ()
DECLARE SUB ShowTable ()
```

There is one DECLARE statement for each procedure you've written. (The order of these statements is not important and does not necessarily match the alphabetical order of the procedures in the program. You can rearrange the order of the DECLARE statements if you want.) Each statement indicates the type of procedure (all SUB procedures in this program), the name of the procedure, and any arguments that the procedure expects to receive. None of the procedures in this program takes arguments, so each procedure name is followed by a pair of empty parentheses.

You don't have to worry much about the DECLARE statements in this program. They need to be there, QBasic supplies them, and that's that. The only thing you might want to do is move them around a bit in the listing. They currently precede the two comment lines you originally entered at the top of the listing. For clarity, it would be nice to move the DECLARE statements to the position just after the comments. Use the Cut and Paste commands in the QBasic Edit menu for this task, as follows:

1. Move the cursor to the beginning of the first DECLARE statement. You can do this by pressing the arrow keys on your keyboard, by clicking the mouse at the position where you want to move the cursor, or by pressing Ctrl-Home.

2. Highlight the four DECLARE statements. To do this, hold down the Shift key while you press the down-arrow key four times. Alternatively, hold down the left mouse button and drag the mouse from the first line to the last.

3. Pull down the Edit menu and choose the Cut command. The four statements disappear from the listing.

4. Position the cursor just above the ShowTable call, where you want to move the four DECLARE statements.

5. Pull down the Edit menu and choose Paste. The four DECLARE statements reappear in their new location.

6. Add a blank line after the last statement.

7. Save the revised listing to disk.

Don't move DECLARE statements indiscriminately in your program. They must appear before the first executable line of code. DECLARE statements can appear after comments, however. ▨

Running the Program — If You're Lucky

You've entered all the code and responded to any syntax errors that the smart editor has pointed out to you along the way. You've carefully planted a nice crop of comments between the rows of code. But you're probably not finished yet. However carefully you develop programs, they rarely run successfully on the first try.

When you give the command to run a program, QBasic quickly checks all the code for consistency and completeness. If QBasic finds any problems, it refuses to even begin running the program. Instead, it tries its best to let you know what's wrong. The following events take place:

- ✔ The View window displays the procedure where a problem has been found.
- ✔ QBasic highlights the line in which the error is apparently located.
- ✔ An error message appears on the screen.

The most common type of error at this point in your work is a misspelled procedure name. For example, suppose you entered the ShowHeadings procedure as follows:

```
SUB ShowHeadings
  ' Display the column headings.

  CLS
  ShowLine
  PRINT "Country", "Currency", "In Dollars", "$ In Currency"
  ShoLine

END SUB  ' ShowHeadings
```

Can you see the error? The second call to the ShowLine procedure is spelled incorrectly. If you tried to run the program in this condition, QBasic would display this procedure in the View window, highlight the call to ShoLine, and display an error box with a Syntax error message.

Why didn't the editor catch this error when you originally entered the line? It assumed you were planning to write a procedure named ShoLine. QBasic discovers that ShoLine doesn't exist only when you attempt to run the program.

So, take a deep breath and give the program a try. Pull down the Run menu and choose the Start command, or simply press F5. If QBasic finds a mistake in your code, check it carefully against the listing in this chapter. After you make changes, save the program to disk. You may have to repeat these steps several times before you find and correct all the errors.

When everything is finally all right, QBasic prepares the code for a run. The output screen appears, and voilà, there's the currency exchange table.

Your next job is to check the output carefully and make sure the information appears as you intended. Sometimes, QBasic completes a program run successfully but produces erroneous or inappropriate output. So, as with any endeavor, you just have to keep working at it until it comes out right. In the next chapter, you explore techniques you can use to ferret out the bugs in a program that is not behaving.

Chapter 3
And We're Off — Almost

*B*efore the first run of a new program, you'll probably spend a lot of time revising, adjusting, and fine-tuning your code. As you saw in Chapter 2, QBasic forces you to confront some categories of errors before you try to run a program.

First, if you make errors while typing the program, the smart editor displays a variety of error messages. You correct each error before moving to the next line of code. Then when you press F5 to start the program, QBasic highlights any other errors.

Doggedly you keep working on your code and making attempts to run it. A misspelled procedure call here, a missing argument there, and an incomplete declaration in the main module are all simple mistakes that can prevent you from running your program. But eventually the moment comes when you correct the last problem, press F5, and see your program's output for the first time. As you watch your program in action, you relish the moment. Finally your work is finished! Right?

Wrong. The action is just beginning. Your next job is to examine every detail of your program's performance — every line of output and every possible turn of events — to see whether the program is really doing what you've designed it to do. Oddly, this stage of your work can be the most mysterious and exasperating. You can rely on QBasic to perform each statement just as you've written it. The tough part is figuring out why your code isn't producing the results you intended — sort of like raising kids.

When something goes wrong, you're faced with the tasks of following through the logic of your program, identifying the statement that's causing the problem, and figuring out how to correct it. This can be a daunting and time-consuming job. You may be only mildly consoled to learn that every programmer, no matter how skilled, goes through this process with every new program.

Tools of the Trade

Fortunately, modern programming environments include tools designed to help you *debug* a running program — to find the errors that are keeping the program from performing its job correctly. In QBasic, these tools are listed in the Debug menu. They are

- ✔ Step and Procedure Step. You use these two commands to step through a program one statement at a time, pausing to analyze the effect of individual lines of code. The Step command goes through every line of code in every procedure. The Procedure Step command performs a procedure call as a single statement without taking you step-by-step through the lines of the procedure.

- ✔ Trace On. The *trace mode* highlights each line in your listing while the program is running. This gives you a broad view of your program's flow as the action is taking place. You activate and deactivate the trace mode by choosing the Trace On command in the Debug menu.

- ✔ Toggle Breakpoint. A *breakpoint* stops the program run so that you can investigate the data and output at a particular point in the action. The Toggle Breakpoint command creates temporary breakpoints at statements you select in your program.

In addition, the Immediate window is one of the most significant of all debugging tools. When your program is interrupted — either by a breakpoint you've established or by an unexpected turn of events — you can use the Immediate window to examine the data that the program is currently working with. This is often the clearest and easiest way to find out what's going wrong.

In this chapter, you experiment with debugging tools while you work on a new project, a simple program that prints mailing labels. You start your work by typing the Mailing Labels program into the QBasic editor and saving it to disk.

Signed, Sealed, and Delivered

A typical mailing list application reads different addresses from a database and prints each address on a gummed label that you can stick on an envelope. You might use this type of program to prepare mailings to large groups of customers.

But sometimes you may have a simpler use in mind for labels. You may need to print whole pages of labels with a single repeated address. For example, suppose you're getting ready for an international business trip. You've reserved hotel rooms in all the cities where you'll be doing business. Before leaving, you want to send to each of these hotels several packages of business materials, which will be held for your arrival. You also want to prepare mailing labels for materials that will be forwarded to you while you're gone. In short, you'd like to avoid surprises on your trip — like arriving in Paris to discover that the materials you've prepared for an important presentation are waiting safely for you at your hotel in Ouagadougou.

You need a quick way to produce a page or two of labels addressed to yourself at each stop of your trip. This is the task of the Mailing Labels program (LABELS.BAS).

Making labels

When you run the Mailing Labels program, it begins by requesting the lines of an address. Here's what the dialog might look like as you enter the address of one of the hotels:

```
Line # 1 : J. Smith
Line # 2 : l'Hotel Baobab
Line # 3 : Place de l'Independence
Line # 4 : Dakar, SENEGAL
Line # 5 :

Print the labels? y
```

Your responses are shown in boldface. After you type each line, you press Enter. After the last line of the address, you press Enter again in response to the next Line prompt; the blank line signals the program that the address is complete. (The address is limited to a maximum of five lines.) When you see the Print the labels? prompt, you load a sheet of blank labels into your printer. Then you type Y and press Enter. The program prints a page of labels with the address you've typed.

Gummed labels come in many sizes and arrangements. The Mailing Label program is designed to print addresses on a standard three-column by ten-row page of labels.

Figure 3-1 shows how the first few rows of labels will be printed.

```
J. Smith            J. Smith            J. Smith
l'Hotel Baobab      l'Hotel Baobab      l'Hotel Baobab
Place de l'Independence  Place de l'Independence  Place de l'Independence
Dakar, SENEGAL      Dakar, SENEGAL      Dakar, SENEGAL

J. Smith            J. Smith            J. Smith
l'Hotel Baobab      l'Hotel Baobab      l'Hotel Baobab
Place de l'Independence  Place de l'Independence  Place de l'Independence
Dakar, SENEGAL      Dakar, SENEGAL      Dakar, SENEGAL

J. Smith            J. Smith            J. Smith
l'Hotel Baobab      l'Hotel Baobab      l'Hotel Baobab
Place de l'Independence  Place de l'Independence  Place de l'Independence
Dakar, SENEGAL      Dakar, SENEGAL      Dakar, SENEGAL
```

Figure 3-1:
Output from
the Mailing
Labels
program.

To print another page of labels, you run the program again and enter the next address.

Code it

The Mailing Labels program consists of a main module followed by two short procedures. Here is what the correct listing will look like when you complete the various debugging exercises in this chapter:

```
' Mailing Labels.  (LABELS.BAS)
' Prints a page of labels
' for a single address.

DECLARE SUB CreateLabels ()
DECLARE SUB PrintLabels ()

' The Label array stores the label;
' n% is the number of lines of text.
DIM SHARED Label(5) AS STRING
DIM SHARED n%

CreateLabels
END  ' LABELS.BAS
```

```
SUB CreateLabels

  ' Accept up to 5 lines of text.
  CLS
  n% = 0
  DO
    n% = n% + 1
    PRINT "Line #"; n%; ": ";
    LINE INPUT Label(n%)
  LOOP UNTIL Label(n%) = "" OR n% = 5

  ' Send label to printer.
  PRINT
  INPUT "Print the labels"; yesNo$
  IF UCASE$(LEFT$(yesNo$, 1)) = "Y" THEN PrintLabels

END SUB  ' CreateLabels

SUB PrintLabels

  ' Print 10 rows of labels
  LPRINT
  FOR i% = 1 TO 10       ' Rows of labels.
    FOR j% = 1 TO n%     ' Lines of text in a label.
      FOR k% = 1 TO 3    ' Columns of labels.
        nextTab% = 2 + (k% - 1) * 27
        LPRINT TAB(nextTab%); Label(j%);
      NEXT k%
      LPRINT
    NEXT j%

    ' Leave blank lines between labels.
    FOR blank% = 1 TO 6 - n%
      LPRINT
    NEXT blank%
  NEXT i%

END SUB  ' PrintLabels
```

The main module makes one call to the CreateLabels procedure. This procedure conducts the input dialog for an address label. Then it calls the PrintLabels procedure, which prints the page of labels.

To print identical information for each of the thirty labels on a three-column page, PrintLabels uses a sequence of FOR loops. These detailed loops are an easy target for bugs that can creep into your code as you type the listing.

Entering the Code — with Mistakes!

In the first version of the Mailing Labels program you create, you'll do something unusual: You'll fabricate some common bugs by entering two intentional errors into the code. Then you'll use these mistakes to experiment with the commands in the QBasic Debug menu.

Start QBasic and press Esc to clear the welcome message. Type the program's main module into the View window, as follows. (You'll probably spend more time typing the comments than typing the code.)

```
' Mailing Labels.  (LABELS.BAS)
' Prints a page of labels
' for a single address.

' The Label array stores the label;
' n% is the number of lines of text.
DIM SHARED Label(5) AS STRING
DIM SHARED n%

CreateLabels
END  ' LABELS.BAS
```

The DIM SHARED statements define names to represent the program's input data: an array named Label and a simple variable named n%.

A *simple variable* represents one data item that is stored in memory for the program to work with. An *array* represents a list or table of data. Each variable in a program is defined to represent one *type* of data, such as an integer, a real number, or a string. An integer variable is identified by a percent sign at the end of a name (as in n%). A string variable is designated by a dollar sign (as in yesNo$, a variable you see later in the program). Chapter 7 discusses variables in detail. ▪

The integer variable n% in the Mailing Labels program records the number of lines in the input address. Be careful to include the percent sign suffix wherever you type the variable name.

The main module's call to the CreateLabels procedure initiates the program's action. The next line, END, marks the end of the main module. Remember that QBasic adds DECLARE statements to the main module when you complete the two procedures and save your program to disk.

Now pull down the Edit menu and choose the New SUB command. In the New SUB dialog box, enter CreateLabels as the name of the first procedure, and press Enter. In the View window, QBasic displays the first and last lines of the new procedure. Press Enter twice (once to move the cursor to a new line after SUB CreateLabels and again to create a blank line). Then start typing the following comments and code:

```
SUB CreateLabels

  ' Accept up to 5 lines of text.
  CLS
  n% = 0
  DO
    n% = n% + 1
    PRINT "Line #"; n%; ": ";
    LINE INPUT Label(n%)
  LOOP UNTIL Label(n%) = "" OR n% = 5

  ' Send label to printer.
  PRINT
  INPUT "Print the labels"; yesNo$
  IF UCASE$(LEFT$(yesNo$, 1)) = "Y" THEN PrintLabels

END SUB  ' CreateLabels
```

A DO loop conducts the input dialog. Each time around the loop, the procedure increases the value of n% by 1 and stores a new line of the address in the Label array.

The variable n% plays a central role in controlling the loop. The looping ends when the user enters a blank line or when n% reaches a value of 5.

When the input dialog is over, the procedure uses an INPUT statement to ask whether you want to print the label. If you answer y (or yes), an IF decision statement calls the PrintLabels procedure. (If you answer n, the program ends without printing the labels.)

The IF statement uses two QBasic built-in functions — named UCASE$ and LEFT$ — to examine your response and determine whether you want to go ahead with the printing. Notice the matched parentheses that are required in this statement.

Bugs, bugs, bugs

In this section, you complete the program by typing the PrintLabels procedure, but with a few adjustments. In its final form, the procedure uses the QBasic LPRINT statement to send information to your printer. But for now, you'll temporarily use the PRINT statement instead to send the output to the screen. In this way, you won't waste paper during the early stages of program development. Later, when the program is working properly, you'll change the PRINT statements in this procedure to LPRINT statements.

In addition, you'll enter the PrintLabels procedure with a couple of "small" typographical errors. As you've already seen, no typo is really small in QBasic. These mistakes cause dramatic — and unwanted — changes in the output, but they also provide interesting material for the upcoming debugging exercises.

Enter the procedure exactly as follows. Don't worry if you can't spot the mistakes right away — you'll find them soon enough.

```
SUB PrintLabels

  ' *** Watch for bugs in this version! ***

  ' Print 10 rows of labels
  PRINT
  FOR i% = 1 TO 10      ' Rows of labels.
    FOR j% = 1 TO n%     ' Lines of text in a label.
      FOR k% = 1 TO 3    ' Columns of labels.
        nextTab% = 2 + (k - 1) * 27
        PRINT TAB(nextTab%); Label(k%);
      NEXT k%
      PRINT
    NEXT j%

    ' Leave blank lines between labels.
    FOR blank% = 1 TO 6 - n%
      PRINT
    NEXT blank%
  NEXT i%

END SUB   ' PrintLabels
```

Now pull down the File menu and choose the Save As command. Save the program as LABELS.BAS. Press F2 to view the SUBs dialog box. You see the names of the main module and the two procedures you've created. Highlight LABELS.BAS in the list and press Enter to display the main module in the View window.

QBasic has added the two required DECLARE statements to the top of the listing. Use the Cut and Paste commands in the Edit menu to move these two lines below the first three comment lines. Your main module should now look like this:

```
' Mailing Labels.  (LABELS.BAS)
' Prints a page of labels
' for a single address.

DECLARE SUB CreateLabels ()
DECLARE SUB PrintLabels ()

' The Label array stores the label;
' n% is the number of lines of text.
DIM SHARED Label(5) AS STRING
DIM SHARED n%

CreateLabels
END   ' LABELS.BAS
```

Pull down the File menu and choose Save to update the program on disk.

Erroneous output

Now that you've saved the program — with mistakes — it's time to try to run it.
Press F5 to start a run of the program. QBasic switches to the output screen
and begins the dialog. Enter the address of the first hotel as follows. (Or enter
an address of your own choice.)

```
Line # 1 : J. Smith
Line # 2 : l'Hotel Baobab
Line # 3 : Place de l'Independence
Line # 4 : Dakar, SENEGAL
Line # 5 :

Print the labels? y
```

After you enter y in response to the `Print the labels?` prompt, the output
scrolls by rapidly. You can see right away that something is wrong with the
program. The labels are arranged in a single column rather than in three
columns, and the last line of the address is missing from each label:

```
J. Smith
l'Hotel Baobab
Place de l'Independence
J. Smith
l'Hotel Baobab
Place de l'Independence
J. Smith
l'Hotel Baobab
Place de l'Independence
J. Smith
l'Hotel Baobab
Place de l'Independence
J. Smith
l'Hotel Baobab
Place de l'Independence
J. Smith
l'Hotel Baobab
Place de l'Independence
```

What has gone wrong? Well, in this exercise you *know* what's gone wrong —
you've intentionally introduced some typos into the listing. But for the moment,
pretend that you've just developed the Mailing Labels program and are now
faced with the task of debugging it. The bugs could be anywhere, and your job
is to find them.

Knowing Where to Look

Where do you start? You know that your program is organized into two procedures that do all the work. CreateLabels conducts the input dialog, and PrintLabels produces the output. You can reasonably speculate that one or both of these procedures are flawed:

✔ CreateLabels may be storing the input information incorrectly in the `Label` array.

✔ PrintLabels may be using the information incorrectly to produce the output.

It makes sense to begin by looking at the procedure that initially accumulates the data. If you can show that the program's data is stored correctly by the time CreateLabels is finished, you know that the problem lies exclusively in PrintLabels.

Gimme a break

In the first part of the investigation, you learn how to designate a temporary breakpoint in your program and how to take advantage of the Immediate window during a break in the run.

If the Output screen is still displayed, press any key to return to the View window. Then proceed as follows:

1. Press F2 to open the SUBs dialog box.

2. Highlight the name of the CreateLabels procedure in the SUBs list and press Enter. QBasic displays the procedure in the View window.

3. Press the down arrow key until the cursor is on the IF line near the bottom of the procedure (if it's not already there). The IF line is

   ```
   IF UCASE$(LEFT$(yesNo$, 1)) = "Y" THEN PrintLabels
   ```

   This statement makes the call to the PrintLabels procedure. What you'd like to do is interrupt the run just before this call, and examine the input data that the program has accumulated.

4. Pull down the Debug menu and choose the Toggle Breakpoint command. (Notice that F9 is the shortcut key for this command; you'll use this shortcut next time.) In the View menu, QBasic highlights the IF statement. This highlighting indicates that you've established a breakpoint. When you run the program, it will stop just before this statement is performed.

5. Press F5 to run the program. As before, enter the four-line address for the first hotel stay in your upcoming business trip, and press Enter in response to the last `Line` prompt. Press Y when asked whether to print the labels, and then press Enter. At this point, QBasic stops the program and returns to the View window, where the breakpoint is still highlighted.

Your program isn't over yet; the breakpoint has temporarily paused the action. All the program's data is still stored in memory, and you can now use the Immediate window to take a look. If the CreateLabels procedure has performed its job correctly, the four lines that you entered for the address should be safely stored in the following four indexed elements of the Label array:

```
Label(1)
Label(2)
Label(3)
Label(4)
```

Don't worry about the details of an array right now. Just notice that the elements of an array are represented by index numbers that appear in parentheses after the name of the array. You learn more about arrays in Chapter 15.

Getting immediate feedback

Your next task is to switch to the Immediate window and examine the four data items. Press F6 to activate the Immediate window. As you saw in Chapter 2, any statement you type in this window is performed as soon as you press Enter. Type the following PRINT statement to view the current contents of the Label array:

```
PRINT Label(1), Label(2), Label(3), Label(4)
```

Press Enter and QBasic switches back to the Output window. The following information appears on the screen:

```
J. Smith       l'Hotel Baobab          Place de l'Independence  Dakar, SENEGAL
```

As you can see, the CreateLabels procedure has performed its job. The four lines of the input address are stored in memory just where they're supposed to be. You can now safely assume that the program's flaws are in the other procedure, PrintLabels. This is the next focus of your investigation.

Press any key to return to the QBasic environment from the output screen. Because the Immediate window is still active, press F6 to switch to the View window. The cursor should still be located at the IF statement near the bottom of the CreateLabels procedure. Press F9 to clear the breakpoint from this line.

Now switch to the PrintLabels procedure: Press F2, highlight the procedure's name in the SUBs list, and press Enter.

Watch where you step

You've identified two problems with the program's current output: the information is arranged in a single column rather than three columns, and the last line of each address is missing. You can probably assume that these problems are caused by two different bugs in the code.

The column format is defined by tab settings calculated by a statement near the middle of the PrintLabels procedure. Here's what the statement currently looks like:

```
nextTab% = 2 + (k - 1) * 27
```

As the printing procedure moves from one column to the next on the label sheet, this statement should produce numeric tab settings that are 27 spaces apart. In other words, the value of `nextTab%` should be 2, 29, and 56 for the three column tab settings. You need to find out whether the statement is calculating these settings correctly. To do so, you'll set a breakpoint just after this statement so that you can look at the successive values of `nextTab%`. Follow these steps:

1. Move the cursor to the PRINT statement immediately after the `nextTab%` calculation.

2. Press F9 to set a breakpoint. QBasic highlights the statement.

3. Press F5 to continue the program run. QBasic continues where it left off after the previous break in the program. The CreateLabels procedure calls PrintLabels, which begins the output process. After the first tab calculation, the program stops, thanks to the new breakpoint you established.

4. Press F6 to activate the Immediate window, type the following new statement into the window (beneath the previous statement you entered), and press Enter:

```
PRINT nextTab%
```

When you press Enter, QBasic switches to the Output window and displays the current value of the `nextTab%` variable. The value is –25, a negative number. A tab setting should never be negative; clearly something is wrong with this calculation.

5. Press any key to return to QBasic. Press F6 to activate the View window. Then pull down the Debug menu and choose the Step command. In response, QBasic performs the current statement in the PrintLabels procedure, and then highlights the next statement by displaying it in bold type. (Note that the shortcut for the Step command is F8.)

6. Press F8 twice to step through the next two commands. Then press F6 to activate the Immediate window, and run the `PRINT nextTab%` statement again. To rerun a statement that is already displayed in the Immediate window, you don't need to retype the statement. Instead, you can simply move the cursor back up to the statement and press Enter.

Repeat steps 5 and 6 several times to display additional interim values of `nextTab%`.

As you continue, you'll find something like this on the output screen:

```
-25
J. Smith-25
l'Hotel Baobab-25
Place de l'Independence
-25
J. Smith-25
```

By studying this output, you can learn two important things about the current version of your program:

- ✔ The procedure repeatedly calculates the same incorrect value for `nextTab%` before displaying each output item.
- ✔ The procedure's innermost loop should display three identical lines of information across the page. Instead, it is displaying three different lines of the address.

As you learn more about FOR loops and arrays (in Chapters 13 and 15, respectively), facts like these become important clues in your search for bugs in a program. In short, they tell you that the procedure is using variables incorrectly during the looping.

The Last of the Bugs

You can probably already imagine how to use these clues. Taking a closer look at the lines of code you've been stepping through, you notice that the `nextTab%` calculation uses an undefined variable named k rather than the loop's correct control variable, `k%`. There's a missing percent sign (%) in the variable name. To correct this problem, insert the character at the appropriate position in the line, as follows:

```
nextTab% = 2 + (k% - 1) * 27
```

The next bug is a little more elusive. But after studying the code carefully, you realize that the subsequent PRINT statement should be using `j%`, not `k%`, to access successive address lines from the Label array. To make this correction, delete the k and replace it with j, as follows:

```
PRINT TAB(nextTab%); Label(j%);
```

Move the cursor down to the next line to complete the edit. As you see, a breakpoint is still defined on this line.

After completing these two corrections, you can try rerunning the program from the beginning. In the View window, press F9 to clear the breakpoint at the PRINT statement.

Then pull down the Run menu and choose the Start command. On the output screen, enter the four address lines again, and enter Y in response to the Print the labels? prompt.

Finally, the program produces the correct output, as shown in Figure 3-2. The address labels are correctly arranged in columns across the screen, and each label contains all four lines of the address.

Figure 3-2:
Corrected
label output.

```
J. Smith                    J. Smith                    J. Smith
l'Hotel Baobab              l'Hotel Baobab              l'Hotel Baobab
Place de l'Independence     Place de l'Independence     Place de l'Independence
Dakar, SENEGAL              Dakar, SENEGAL              Dakar, SENEGAL
```

In summary, here are the QBasic tools that have helped you debug the program:

✔ The Toggle Breakpoint command (with a shortcut key of F9) enables you to designate specific lines where the program will stop temporarily so that you can investigate the status of variables.

✔ The Step command (F8) performs lines of code one at a time so you can focus on a small passage of code.

✔ The Immediate window gives you a simple way to display values of selected variables on the output screen during breaks in the program run.

As you've seen, major output problems can result from tiny typographical errors in a listing. The output of the Mailing Labels program was spoiled by two small mistakes in the code: a missing character and a mistaken one-letter variable name. Errors like these can be the hardest to find. But the QBasic debugging tools are designed to help you focus quickly on suspicious passages of code and make intelligent guesses about the lines that are causing trouble.

You may not always be able to correct a program as quickly as you did this one. Sometimes it can take many hours — or many days — to find a stubborn bug. But the more experience you gain with these debugging features, the more adept and efficient you'll become at locating errors.

You're Golden

Now you're ready to produce the final version of your program — or *gold code,* as programmers say. You used four PRINT statements in the PrintLabels procedure to send the program's output to the screen instead of the printer. Now it's time to change these to LPRINT statements so you can print your labels.

This is a good opportunity to use the QBasic Change command. Move the cursor to the top of the PrintLabels procedure, and follow these steps:

1. Pull down the Search menu and choose Change. The resulting Change dialog box contains the Find What and Change To text boxes along with other options.

2. In the Find What box, enter PRINT. Then press Tab to activate the Change To box, and enter LPRINT. These entries tell QBasic to replace occurrences of PRINT with LPRINT.

3. Press Alt-M to place an X in the Match Upper/Lowercase checkbox. Press Alt-W to mark the Whole Word checkbox. These options ensure that QBasic will change only uppercase whole-word occurrences of the PRINT statement.

4. Press Enter to find the first occurrence. QBasic highlights the first PRINT statement in the procedure. The Change dialog box now displays only four options: Change, Skip, Cancel, and Help. Press Enter to change the highlighted statement.

5. Press Enter three more times to change the remaining three PRINT statements in the procedure. Then press Esc to avoid revising any other part of the program.

The Change command is a great convenience, but also a bit of a hazard. If you're not careful, you can end up making changes that you didn't intend. ▣

Now choose the Save command from the File menu to save all these changes to disk. Then turn your printer on and run your program again, but this time use a real address that you want to print onto labels. The program finally sends the correct output to the printer as planned. It's alive!

Chapter 4

Help!

*A*s you get started with QBasic, you'll notice an important feature that distinguishes it from almost any other software package: it comes with no ponderous and soporific manuals designed to gather dust on your bookshelf.

In fact, there's no printed documentation. At first, you may think this "feature" sounds suspiciously like the *no soggy undercrust* claim for chicken pot pies. Does it mean they've finally found a way to keep the undercrust flaky and light, or have they just poured the pie filling directly into the tin without giving you an undercrust at all?

For QBasic the answer is simple. The undercrust is included, and it's remarkably easy to digest. QBasic's documentation comes in the form of a complete online help system that you can consult at any time during your work on a program. The Help window supplies complete information about all aspects of QBasic: the programming environment, the menu commands, and the language itself. What's more, there are several convenient ways to open the Help window and go directly to the information you need. The online help system is elaborately cross-referenced so that you can move easily from one topic to another to find interrelated information.

The more familiar you are with this important resource, the more efficient you'll be at programming. This chapter surveys the information available to you in the Help window and shows you the quickest ways to get help.

Getting Help with the Menu

QBasic's pull-down menus contain three dozen commands you can use to develop, view, edit, debug, save, and run a program. You've already practiced working with the most important commands. Although the menu commands are generally easy to use and remember, you occasionally may want a quick review of the details. You can rely on the Help window to supply this information when you need it.

Follow these steps to get help with any command in a pull-down menu:

1. Press Alt to activate the menu bar.

2. Press the first letter of the menu you want to pull down.

3. Use the up- or down-arrow key to highlight the command that you need information about.

4. Press F1.

In response, QBasic opens a Help window and displays information about the command you've chosen. When you finish reading the help topic, press Enter to close the window. Press Enter again if you want to carry out the menu command, or press Esc to close the pull-down menu.

You can get help at any time for any command. You can open a Help window even for a command that is dimmed, which means it is currently unavailable. (Some commands are dimmed, or displayed in light gray text, when their use is inappropriate in the context of your current activity.) Just follow the same steps as you would for an undimmed command.

Help with dialog boxes

Menu commands that result in the display of a dialog box are always followed by an ellipsis (...) in a pull-down menu. For example, the New SUB and New FUNCTION commands are listed as follows in the Edit menu:

```
New SUB...
New FUNCTION...
```

Every dialog box contains a Help button. If you want specific information about the options and requirements of a dialog box, you can click the Help button or simply press F1 while the dialog box is active on the screen. The resulting help topic is more detailed than the one you get when you request help directly from a pull-down menu.

It's Greek to Me

No one can remember all the ways to use every keyword in a programming language. Occasionally, you need to look up a statement or function to find out exactly what you're supposed to do.

As you enter lines of code into the View window, you may suddenly find that you can't recall the punctuation required in a statement, the order of arguments needed in a built-in function, or the options available for a particular QBasic structure. In short, you know which keyword you want to use (such as INPUT, PRINT, or DIM), but you need to review the syntax.

QBasic gives you two easy techniques for displaying a help topic on the language:

✔ Type the keyword into the View window and press F1 while the cursor is still located next to the word.

✔ Position the mouse pointer over the keyword and click the right mouse button.

The resulting Help window shows a variety of information about the statement or function you've selected, including the following:

✔ A brief description

✔ A general representation of the syntax

✔ Explanations of arguments and other syntactical elements

✔ Additional information that will help you use the keyword

✔ A short sample program that illustrates the statement or function in action

✔ Cross-references to related statements or functions

To activate the Help window, press Shift-F6. When the window is active, you can use the PgUp and PgDn keys to scroll through the topic.

At the top of the Help window are three help topics, each enclosed in highlighted arrowheads: Contents, Index, and Back. Press C, I, or B to move the cursor to one of these topics, and then press Enter to switch to the selected topic in the Help window. Alternatively, click the Contents, Index, or Back option with the right mouse button.

The Contents option is a list of general help topics that you can select for an overview of QBasic. The Index option is an alphabetized list of QBasic language topics. (You can choose the Contents and Index topics also directly from the Help menu. You learn more about these topics later in this chapter.) The Back option returns you to a previous help topic; QBasic remembers the last twenty help topics you've selected. ■

It's OK to copy

The sample code included in a help topic is designed to illustrate the details of a particular statement or function. You may want to copy the sample code from a help topic to the View window so you can run the code. To do so, you highlight the code, copy it, and then paste it.

Begin by dragging the mouse from the beginning to the end of the code to highlight it. (Or hold down the Shift key while you press the arrow keys to highlight the code.) Then pull down the Edit menu and choose Copy; this action copies the code to the QBasic Clipboard.

Press Esc to close the Help window. When the View window is active, pull down the Edit menu and choose Paste. The sample code appears in the View window. You can now press F5 to run the code.

Cross-references are listed in the See Also section at the bottom of each help topic. To jump to a related topic, click the reference with the right mouse button. If a programming topic includes sample code, you can copy the code to the View window and run it. (See the "Copying code from a help topic" sidebar for details.)

To close a language help topic, press Esc. The View window displays your program just as it was before you requested help.

Check Contents Carefully

The Contents list contains twenty general-interest help topics you can select. To view the Contents list, pull down the Help menu and choose Contents, or select the Contents option at the top of any Help window.

There are two ways to select a topic in the Contents list:

- ✔ From the keyboard, press the key corresponding to the first letter of the topic you want to go to. (If more than one topic begins with the same letter, press the key multiple times until the cursor is displayed over the topic you want.) Then press Enter.
- ✔ Position the mouse pointer over the topic you want to see, and click the right mouse button.

When you take either of these actions, the Help window displays the topic you selected.

The Contents list is divided into four categories of help topics. Here are the highlights of the list:

🡒 The Orientation topics provide introductory information about the QBasic environment: how to get help, how to use menus, commands, and dialog boxes, and how to read the syntax templates that appear in language help topics.

🡒 The Using QBasic topics contain detailed technical information about the language itself, including options, limits, and version differences. One of the most valuable topics in this group is Keywords by Programming Task. This topic gives you an overview of the QBasic language, organized by the kinds of tasks you may want to perform in a program.

🡒 The Keys topics provide lists of shortcut keys in the QBasic environment. You may be particularly interested in the topic named Editing Keys, which shows you a variety of shortcuts you can use in the QBasic editor.

🡒 The Quick Reference topics contain three special code tables (ASCII, keyboard, and error codes) along with the QBasic copyright notices.

The Contents list gives you access to a lot of important reference material. Take a look at this material now so that you know what information is available.

Use the Index

The Index help topic is an alphabetized list of all the keywords in the QBasic language. This list has all the statements (such as FOR, PRINT, and DO), built-in functions (such as INT, MID$, or RND), and operators (such as MOD, AND, and OR), along with additional keywords required in the syntax of QBasic statements. To view the Index, pull down the Help menu and choose the Index command, or click the Index option at the top of an open Help window.

To jump to an Index topic, you can use the keyboard or the mouse:

🡒 From the keyboard, press the key corresponding to the first letter of the keyword you want to select. (If necessary, press the key repeatedly until the cursor appears over the keyword you want.) Then press Enter or F1.

🡒 Use the mouse to scroll through the list of topics. (Click the up or down arrows in the scroll bar at the right side of the Help window, or drag the scroll box up or down in the scroll bar.) When you see the topic you want to select, click it with the right mouse button.

Either way, the Help window immediately displays the topic you selected.

You can display a language help topic also by clicking a keyword in the View window with the right mouse button. This is an easier technique when you've begun entering code. But the Index list is a valuable resource when you want to browse through the keywords available in the language. ▪

Get It in Writing

When you want to print a copy of a help topic, just display the topic in the Help window and choose the Print command from the File menu. The Print dialog box enables you to print the entire contents of the current Help window or a portion of the window that you select. (To print a selection, use the mouse or the keyboard to highlight the information you want to print before you choose the Print command.) Press Enter, and QBasic sends the help topic to your printer.

Your printer may be unable to print some characters that appear in the Help window. such as underline characters, arrowheads, or bullets. These may appear as strings of unusual characters in the resulting printout. To avoid this, select only the *text* that you want to print and then choose the Print command from the File menu. In the Print dialog box, the Selected Text Only option will be selected. Press Enter to proceed with the printing. ▪

You may want to print a small collection of the language topics you use most often. For example, you might print the Help windows for built-in functions you have a difficult time remembering or for commands that frequently give you trouble.

Part II
Using a New Language: Input and Output

In This Part...

*N*ow you're ready to turn your attention to the QBasic programming language. In this part, you learn how a program orchestrates a dialog. You've already seen the typical pattern. A program displays a prompt on the screen, asking for a particular item of data. The user types the information at the keyboard and presses the Enter key. In response, the program performs a calculation or reorganizes the input data in some way, and then displays the output on the screen.

QBasic gives you a variety of tools for planning this kind of dialog, and for working with the data that a program receives as input. To illustrate these features, Part II presents a group of programs designed to help you keep track of travel expenses during business trips. *Bon voyage!*

Chapter 5
Can We Talk?

*I*nput is any information a program receives from an outside source. One of your important jobs as a programmer is to plan ways for your program to receive input. In an *interactive* program, the data often comes from the keyboard or, to be more precise, from the person sitting at the keyboard with fingers poised over the keys. This person is known affectionately as the *user*.

Sometimes, the user may be someone you know rather well: *you*. If your goal is to use QBasic to build software tools for your own work, you are both the programmer and the user. In this case, designing a program can be easy. You know what you want the program to do, and you know how you want to provide the data for the program to work with.

But you may eventually find yourself programming for someone else: a colleague, a family member, or — gulp — someone who has actually agreed to pay you for your work. Here the job takes on a different quality, with new responsibilities and pressures. Suddenly you need to consider how another user will interact with the program you build. In particular, you must think carefully about the problems of getting input from the user:

✔ What types of information must the user supply? For example, will items be entered as text, numbers, or dates?

✔ How should your program ask the user for each item of information? Is a simple question — or even a single word — sufficient as an input prompt, or should your program provide a detailed explanation of the input requirements?

✔ What are the easiest and most reliable ways to respond from the keyboard? In some situations, a single keystroke may be the best way for a user to answer a question. Other times, the user needs to supply more information, such as a line of text or a number; in this case, pressing the Enter key completes the input.

✔ What happens when the user makes a mistake while entering data? For example, what happens if the user enters a word when the program is expecting a number?

✔ How will the user select options that your program offers? Will the user enter a number corresponding to an option in a list, or will your program provide some other way of expressing a choice?

These problems take time to solve and can require many adjustments in your code to simplify and clarify the data-entry process.

QBasic's main tool for getting information from the user is the INPUT statement. In this chapter, you learn how this statement works and what options it provides. Along the way, you develop a new project called the Travel Expense Log program, which records expenses during an international business trip. This program has several examples of INPUT and also illustrates other QBasic tools for accepting responses from the keyboard. Using a variety of techniques, the program successfully gets all the information it needs from the user and smoothly allows for small but important variations in the data entry process.

Having a Dialog

The Expense Log program elicits several items of information about a given travel expense, and then saves all the information to disk as a single expense record. The user supplies the following items:

✔ The date of the expense

✔ The location (that is, the place where the money was spent)

✔ A description of the expense

✔ The amount spent in local currency

✔ The exchange rate on the day of the expenditure

For each of these items, the program displays on the screen an input prompt (a line of text that tells the user what to enter) and waits for an appropriate response. When the user types a data item and presses the Enter key, the program displays the prompt for the next item.

For example, suppose that you're nearing the end of a four-day business trip to
Paris, where you've been meeting with clients. You stayed at a pricey but
conveniently located Left Bank hotel, and you've just paid the bill. The following
dialog shows how you might enter your hotel expense record:

```
Expense Log
------- ---

Date (Enter for today): 12-07-1993
Location:      Paris
Description:   l'Hotel du Jardin, four nights
Amount spent:  3480
Exchange rate: 5.75

Save this record? Y
Another expense?  Y
```

Your input responses are shown here in bold. The program displays a total of
seven input prompts on the screen: five for specific data items and two for
issuing instructions to the program itself. The expense record consists of a
date, two text entries, and two numbers. The final two keystrokes instruct the
program to save the record to disk and then restart the dialog for another
expense record entry.

Keep your options open

Short as it is, the preceding dialog requires precise programming. As you write
the code that elicits and receives the expense data, you need to think carefully
about the details of the input process. How do you like to enter data? What are
your quibbles with other programs? Whether the user will be you or someone
else, the success of the program depends on the design and reliability of the
input dialog.

Consider the first input item, the date of the expense. Some business travelers
may want to record expense information contemporaneously, that is, on the
day the money is spent. In this case, it would be a bother to have to enter the
current date for each new record; instead, the program should be able to
provide this information automatically. But another user may not get around to
entering expense records until several days have passed. This user needs the
option of entering the date of a given expense.

The Expense Log program allows for these two possibilities in a simple way.
The date prompt appears on the screen as follows:

```
Date (Enter for today):
```

To enter today's date, the user simply presses the Enter key. In response, the program displays the date on the screen and, more importantly, records the date in the expense record.

Alternatively, to enter a date other than today's date, the user types the date directly from the keyboard and then presses Enter. As you see shortly, these two techniques for entering the date are made possible by a special format of the QBasic INPUT statement.

Other data items in the input dialog have their own contingencies. For example, the text entered for the Location and Description fields may include punctuation such as quotation marks and commas:

```
Description:   l'Hotel du Jardin, four nights
```

In some contexts, QBasic reads this kind of punctuation as a separator between two input items on the same line. But in this program, you must make sure that the entire line is accepted as a single input item, regardless of any punctuation the user may include in the text. Again, you do this with a special form of the INPUT statement.

Numeric entries have their own particular dangers. Suppose that the user types a nonnumeric response when the program is expecting a number, as follows:

```
Amount spent:   Ten Francs
```

In some programming environments, this error might be catastrophic. The program could stop dead in its tracks, and the user could lose any data entered up to that point. But the QBasic INPUT statement handles this situation more gracefully. If the user enters information that doesn't work in the context of the current program, QBasic simply displays the message Redo from start and gives the user another chance to provide the correct input:

```
Amount spent:   Ten Francs

Redo from start
Amount spent:   10
```

What say you?

Finally, the Expense Log program asks two questions that require only yes-or-no answers. The user's responses determine how the program proceeds. The first question gives the user the chance to pause and look back at the dialog for a particular expense record:

```
Save this record?
```

If everything in the expense record is correct, the user can go ahead and save the record to disk. But if there is an error in the input, this prompt gives the user the opportunity to abandon the record and reenter it correctly.

To issue instructions to the program at this point, the user presses only Y for yes or N for no. One keystroke is sufficient in this case; the user does not press Enter to complete the answer.

The Expense Log program conducts a repeating dialog so that the user can enter as many records as necessary during a given run of the program. Accordingly, when the user completes one record entry, the program needs to know whether there are more expenses to receive:

```
Another expense?
```

Again, the user simply presses Y to continue or N to quit the program. In response to Y, the program clears the screen and starts all over again. When the user eventually presses N, the program is over.

In summary, a well-designed program hides the complexities of data input, enabling the user to concentrate on the information itself rather than the details of data storage. When you design an interactive program, you therefore have two goals to meet:

- ✔ Provide the program with accurate data
- ✔ Give the user a simple and convenient way to enter the data

QBasic gives you some good tools for meeting both these goals.

Code it

Take a first look at the listing of the Travel Expense Log program now. It contains two procedures, plus the main module:

```
' Travel Expense Log (EXPLOG.BAS)
' Records expenses during
' a business trip.

DECLARE SUB GetExpenseRec ()
DECLARE FUNCTION YesOrNo$ (question$)

' Open expense log file.
OPEN "\EXPLOG.TXT" FOR APPEND AS #1

' Read expense records from keyboard.
DO
  GetExpenseRec
LOOP UNTIL YesOrNo$("Another expense?  ") = "N"

END  ' EXPLOG.BAS
```

(continued)

```
SUB GetExpenseRec

  ' Reads one expense record from the keyboard.

  CLS
  PRINT "Expense Log"
  PRINT "------- ---"
  PRINT

  ' Accept the user's date input or
  ' supply today's date as the default.
  INPUT ; "Date (Enter for today): ", expDate$
  IF LTRIM$(expDate$) = "" THEN
    PRINT DATE$
    expDate$ = DATE$
  ELSE
    PRINT
  END IF

  ' Get the remaining fields.
  LINE INPUT "Location:      "; city$
  LINE INPUT "Description:   "; descript$
  INPUT "Amount spent:  ", amount
  INPUT "Exchange rate: ", rate

  ' Save the record to the expense file.
  PRINT
  IF YesOrNo("Save this record? ") = "Y" THEN
    WRITE #1, expDate$, city$, descript$, amount, rate
  END IF

END SUB   ' GetExpenseRec


FUNCTION YesOrNo$ (question$)

  ' Display a question and wait
  ' for the user to type Y or N.

  PRINT question$;
  DO
    answer$ = UCASE$(INKEY$)
  LOOP UNTIL answer$ = "Y" OR answer$ = "N"
  PRINT answer$

  YesOrNo$ = answer$

END FUNCTION   ' YesOrNo$
```

The main module begins by opening a data file named EXPLOG.TXT in the root directory of your hard disk. If the file doesn't exist, the program creates it. If it does exist, the program prepares to add new expense records to it. Then the program makes repeated calls to a procedure named GetExpenseRec. This procedure conducts the input dialog for each expense record.

Looking through the listing of the GetExpenseRec procedure, you can see an input statement for each of the five data items that make up an expense record: date, location, description, amount spent, and exchange rate. Calls to this procedure continue until the user presses N in response to the question `Another expense?` The program's second procedure, a function named YesOrNo$, is in charge of displaying a yes-or-no question on the screen and accepting the user's one-key response. You focus on both of these procedures in later sections of this chapter.

Getting INPUT

The INPUT statement has two jobs:

 ✔ It displays a prompt on the screen explaining what information the program is expecting to receive, and then waits for the user's response.

 ✔ As soon as the user types the information and presses the Enter key, INPUT stores the information in the computer's memory, where the program can conveniently gain access to it.

When you write an INPUT statement, you write the prompt that will appear on the screen and define a variable to represent the data entered from the keyboard. In one typical form of the statement, you enclose the input prompt in quotes, and use a comma to separate the prompt from the variable:

```
INPUT "Input prompt ", inputVar
```

Notice that the comma separating the prompt from the input variable is *outside* the quotation marks. ■

Here's an example from the Expense Log program:

```
INPUT "Amount spent:   ", amount
```

You've seen that `Amount spent:` appears on the screen when the program is ready for this input item; `amount` is the variable that represents the number the user enters.

What's in a name?

As you first learned in Chapter 3, a variable is a name you devise to represent information in a program. It's generally a good idea to create variable names that clearly identify the data they represent; this practice makes your program easier to understand. For example, here are the five variables used in the Expense Log program to represent the data entered for a particular expense record:

expDate$	Date of the expense
city$	Location of the expense
descript$	Description
amount	Amount spent
rate	Exchange rate on the day of the expense

After the INPUT statements are performed, the program uses expDate$, city$, descript$, amount, and rate to represent the information that the user has entered from the keyboard.

The data stored in these five variables changes each time the user enters a new expense record. But the *type* of data that each variable can store does not change. The amount and rate variables always represent numbers; expDate$, city$, and descript$ always represent text entries, commonly known as *strings* in QBasic.

One simple way to define the type of information a variable will store is to add a special character to the end of the variable name. The dollar sign ($) designates a string variable; a name that contains no special character at the end represents a numeric value. (You learn a lot more about variables and data types in Chapter 7.) ▪

How does INPUT determine what type of data should be received from the keyboard? The input data must match the type of the variable you include in the statement. For the expDate$, city$, and descript$ variables, the program accepts the input as text. For amount and rate, INPUT expects to receive numeric values from the keyboard. You've seen what happens when there's a discrepancy between the data expected and the data received: INPUT displays the Redo from start error message, and then repeats the input prompt for another try.

Proper names and nicknames

QBasic doesn't care what names you choose for your variables, as long as you follow a few simple rules for the format of names. A variable name must begin with a letter and may consist of letters, digits, and periods.

Keyboard-averse programmers sometimes opt for the shortest variable names possible. For example, a programmer who hates to type might replace the five input variables of the Expense Log program with one-letter names: *e$, c$, d$, a,* and *r.* But a program containing these abbreviated variable names is more difficult to understand — and debug — than one that uses more meaningful names.

Subtle Input

You can vary the way INPUT works by changing the punctuation in the statement. This is one of those times when you must watch carefully for details in your code; tiny differences in punctuation can produce significant changes in your program's behavior.

One of the options you can control is the way INPUT displays a prompt on the screen. In the Expense Log program, prompts appear exactly as they are supplied in the INPUT statements. For example, the following statement elicits the current exchange rate from the user:

```
INPUT "Exchange rate: ", rate
```

When QBasic gets to this statement, the prompt is displayed on the screen as follows:

```
Exchange rate: _
```

A cursor appears just after the prompt, but INPUT supplies no punctuation other than what you place between quotation marks in the statement itself.

Sometimes you might want your prompt to end in a question mark. In this case, you can let INPUT modify your prompt a little. By placing a semicolon rather than a comma after the prompt string in the INPUT statement, you instruct QBasic to supply a question mark and a space at the end of the prompt. For example, here is a variation of the exchange rate input prompt:

```
INPUT "Exchange rate"; rate
```

This statement displays the input prompt as follows:

```
Exchange rate? _
```

The prompt string in the INPUT statement contains no ending punctuation, but the prompt appears on the screen with a question mark and a space before the cursor.

Guard against a confusing combination of your punctuation and QBasic's. For example, you wouldn't want to write the INPUT statement like this:

```
INPUT "Exchange rate: "; rate
```

This statement produces the following awkward prompt:

```
Exchange rate: ? _
```

If you supply punctuation inside the input prompt, follow the prompt with a comma rather than a semicolon in the INPUT statement. ▪

Multiple inputs

You can use a single INPUT statement to ask the user to enter multiple input values on a single line. To do so, you change the statement in two ways:

✔ Write an input prompt that clearly tells the user the number and type of input values your program is expecting.

✔ In the INPUT statement, include a list of variables — one for each input value.

For example, suppose that you want the user to enter a description of an expense item followed immediately by the amount of the expense. You could write the INPUT statement like this:

```
INPUT "Description, amount: ", descript$, amount
```

With this statement, QBasic displays the prompt on the screen and then waits for the user to enter *two* input items: a text description of an expense, followed by the amount of the expense. On the input line, the user must separate the two data items with a comma:

```
Description, amount: Taxi to airport, 285
```

You might think that this arrangement simplifies your program, but the reverse is true. Multiple input values on a single line make your program more confusing to the user and increase the likelihood of input errors. For example, the user might enter incorrect data types for one or more items or forget to enter a comma between individual data items. It's usually better to write a separate INPUT statement for each input value that your program needs.

The preceding variation alerts you to another important characteristic of the INPUT statement. When a line of input contains a comma, INPUT reads that punctuation as a separator between two input values. An INPUT statement that is prepared to read only one input value displays the `Redo from start` message if the input line contains a comma.

For example, suppose that a program contains the following statement:

```
INPUT "Enter your full name: ", fullName$
```

You run the program, and the prompt appears on the screen:

```
Enter your full name: _
```

If you enter a name without commas, the statement works just fine:

```
Enter your full name: Sally J. Smith
```

INPUT accepts the full string as the value of the `fullName$` string variable. But suppose you instead enter a name in the *last name, first name* format:

```
Enter your full name: Smith, Sally J.
```

In this case, QBasic reads the input line as two separate string values: `Smith` and `Sally J`. Because the INPUT statement contains only one variable, it can't accept this input and instead displays the `Redo from start` message on the screen.

If you are expecting the user to enter a string that may contain commas as part of the input text, you can solve this problem by using the LINE INPUT command, which is described next.

Successful one-liners

The LINE INPUT command reads an entire input line as a single data entry, regardless of any punctuation that the input contains. Except for the keyword LINE, the syntax is similar to the INPUT statement:

```
LINE INPUT "Input prompt: "; inputVar$
```

Notice that the input variable must be a string type variable in this case. You can't use LINE INPUT to receive numeric data from the keyboard. In addition, LINE INPUT never adds a question mark to the end of the prompt. You can use either a semicolon or a comma to separate the prompt from the input variable; the prompt on the screen remains the same.

For example, here are the two LINE INPUT statements that elicit the location and description of a travel expense item:

```
LINE INPUT "Location:      "; city$
LINE INPUT "Description:   "; descript$
```

These statements enable the user to use any kind of punctuation in the input string:

```
Location:      Paris, France
Description:   l'Hotel du Jardin, four nights
```

The program successfully assigns these two lines of text to the city$ and descript$ variables, respectively.

Give me a default value

The date input in the Expense Log program illustrates a neat trick you can perform with the INPUT statement. As you might recall, the date input works as follows. If you want to enter today's date, you simply press the Enter key, and the program provides the date automatically. If you want to enter a date other than today's date, you type the date from the keyboard and press Enter.

Actually, INPUT's role in this trick is small. A variation in the statement's syntax enables you to keep the cursor on the same line as the input after the user completes a data entry. To make this happen, you include a semicolon between INPUT and the prompt string:

```
INPUT ; "Input prompt ", inputVar
```

For example, here is how the Expense Log program elicits the date:

```
INPUT ; "Date (Enter for today): ", expDate$
```

This statement displays the expected prompt on the string, and waits for the user's input:

```
Date (Enter for today): _
```

The user either presses Enter or types a date and then presses Enter. Thanks to the semicolon after the INPUT keyword, the cursor remains on the input line when the entry is complete.

After the user's action, the program takes a look at the value of the `expDate$` input variable. If the variable is empty — that is, the user entered nothing from the keyboard — the program displays today's date on the input line. Otherwise, the program skips to the next line and continues with the next input line. This action is carried out by a decision statement:

```
INPUT ; "Date (Enter for today): ", expDate$
IF LTRIM$(expDate$) = "" THEN
  PRINT DATE$
  expDate$ = DATE$
ELSE
  PRINT
END IF
```

You don't need to figure out this code yet (although you may find it intuitive if you take a brief look). The main thing to understand is that this format of the INPUT statement allows your program to control the input line *after* the user has completed the input. The Expense Log program uses this opportunity to supply today's date as the *default* input value in the event that the user does not supply a different date.

On Key

All the forms of the INPUT and LINE INPUT statements have one interesting feature in common: they require the user to press the Enter key to complete the input. In other words, Enter becomes the user's way of signaling that the current input is complete. This is a reasonable approach whenever the user is asked to enter strings of text or numbers.

But when a program offers a user simple options — yes-or-no alternatives or menu choices, for example — it may be more convenient to express those choices as single-key responses. You've seen an example in the two yes-or-no questions posed by the Expense Log program:

```
Save this record? Y
Another expense?  Y
```

After the user has completed an expense record, these two questions provide a quick way to make decisions about what to do next. Because the user doesn't have to press Enter after each response, the process is streamlined.

The QBasic tool that allows this type of single-key input is a function rather than a statement. Its name is INKEY$. This function reads a single character from the keyboard, if a key has been pressed. If no key has been pressed, INKEY$ returns an *empty* string, that is, a string that contains no characters.

To use INKEY$ effectively, you generally put it in a loop that makes repeated calls to the function until a particular response is received from the keyboard. In the Expense Log program, this operation takes place in the YesOrNo$ function:

```
PRINT question$;
DO
   answer$ = UCASE$(INKEY$)
LOOP UNTIL answer$ = "Y" OR answer$ = "N"
PRINT answer$
```

You don't have to try to understand this code yet in its entirety. But here is an outline of how the code works:

1. The program displays an input prompt (represented by the string variable `question$`) on the screen.

2. A DO loop makes repeated calls to the INKEY$ function until the user presses either the Y key or the N key. (Before examining the value returned by INKEY$, the program uses the UCASE$ function to convert the value to an uppercase letter.)

3. The program displays the user's one-character response on the screen, just to the right of the input prompt.

As you learn more about the features of QBasic — loops, built-in functions, and output statements — you'll see many versatile uses for the INKEY$ function. For now, just remember that it provides a different mode of input than the INPUT statement.

Chapter 6

Here It Is

*O*utput is the information a program provides to the user. Output can be sent to a variety of devices attached to your computer, such as the display screen, the printer, a disk, or even sound speakers. QBasic programs supply information in various forms, including text, tables of numbers, charts, graphs, pictures, or sound.

From the user's point of view, the output *is* the program. The essence of a program is the information it provides. In this sense, the goal of programming is to separate the process from the result: A user doesn't care, or shouldn't have to care, about the detailed steps involved in creating output. Only the result matters.

Given the importance of a program's output, you'll want to master the QBasic tools that give information to the user. This chapter focuses on statements that display text and numeric output on the screen (PRINT and PRINT USING) and send output to the printer (LPRINT and LPRINT USING). To demonstrate these tools in action, the chapter presents a new project called the Travel Expense Table program. You can think of this project as Part Two of the Travel Expense Log program presented in Chapter 5.

As you recall, the Expense Log program conducts an input dialog, accepting expense records from the keyboard and saving the records in an expense data file on disk. By contrast, the Expense Table program performs an output operation. It opens that expense data file, reads the information the file contains, and produces a data table on the screen. (At the end of this chapter, you learn how to revise the program to send the output to the printer instead of the screen.)

Like the INPUT statement, PRINT requires you to pay careful attention to details. As you learn how to use output statements, you'll once again find yourself struggling over minute and cryptic syntactical options such as commas, semicolons, and other special characters. PRINT is almost like a language in itself—an output language. Master the PRINT statement and you can produce exactly the results you want in a program's output.

Table It

The Expense Table program begins by opening the data file named EXPLOG.TXT, which was originally created by the Expense Log program and stored in the root directory of your hard disk. If you want to examine this file, you can display its contents on your screen by loading it into a text editor such as EDIT or by simply entering the following command from the DOS prompt:

```
TYPE \EXPLOG.TXT
```

When you do so, you see all the expense records you've recorded in the file. For example, suppose you've entered a dozen or so records from a recent business trip to France; your file might look like Figure 6-1.

```
"11-30-1993","Paris","l'Hotel du Pont, two nights",2480,5.8
"11-30-1993","Paris","Lunch with G. Lepoint, Chez Agnes",680,5.8
"11-30-1993","Paris","Taxi to airport",240,5.8
"11-30-1993","Strasbourg","Dinner with C. Muller, Cafe Berthe",680,5.8
"12-01-1993","Strasbourg","l'Hotel Central, one night",750,5.85
"12-01-1993","Strasbourg","Miscellaneous supplies",665,5.85
"12-02-1993","Caen","Conference room, l'Hotel du Chateau",1750,5.85
"12-03-1993","Caen","l'Hotel de la Gare, one night",850,5.85
"12-04-1993","Paris","Car rental",1850,5.85
"12-05-1993","Chartres","Lunch meeting with M. Lenoir",455,5.8
"12-06-1993","Chartres","Grand Hotel, one night",825,5.75
"12-07-1993","Paris","Books and supplies",585,5.7
"12-07-1993","Paris","l'Hotel du Jardin, four nights",3480,5.7
```

Figure 6-1: Contents of the EXPLOG.TXT file.

The information is not easy to read in this format. All the same, you can recognize each line in the file as a single expense record, entered from the keyboard during a run of the Expense Log program. A given line contains five items of information: the date of an expense, the location, a description, the amount, and the exchange rate on the day of the expense.

The job of the Expense Table program is to read this file from the root directory and display its information on the screen in a useful and coherent way. (Of course, you shouldn't try to run this chapter's program until you've created the file by running the Expense Log program from Chapter 5.) The program accomplishes the following tasks:

✔ *Organizes the information in table format.* Each "field" of data appears in its own column in the table. The columns must be spaced in an orderly way, and the information in each column should be aligned appropriately (left alignment for text, and right alignment for numbers).

✔ *Displays a title and column headings.* The title and column heads identify the information that the table contains.

✔ *Performs calculations from the raw data.* For example, the program computes the dollar equivalent of each expense amount and displays this calculated field in a separate column.

✔ *Displays numeric values in readable formats.* For example, the dollar amounts appear in dollar-and-cent format, such as $2,641.10 rather than 2641.10.

✔ *Summarizes the data.* The program keeps a running total of all the dollar expense amounts, and displays the grand total at the bottom of the table.

To accomplish these tasks, the program reads the expense log file record-by-record and displays each record on the screen in a consistent format. Figure 6-2 is the program's output for the EXPLOG.TXT example shown previously.

```
                           Travel Expense Log
                           ====== ======= ===

       City          Date         Amount   Dollars  Description
       ----          ----         ------   -------   -----------
       Paris         11-30-1993    2480    $427.59   l'Hotel du Pont, two nights
       Paris         11-30-1993     680    $117.24   Lunch with G. Lepoint, Chez Agnes
       Paris         11-30-1993     240     $41.38   Taxi to airport
       Strasbourg    11-30-1993     680    $117.24   Dinner with C. Muller, Cafe Berthe
       Strasbourg    12-01-1993     750    $128.21   l'Hotel Central, one night
       Strasbourg    12-01-1993     665    $113.68   Miscellaneous supplies
       Caen          12-02-1993    1750    $299.15   Conference room, l'Hotel du Chateau
       Caen          12-03-1993     850    $145.30   l'Hotel de la Gare, one night
       Paris         12-04-1993    1850    $316.24   Car rental
       Chartres      12-05-1993     455     $78.45   Lunch meeting with M. Lenoir
       Chartres      12-06-1993     825    $143.48   Grand Hotel, one night
       Paris         12-07-1993     585    $102.63   Books and supplies
       Paris         12-07-1993    3480    $610.53   l'Hotel du Jardin, four nights

       Total in dollars .....              $2,641.10
```

Figure 6-2: Output from the Expense Table program.

Examining this output, you can see several important changes that the program has made in the presentation of data. The columns of information in the table are in a different order than the data in the file. The exchange rate field is missing, and is replaced by a column of more relevant information, the dollar equivalent of each expense amount. The program provides a title centered over the table and column headings aligned correctly with the data beneath them. And at the bottom of the table you see the total of the dollar expense amounts, a simple but important summary of the data.

Details like these do not happen by accident. When you write a program that produces an output table, you're in charge of making sure each part of the table looks exactly the way it should. The tools for accomplishing this are the various PRINT statements you examine in this chapter.

Code It

Take a first look at the listing of the Travel Expense Table program now:

```
' Travel Expense Table (EXPTABLE.BAS)
' Displays a table of travel
' expenses with totals.

DECLARE SUB ShowExpenseRec ()
DECLARE SUB ShowTotals ()
DECLARE SUB ShowHeadings ()

DIM SHARED totDollars

' Open the expense log file.
OPEN "\EXPLOG.TXT" FOR INPUT AS #1
totDollars = 0

' Read expense records from the file
' and show them on the screen.

ShowHeadings
DO WHILE NOT EOF(1)
  ShowExpenseRec
LOOP

ShowTotals  ' Show total expenses.

END  ' EXPTABLE.BAS



SUB ShowExpenseRec

  ' Read and display one expense record.

  INPUT #1, expDate$, city$, descript$, amount, rate
  PRINT city$, expDate$,
  PRINT USING "####"; amount;

  ' Calculate and display the dollar amount.
  PRINT USING "$$#,###.##"; amount / rate;
  PRINT "  "; descript$
```

```
    ' Accumulate the total in dollars.
    totDollars = totDollars + amount / rate

END SUB   ' ShowExpenseRec



SUB ShowHeadings

  ' Display a title.
  CLS
  PRINT TAB(25); "Travel Expense Log"
  PRINT TAB(25); "====== ======= ==="
  PRINT

  ' Display the column headings.
  PRINT "City", "Date";
  PRINT TAB(27); "Amount    "; "Dollars  "; "Description"
  PRINT "----", "----";
  PRINT TAB(27); "------    "; "-------  "; "-----------"

END SUB   ' ShowHeadings



SUB ShowTotals

  ' Show the total in dollars.

  PRINT
  PRINT "Total in dollars ....."; TAB(32);
  PRINT USING "$$##,###.##"; totDollars

END SUB   ' ShowTotals
```

The program's action is simple. After opening the expense file, the main module makes calls to the program's three procedures. The ShowHeadings procedure displays the title and column headings on the screen. ShowExpenseRec displays one expense record on the screen each time it's called. ShowTotals displays the calculated total expense amount at the bottom of the table.

Looking through the listing, you can see many examples of PRINT and PRINT USING. Both of these statements are designed to display on the screen individual data items or several items in a row. Whereas PRINT sends information to the screen without any special changes in appearance, PRINT USING lets you apply custom formats to your output data. For example, the Expense Table program uses PRINT USING to display two columns of numbers on the screen: the original expense amounts and their dollar equivalents. You see how this works as you look at the program in more detail.

Even Kids Can Print

In one of its simplest forms, PRINT displays a single data item on the screen, as follows:

```
PRINT dataItem
```

In this statement, *dataItem* can appear in a variety of forms:

- ✔ As a *literal string value,* that is, a sequence of characters enclosed in quotation marks. For example, the following statement displays a two-word string:

  ```
  PRINT "Business Itinerary"
  ```

- ✔ As a *literal numeric value,* for example:

  ```
  PRINT 2001
  ```

- ✔ As a *variable.* In this case, the PRINT statement displays the variable's current value. For example, the following statement displays the value of the variable totValue:

  ```
  PRINT totValue
  ```

- ✔ As an *arithmetic expression* using operations such as addition, subtraction, multiplication, and division. QBasic performs the calculation, and then PRINT displays the result. For example, the following statement displays the result of dividing amount by rate:

  ```
  PRINT amount / rate
  ```

Each of these PRINT statements displays a data item on the screen and automatically performs a *carriage return* and *line feed.* These archaic terms come from manual typewriter operations: A carriage return moves the roller to the left so you can begin typing at the beginning of a line; a line feed advances the paper up so you can start typing a new line of text. On the computer, the carriage-return and line-feed operations simply move the cursor to the beginning of the next screen line. As a result, the *next* PRINT statement displays its information on a new line.

When you write several PRINT statements in sequence, the output appears on separate lines of the screen. For example, these statements:

```
PRINT "Tourist stops:"
PRINT
PRINT "The Eiffel Tower"
PRINT "The Cathedral of Notre Dame"
PRINT "The Louvre Museum"
```

produce the following output:

```
Tourist Stops:

The Eiffel Tower
The Cathedral of Notre Dame
The Louvre Museum
```

Each PRINT statement produces one line of output. Notice that the PRINT statement by itself, with no output value, creates a blank line.

Printing values

You can use PRINT also to display two or more values as a single line of output on the screen. To do so, you separate the data items by semicolons in the PRINT statement, as follows:

```
PRINT dataItem1; dataItem2; dataItem3
```

Again, each data item can appear in any acceptable form: a literal string in quotation marks, a literal numeric value, a variable, or an expression. For example, the following statement displays two strings and the value of a numeric variable, all on one line:

```
PRINT "Today's exchange rate is"; rate; "francs to the dollar."
```

Suppose the variable `rate` contains the value 5.75. The resulting line of output is

```
Today's exchange rate is 5.75 francs to the dollar.
```

In general, a semicolon between PRINT items instructs QBasic to display the items side-by-side on the screen. But PRINT conveniently inserts a space before and after a numeric value, as you can see in the preceding example. In a statement that displays two strings on the screen, you must supply a space if you want one. Here's an example:

```
PRINT city$; " "; country$
```

If the `city$` string variable contains the value "Strasbourg" and `country$` contains "France", the preceding statement would display its output as

```
Strasbourg France
```

Here the space between the two words is supplied as a literal string (" ") in the PRINT statement. Without this, the two words would appear on the screen side-by-side without any spacing. For example, the following statement:

```
PRINT city$; country$
```

results in

```
StrasbourgFrance
```

You can use a semicolon at the end of a PRINT statement to suppress the usual carriage-return and line-feed operation. You might do this if you want to display on the same line the information from several PRINT statements. For example:

```
PRINT "In "; country$;
PRINT " the exchange rate is";
PRINT rate; currency$;
PRINT "s to the dollar."
```

Suppose that `country$` contains the string "France", `rate` contains 5.75, and `currency$` contains "franc". These four PRINT statements result in the following line of output on the screen:

```
In France the exchange rate is 5.75 francs to the dollar.
```

As you can see, the ending semicolon is a useful feature when you want to use several PRINT statements to build a single line of output text.

You are now entering the print zone

To display information on the screen in table form (in columns and rows of numbers and text), you must place items at designated positions across the width of the screen. One way to do this is to use a comma rather than a semicolon to separate data items in a PRINT statement. The comma instructs QBasic to advance across the screen to the beginning of the next *print zone* before displaying the next data item:

```
PRINT dataItem1, dataItem2, dataItem3
```

QBasic print zones are 14 characters wide. There are five print zones across the screen, beginning at character positions 1, 15, 29, 33, and 47. Here's a simple way to explore this feature:

```
PRINT 1, 2, 3, 4, 5
PRINT 6, 7, 8, 9, 10
PRINT 11, 12, 13, 14, 15
PRINT 16, 17, 18, 19, 20
```

These lines produce a table of numbers across the screen, as follows:

```
1               2               3               4               5
6               7               8               9               10
11              12              13              14              15
16              17              18              19              20
```

Each PRINT statement displays one number in each print zone. The numbers in a given zone automatically form a column on the screen.

The Expense Table program uses print zones to create the first two columns of its output table — the columns for the city and date of a given expense. The following line is in the ShowExpenseRec procedure:

```
PRINT city$, expDate$,
```

The city appears at the beginning of the line for each expense record; then the date appears at the beginning of the next print zone. (The comma at the end of this PRINT statement instructs QBasic to advance by another print zone for the data that comes next.) Here is a sample of the output produced by this statement:

```
Paris          11-30-1993
Paris          11-30-1993
Strasbourg     11-30-1993
Strasbourg     12-01-1993
Strasbourg     12-01-1993
Caen           12-02-1993
Caen           12-03-1993
Paris          12-04-1993
```

Tab It

Sometimes print zones are not ideal for the columns in a table. In this case, you can use the QBasic built-in TAB function to create columns of data. A tab is simply a horizontal screen position identified by a number; you create columns by aligning multiple data items at the same tab stops. (Once again, *tab* is a term from typewriter days.)

TAB instructs QBasic to advance to a specified horizontal position across the screen:

```
PRINT TAB(colNum); dataItem
```

The *dataItem* is displayed at the horizontal screen position identified as *colNum*.

The Expense Table program uses TAB in a variety of ways. First the ShowHeadings procedure centers the title horizontally across the screen by displaying it at tab position 25, as follows:

```
PRINT TAB(25); "Travel Expense Log"
PRINT TAB(25); "====== ======= ==="
```

The strings of equal signs (=) produce a double-underline effect to highlight the title. ShowHeadings uses TAB two more times to orient the column headings properly, as follows:

```
PRINT "City", "Date";
PRINT TAB(27); "Amount    "; "Dollars   "; "Description"
PRINT "----", "----";
PRINT TAB(27); "------    "; "-------   "; "-----------"
```

The first two PRINT statements display the line of column headings; the second two PRINT statements display strings of hyphens to underline the headings. As this passage shows, you may sometimes end up using a combination of different PRINT features to display information just where you want it on the screen. The City and Date headings appear in the first two print zones across the screen, but the remaining headings are positioned at a tab stop.

The TAB function can appear in other positions in a PRINT statement. For example, the ShowTotals procedure contains the following statement:

```
PRINT "Total in dollars ....."; TAB(32);
```

This statement displays text that identifies the information on the bottom line of the table, and then tabs to position 32 on the screen. A semicolon at the end of the line prevents a carriage-return and line-feed operation. The *next* PRINT statement in the procedure displays the total expense amount at the tab position.

TIP

Start with a clean slate

You may be wondering how the Expense Table program manages to begin its output at the top of the screen. What happens if information is on the output screen when the program begins?

When you want your program's output to appear as the only information on the output screen, you start by clearing the screen of existing information. QBasic supplies a simple tool for doing this: the CLS statement, which stands for *clear screen*.

For example, here's how the ShowHeadings procedure displays the title at the top of the screen:

```
CLS
PRINT TAB(25); "Travel Expense Log"
PRINT TAB(25); "====== ======= ==="
PRINT
```

After clearing the output screen, CLS positions the text cursor at the upper-left corner of the screen. The first two PRINT statements create the title and the underlining. The third PRINT creates a blank line between the title and the column headings.

Getting Numbers in Shape

In a program that displays numeric output, you often need precise control over the format of individual numbers on the screen. For example, you may want to be able to specify some of the following characteristics:

- The number of digits appearing after the decimal point
- The alignment of numbers in a column
- The use of commas to separate every three digits located before the decimal point
- The appearance of a dollar sign in a number that represents a dollar-and-cent amount

The PRINT USING statement gives you a simple way to handle all these details by creating a special format string to represent the appearance of your numeric output. For example, in the following syntax, the format string controls the output of a single data item:

```
PRINT USING "formatString"; dataItem
```

You supply the format string in quotation marks at the beginning of the PRINT USING statement. The string is followed by a semicolon and then the data item to format. As always, the data can be represented as a literal value, a variable, or an expression.

The format string consists of a variety of special characters that QBasic recognizes for specific formatting effects. Here are the characters used in the Expense Table program to format the columns of numeric data:

#	Represents a placeholder for a single digit
.	Indicates the position of the decimal point
,	Inserts a comma at every third position before the decimal
$$	Provides a "floating" dollar sign at the beginning of a number

For example, the following statements from the ShowExpenseRec procedure display the original expense amount and the dollar equivalent calculated from each expense record:

```
PRINT USING "####"; amount;
PRINT USING "$$#,###.##"; amount / rate;
```

Study these statements carefully. The first format string contains placeholders for four digits, "####"; the main effect of this format is to right-align the original expense amounts in a column. The second format string is more detailed. It not only contains placeholders, but also indicates the position of the decimal point (with two digits after the decimal), the use of commas before the decimal, and the display of a "floating" dollar sign just before the first digit.

Here are the two columns of data produced by these PRINT USING statements:

```
2480    $427.59
 680    $117.24
 240     $41.38
 680    $117.24
 750    $128.21
 665    $113.68
1750    $299.15
 850    $145.30
1850    $316.24
 455     $78.45
 825    $143.48
 585    $102.63
3480    $610.53
```

Notice that these columns are *right aligned*, that is, the last digit of each number is vertically aligned with all the other final digits. In the second column, the decimal points are aligned, and a dollar sign appears before each expense amount.

To see how the comma symbol works in a format string, look at the statement that displays the total expense amount at the bottom of the table. This PRINT statement is in the ShowTotals procedure:

```
PRINT USING "$$##,###.##"; totDollars
```

The output from the statement appears in this form:

```
$2,641.10
```

When you include a comma in a format string, QBasic automatically displays a comma at every third digit position to the left of the decimal point.

Several other special characters are available for the format string in a PRINT USING command. Here are two of them:

**	Displays a string of asterisks before a number
**$	Displays asterisks and a floating dollar sign

You might see the second of these two features in a program that prints checks. For example, consider this statement:

```
PRINT USING "Pay exactly **$#######,###.##"; payment
```

TIP

Even more PRINT USING possibilities

The QBasic online Help facility contains a complete reference table of the formatting characters available with PRINT USING. Follow these steps to see the table:

1. Move the mouse pointer over the keyword USING in the View window, and click the right mouse button. The Help window displays a general topic about the statements that include USING.

2. In the See Also line, click the PRINT USING, LPRINT USING topic with the right mouse button. The Help screen displays a complete description of these two statements.

3. Look for the cross-reference topic identified as *format specifiers,* and click the topic with the right mouse button. The Help screen displays a table of PRINT USING format characters. This is your definitive source of information about format strings.

For a large `payment` amount, this statement produces output like this:

```
Pay exactly *****$9,876,543.21
```

Notice that the PRINT USING format string can include literal characters. In this example, the words `Pay exactly` are included in the output just as they appear in the format string.

Send It Out

The LPRINT and LPRINT USING statements send data to the printer rather than the screen. Other than the destination of their output, these statements work the same as PRINT and PRINT USING. You can demonstrate this by changing all the PRINT keywords in the Expense Table program to LPRINT. Then run the program, and the expense table is printed on paper rather than displayed on the screen.

If you want to try this experiment, you can use the QBasic Change command to revise your program quickly and efficiently, as follows:

1. Make sure that you've saved the original version of the program as EXPTABLE.BAS. Open the program into the View window.

2. Pull down the Search menu and choose the Change command. The Change dialog box appears on the screen.

3. Enter PRINT in the Find What box. Then press Tab to activate the Change To box.

4. Enter LPRINT in the Change To box.

5. Press Alt-M to activate the Match Upper/Lowercase option. (An X appears in the check box.)

6. Press Alt-W to activate the Whole Word option. (Again, an X appears in the check box.)

7. Press Alt-C to choose the Change All command. QBasic revises your program and then displays `Change Complete` in a message box. Press the Spacebar to close this box.

8. Pull down the File menu and choose the Save As command. Save this revised version of your program under a new name, for example, EXPTABPR.BAS.

9. Turn on your printer and press F5 to run the program. The expense table is printed.

Now you have two versions of the program: one displays the expense table on the screen, and another sends the table to the printer. The format of the output table is identical for both destinations. Life is good.

Chapter 7

Veritable Variables and Exquisite Expressions

• •

In This Chapter

▶ Planning calculations

▶ Creating variable names and defining types

▶ Using DIM declarations

▶ Declaring global and local variables

▶ Writing assignment statements

▶ Understanding arithmetic expressions and precedence

▶ Writing string expressions

▶ Defining symbolic constants

• •

1 n this chapter, you round out your understanding of variables in QBasic. Think about what you already know: A variable is a name you create to represent an item of information in a program.

The value of a variable can change frequently during the run of a program. But the type of data in a variable always remains the same. A numeric variable stores a number, and a string variable contains text.

You can use special characters at the end of a name to indicate a variable's type. For example, the dollar sign suffix ($) defines a string variable, and the percent sign (%) defines an integer variable. You find out more about data types in this chapter. You also learn a more formal way to declare a variable's type, using QBasic's DIM statement.

A program may contain many different variables to represent data. It makes sense to use variable names that clearly indicate the kind of information the variables represent. For example, variables such as `city$`, `amount`, and `rate` make a program listing easy to read and understand. But programmers who hate to type are sometimes tempted to skimp on meaning in favor of brevity; for this reason, you may see very short variable names such as i%, j%, and k% in a program. As you start writing programs, you'll develop your own style of creating variable names.

You've seen that the INPUT statement is one way to assign a value to a variable. For example, the following statement displays an input prompt on the screen. When the user types a response and presses Enter, QBasic stores the input in the variable amount.

```
INPUT "Amount spent:  ", amount
```

An *assignment statement* is another way to store a value in a variable. You can assign the value of an expression to a variable. An *expression* is a set of operations that results in a particular value. When you include an expression in an assignment statement, QBasic performs the calculation represented in the expression and then assigns the result to a variable.

In this chapter, you find many examples of variables, expressions, and assignment statements. Along the way, you work on a project called the Exchange Rate Statistics program, which shows how the expense of a business trip may be affected by the ups and downs of international exchange rates.

Making the Most of Your Money

Suppose that you've returned home from a business trip to France and you're reviewing your expense records. You know that the dollar-to-franc exchange rate changed several times during your trip, but you were too busy to pay attention to the changes. You just exchanged money on a daily basis as you needed it.

Now you're wondering how significant the rate fluctuations were on your total expense amount. Would it have been worthwhile for you to pay more attention to the exchange rate? What if you had managed to exchange more of your dollars at the best exchange rate available during your time in France? How would this have affected the cost of your trip? The Exchange Rate Statistics program helps you answer these questions.

Run it

Like the Travel Expense Table program you worked with in Chapter 6, the
Exchange Rate Statistics program begins by opening the expense data file,
EXPLOG.TXT. (This file is created in the root directory of your hard disk when
you run the Expense Log program, presented in Chapter 5. Don't try to run the
Travel Expense Table program before you've run the Expense Log program.)
But this new program is concerned with only a few fields of information in the
data file: the date of each expense record, the amount of each expense, and the
daily exchange rates. In the list of data records in Figure 7-1, these relevant
items appear in boldface.

```
"11-30-1993","Paris","l'Hotel du Pont, two nights",2480,5.8
"11-30-1993","Paris","Lunch with G. Lepoint, Chez Agnes",680,5.8
"11-30-1993","Paris","Taxi to airport",240,5.8
"11-30-1993","Strasbourg","Dinner with C. Muller, Cafe Berthe",680,5.8
"12-01-1993","Strasbourg","l'Hotel Central, one night",750,5.85
"12-01-1993","Strasbourg","Miscellaneous supplies",665,5.85
"12-02-1993","Caen","Conference room, l'Hotel du Chateau",1750,5.85
"12-03-1993","Caen","l'Hotel de la Gare, one night",850,5.85
"12-04-1993","Paris","Car rental",1850,5.85
"12-05-1993","Chartres","Lunch meeting with M. Lenoir",455,5.8
"12-06-1993","Chartres","Grand Hotel, one night",825,5.75
"12-07-1993","Paris","Books and supplies",585,5.7
"12-07-1993","Paris","l'Hotel du Jardin, four nights",3480,5.7
```

Figure 7-1:
The relevant
fields in
EXPLOG.TXT.

The Statistics program reads the entire data file, but works with only the date
and numeric fields. Two facts make it easy for the program to extract the data it
needs from the file: the expense records in the file are arranged in chronological
order, and the exchange rate remains constant for any given day during the trip.

To provide useful information about the exchange rate fluctuations during your
trip, the program performs the following calculations:

- The number of days for which you recorded expenses
- The average dollar-to-franc exchange rate during your trip
- The best (highest) exchange rate during the trip
- The total expense amount in francs
- The total expense amount in dollars, calculated at each day's actual
  exchange rate
- The percent savings in the total dollar expense amount if you had man-
  aged to exchange all your money at the best rate

When you run the program, these calculations take place instantly and the program displays a report of its findings on the screen. Here's an example:

```
Travel Expense Log: France
Analysis of exchange rate fluctuations
---------------------------------------

Number of days recorded:     8

Average exchange rate:       5.81 Francs per Dollar
Best exchange rate:          5.85 Francs per Dollar

Total expenses in Francs:    15290
Total expenses in Dollars:   $2,641.10


If all your Dollar-to-Franc exchanges had been at the best
rate available during the trip, you would have saved 1.04%
of the total dollar expense amount.
```

During the eight days of this business trip, the average exchange rate was 5.81 and the best rate was 5.85. If you'd exchanged all your money at the best rate, you would have saved only 1.04% of your total dollar expenses: less than $30 in savings. You conclude that rate fluctuations did not have a significant effect on your expenses this time. But you decide to save the Statistics program for use on future international business trips.

Code it

Here is the complete listing of the program:

```
' Exchange Rate Statistics (RATESTAT.BAS)
' Provides information about exchange rate
' fluctuations during an international
' business trip.

DECLARE SUB RateAnalysis ()
DECLARE SUB RateReport ()

' Constant declaration.
CONST country = "France"
CONST currency = "Franc"

' Global variable declarations.
DIM SHARED maxRate, avgRate
DIM SHARED totDollars, totAmount
DIM SHARED numDays AS INTEGER

' Open the expense log data file.
OPEN "\EXPLOG.TXT" FOR INPUT AS #1
```

```
RateAnalysis   ' Perform the statistical calculations.
RateReport     ' Display the report.

END  ' RATESTAT.BAS



SUB RateAnalysis

   ' Calculate the highest rate, the average rate,
   ' and the total amount spent in local currency
   ' and in dollars.

   ' Initialize variables.
   maxRate = 0
   numDays = 0
   totAmount = 0
   totDollars = 0
   prevDate$ = ""

   ' Read all the records of the expense file.
   DO WHILE NOT EOF(1)
      INPUT #1, expDate$, city$, descript$, amount, rate

      ' Calculate the total expense.
      totAmount = totAmount + amount
      totDollars = totDollars + amount / rate

      ' If this record is a new day...
      IF expDate$ <> prevDate$ THEN

         ' Increase the number of days and the total rate.
         numDays = numDays + 1
         totRate = totRate + rate

         ' Find the highest rate up to this point.
         IF maxRate < rate THEN maxRate = rate
      END IF

      ' Assign the current date to prevDate$
      prevDate$ = expDate$
   LOOP

   ' Calculate the average rate.
   avgRate = totRate / numDays

END SUB  ' RateAnalysis



SUB RateReport

   ' Print the results of the rate analysis.
   CLS
   title$ = "Travel Expense Log: " + country
```

(continued)

```
PRINT title$
PRINT "Analysis of exchange rate fluctuations"
PRINT "--------------------------------------"
PRINT
PRINT "Number of days recorded:    "; numDays
PRINT
PRINT "Average exchange rate:     ";
PRINT USING "###.##"; avgRate;
PRINT " "; currency; "s per Dollar"
PRINT "Best exchange rate:         "; maxRate;
PRINT currency; "s per Dollar"
PRINT
PRINT "Total expenses in "; currency; "s:   "; totAmount
PRINT "Total expenses in Dollars: ";
PRINT USING "$$#,###.##"; totDollars

' Calculate and display the percent
' savings at the best exchange rate.
bestExchange = totAmount / maxRate
percentUp = 100 * ((totDollars - bestExchange) / totDollars)
PRINT
PRINT
PRINT "If all your Dollar-to-"; currency;
PRINT " exchanges had been at the best"
PRINT "rate available during the trip, you would have saved";
PRINT USING "##.##%"; percentUp
PRINT "of the total dollar expense amount."

END SUB   ' RateReport
```

The program contains only two procedures: RateAnalysis performs most of the calculations, and RateReport displays the findings on the screen. The job of the main module (at the top of the program) is to open the expense data file and then call each of these procedures in turn.

Look through the listing, and you'll find references to several important variables that represent values calculated during the course of the program. These variables are

numDays	Number of days in the trip
maxRate	Best exchange rate during the trip
avgRate	Average of all the reported exchange rates
totAmount	Total expense amount in francs
totDollars	Total expense amount in dollars

Throughout this chapter, you focus on how these variables are defined and used.

Naming Names

QBasic imposes only a few rules that you must follow when you create a variable name. A name

- ✔ Must begin with a letter
- ✔ May contain any combination of letters from *A* to *Z* and digits from 0 to 9
- ✔ Cannot contain spaces

In addition, you can use periods in variable names, but it's not a great idea to do so. Periods are required in the special notation for record variables and fields, which you learn about in Chapter 16. The use of periods in simple variable names can therefore lead to confusion.

A variable name can be as long as 40 characters in QBasic. This means you can write clever names like these:

```
TheCostOfThatReallyGoodMealLastFriday
TheNameOfMyFavoriteRestaurantInParis$
TheTallLawyerIMetAtTheChristmasParty$
MostImportantNewYearsResolutionOf1994$
```

You can — but you won't. Names longer than about ten or fifteen characters become unwieldy in a program. Remember, after you create a variable, you must spell it consistently throughout your program. If you misspell a variable name, QBasic thinks you've created a *new* variable. This is a major cause of bugs. Try to write variable names that are meaningful but reasonably short.

QBasic uses five symbols to represent variable types. By adding one of the following characters to the end of a variable name, you declare the type of value you intend to store in the variable:

$ *A string variable.* A string in QBasic can contain as many as 32,767 characters, and can include uppercase or lowercase letters, digits, spaces, punctuation characters, and other symbols.

%   *An integer variable.* An integer in QBasic is a positive or negative whole number. Integers range from –32768 to 32767.

&   *A long-integer variable.* Long integers range from approximately –2 billion to 2 billion. That's long!

!   *A single-precision numeric variable.* Single-precision values are sometimes known as *real numbers* or *floating-point values.* They contain digits before and after the decimal point. QBasic stores single-precision numbers in a way that provides up to eight digits of accuracy. The ! character is optional when defining a single-precision variable. A variable that does not contain a type character at the end of its name (and is not declared in a DIM statement) is single-precision by default.

\#   *A double-precision numeric variable.* QBasic provides up to 15 digits of accuracy for double-precision values.

You'll get used to watching for these special characters at the end of variable names. Here are some examples of each type:

```
countryName$
city$
title$
curYear%
numDays%
i%
j%
population&
quantity&
milesToMoon&
maxRate
avgRate
totdollars
nationalDebt#
molecularWeight#
```

TIP

In any case

You can use any combination of uppercase or lowercase letters in a variable name. As you've seen in many examples, uppercase letters can make a name easier for people to read:

```
maxRate
numDays
expDate$
curAmount
countCountries%
firstName$
lastName$
```

The QBasic editor automatically maintains consistency in alphabetic case for each variable you create in a program. For example, suppose you initially create a variable as

```
lastName$
```

Then, in another part of your program, you write the name as

```
lastNAME$
```

The editor recognizes this as an existing variable, and automatically changes all occurrences of `lastName$` to `lastNAME$`.

Looking for the right type

Two other important characteristics of numeric data types are known as precision and range. *Precision* is the number of digits of accuracy provided in a type. The *range* indicates the largest and smallest values that can be represented in the type. For technical descriptions of QBasic's five data types, look in the online Help window:

1. Choose the Help menu, and then choose the Contents command.

2. Click the QBasic Environment Limits topic with the right mouse button. The resulting Help window provides a selection of subtopics.

3. Click the Name, String, and Number Limits topic with the right mouse button. The Help window displays detailed information about data types.

DIM-witted declarations

As an alternate to the special type characters $, %, &, !, and #, you can use the DIM statement to declare the name and the type of a variable formally. Here is the general form of this statement for defining simple variables:

```
DIM variableName AS dataType
```

In this syntax, *dataType* is one of these five keywords:

STRING	String variable
INTEGER	Integer variable
LONG	Long-integer variable
SINGLE	Single-precision numeric variable
DOUBLE	Double-precision numeric variable

For example, the following statements declare an integer variable and a string variable:

```
DIM numDays AS INTEGER
DIM countryName AS STRING
```

You also can declare more than one variable in a single DIM statement, as follows:

```
DIM numDays AS INTEGER, countryName AS STRING
```

After this declaration, you can use the numDays and countryName variables as you would use any other variable, but without the % and $ type characters.

In short, QBasic enables you to declare variables formally in DIM statements, or informally with the use of type characters. The approach you choose may depend on the length of your program, the complexity of the program's data requirements, or your programming style. Some programmers insist on formally declaring *all* variables before using them, as is required in some languages. Other programmers believe coding is easier and more efficient without the requirement of formal variable declarations; they're glad to take advantage of QBasic's looser structure.

In a few cases, however, the DIM statement is not optional. For example, you use DIM to declare arrays and record variables, two topics you examine in Part VI. DIM is essential also for declaring global variables.

Think globally, act locally

The *scope* of a variable determines where it is available for use in your program. In general, variables defined inside a SUB or FUNCTION procedure are *local* to that procedure, and therefore not available to other procedures or to the main module. This is true whether or not you use DIM to declare the variable inside the procedure. If another procedure has a variable of the same name, it is a *different* variable, with its own distinct value.

Local variables are one of the great advantages of procedural programming. They enable you to develop independent procedures that don't interfere with each other's data.

But occasionally you may want to establish a few central variables as *global* — that is, available to the main module and all the procedures in the program. In this case, you use the DIM statement along with the SHARED keyword to declare your variables:

```
DIM SHARED variableName AS dataType
```

The DIM SHARED statement may appear only in a program's main module.

The Exchange Rate Statistics program contains three DIM SHARED statements, which you'll find near the top of the main module. Together, they declare four single-precision variables and one integer variable:

```
DIM SHARED maxRate, avgRate
DIM SHARED totDollars, totAmount
DIM SHARED numDays AS INTEGER
```

As you might recall, these variables represent the central values that the program calculates from the expense record file. The maxRate variable is the best exchange rate, avgRate is the average rate, totDollars is the total expense in dollars, totAmount is the total in francs, and numDays is the length of the business trip in days. They are declared globally for a simple reason: both procedures in the program need access to them. The RateAnalysis procedure initially calculates these five values and assigns the results to the variables. Then the RateReport uses the variables to display the information on the screen.

Don't overdo the use of global variables. That would be counterproductive in a procedural language. Also, there are other ways for procedures to exchange information, which you learn about in upcoming chapters. But declaring a few of the program's central variables as global is a reasonable technique, especially when a majority of the procedures in the program need access to the variables.

After you've declared a program's variables — global or local — your next step is to assign values to the variables.

Writing Assignments

Before an assignment, a numeric variable has a value of zero, and a string variable is empty (that is, it contains no characters). You use assignment statements to change these initial values.

Assignments are among the most common statements in QBasic programs. An equal sign represents the assignment. To the left of the equal sign is the name of the variable that receives the value. To the right is the value that is being assigned:

```
variableName = value
```

The *value* on the right side of the equal sign can appear in any form that produces a value of the appropriate type. For example, it can be a literal numeric value:

```
thisYear% = 1994
```

a literal string value enclosed in quotation marks:

```
title$ = "Travel Expense Log"
```

a variable name:

```
maxRate = rate
```

or an expression that calculates a value:

```
avgRate = totRate / numDays
```

The Exchange Rate Statistics program has many interesting examples of assignment statements. At the beginning of the RateAnalysis procedure, the program initializes four numeric variables to values of zero and a string variable to an empty string (" "):

```
maxRate = 0
numDays = 0
totAmount = 0
totDollars = 0
prevDate$ = ""
```

Four of these variables, maxRate, numDays, totAmount, and totDollars, are declared globally in the program's main module. The fifth, prevDate$, is local to the RateAnalysis procedure. This is the first assignment for all five variables. Why, you might ask, does the program initialize the variables in this way? After all, QBasic already assigns the same values to all new variables, assigning zero to numeric variables and empty strings to string variables.

The short answer to this question is that programmers are suspicious people by nature. They don't like to leave anything to chance, and they always like to know what's stored in their variables. This program relies on these initial values to produce accurate calculations. When this is the case, most programmers like to perform the initialization explicitly, even if doing so is redundant.

Most of the other assignments in the Statistics program involve arithmetic expressions, from the simple to the complex. When you place an expression on the right side of an assignment statement, QBasic first performs the calculation that the expression represents, and then assigns the result of the calculation to the variable.

Let there be no LET

In some old versions of BASIC, assignment statements always began with the keyword LET:

```
LET variableName = value
```

Although QBasic still allows you to write assignments in this way, LET is now optional and seldom used. But you may occasionally see a program that contains this keyword. Programmers sometimes have trouble dropping old habits.

If you want to read the online Help topic for assignment statements, look up LET in the Help Index, or type LET in the QBasic editor and press F1.

It's just an expression

QBasic provides the following operations for arithmetic expressions:

^   Exponentiation. This operation raises a number to the power of an exponent. For example, x ^ 2 finds the value of x squared.

*   Multiplication. Note that the symbol for multiplication is an asterisk, not an *x*.

/   Division. The number on the left of the division symbol is known as the *dividend,* and the number on the right is the *divisor.* The divisor may not be zero in a QBasic program; division by zero is not defined, and results in a run-time error.

\   Integer division. This operation divides one integer by another and drops the remainder. For example, the expression 7 \ 3 results in a value of 2. Notice that the symbol for integer division is the backslash character. The divisor may not be zero.

MOD   Modulo. This operation returns the remainder from the division of two integers. For example, 7 MOD 3 is 1. This is the only arithmetic operation represented by a keyword rather than a symbol.

+   Addition. Finds the sum of two numbers.

−   Subtraction. Finds the difference between two numbers. The minus sign can be used also as the symbol for negation or for a negative number.

Several of these operations are illustrated in the Statistics program. Here is the statement that calculates the average exchange rate for the duration of the trip:

```
avgRate = totRate / numDays
```

To find the average, the program divides the total of all the exchange rates by the number of recorded days in the expense file. The result of the division is then assigned to the avgRate variable.

Sometimes a program must assign a new value to a variable based on the variable's *current* value. In this situation, the variable's name appears on both the left and right sides of the equal sign in the assignment statement. For example, this statement increases the value of numDays by 1:

```
numDays = numDays + 1
```

The expression on the right instructs QBasic to add a value of 1 to the current value of numDays. Then the statement assigns this new incremented value to numDays. As always in an assignment statement, the previous value of numDays is lost.

Here's another example:

```
totRate = totRate + rate
```

In this statement, the value of the `rate` variable is added to the current value of `totRate`. Then the sum is assigned to `totRate`. As the program reads through the expense file, this statement finds the accumulated total of all the daily exchange rates. Similar statements find the total expense amounts in francs and in dollars:

```
totAmount = totAmount + amount
totDollars = totDollars + amount / rate
```

The expression on the right side of this last assignment contains two operations, addition and division. This brings up the question: When an expression contains multiple operations, how does QBasic decide which operation to perform first?

The order of operations makes a big difference in an expression such as `totDollars + amount / rate`. If you don't believe it, try substituting numeric values into the expression and perform the calculation in two ways. For example, suppose that `totDollars` is 1000, `amount` is 500, and `rate` is 5:

```
1000 + 500 / 5
```

If you perform the addition first and the division second, the result is 300. Conversely, if you perform the division first and the addition second, the result is 1100. Which should it be? QBasic answers this question through a default set of rules known as the *order of precedence*.

Who's on first

Given several operations in a single expression, QBasic performs the operations in the following order:

Exponentiation (^)

Negation (-)

Multiplication (*) and division (/), from left to right

Integer division (\)

The `MOD` operation

Addition (+) and subtraction (-), from left to right

Following this order, you can see how the total dollar expense amount is calculated:

```
totDollars = totDollars + amount / rate
```

First the division is performed (`amount / rate` is the dollar exchange value of the current expense), and then the addition is performed.

Clearly, you need to pay attention to the order of precedence when you write expressions in QBasic. Making false assumptions about the default order can result in big mistakes.

If you're ever in doubt about how QBasic will carry out a calculation, or if you simply want the calculation to be performed in a nondefault manner, you can *override* the order of precedence. To do this, you use parentheses in an expression. QBasic performs operations enclosed in parentheses first. You can even place one set of parentheses inside another (*nested* parentheses). QBasic performs the operation in the innermost parentheses first, and then works its way step by step to the outermost parentheses.

For example, consider the following assignment from the RateReport procedure:

```
percentUp = 100 * ((totDollars - bestExchange) / totDollars)
```

This statement finds the percent savings in dollar expenses if all dollar exchanges had been made at the best exchange rate. The subtraction in the innermost parentheses finds the difference between the actual dollar expense amount and the hypothetical "best" dollar expense amount. The division in the next level of parentheses divides the difference by the actual dollar expense amount. Then the operation outside the parentheses multiplies the result by 100. Without the parentheses, this expression would be evaluated quite differently.

Feel free to use parentheses even when they are not strictly needed. Sometimes parentheses can help you formulate a complex expression, even when the default order of precedence would evaluate the expression correctly. You might also use parentheses when you simply can't remember the QBasic default rules of precedence. Extraneous parentheses are always better than an incorrect calculation. ∎

Concatenatin' Strings and Syncopatin' Rhythm

You've looked at the operations that apply to arithmetic expressions. What operations are defined for other types of data?

Ernestine and other types of operators

QBasic has two other categories of operators:

- The *relational* operators perform comparisons between values. The expression x > y, for example, is true if x is greater than y, or false if y is greater than or equal to x.

- The *logical* operators (sometimes known as Boolean operators) provide ways to combine true or false values. The most commonly used logical operators are AND, OR, and NOT.

You may have noticed a few relational and logical operations in the sample programs you've already worked with. You study these operations formally in Chapter 11.

You can use an operation known as *concatenation* to combine two strings. The symbol for concatenation is the plus sign. Here's an example from the Statistics program:

```
title$ = "Travel Expense Log: " + country
```

In this statement, country represents the string France. The expression on the right side of the assignment therefore combines a literal string with the string country to form a title for the output report. The result of the concatenation is assigned to the title$ string variable and then displayed on the screen:

```
PRINT title$
```

Here's what you see at the top of the screen:

```
Travel Expense Log: France
```

Using Symbolic Constants

Another kind of name you can define for use in a QBasic program is known as the symbolic constant. Unlike variables, *symbolic constants* represent fixed values throughout a program's performance. Symbolic constants are convenient for representing commonly used values in a program.

You define a symbolic constant in a CONST statement:

```
CONST constantName = value
```

The *value* on the right side of the equal sign can be a literal numeric value, a literal string (enclosed in quotation marks), another symbolic constant, or any arithmetic operation *except* exponentiation (^).

The Statistics program has two examples of symbolic constants, representing the country name and the currency name for the current business trip. The following two statements appear near the top of the program's main module:

```
CONST country = "France"
CONST currency = "Franc"
```

Constants defined in the main module are available for use throughout the program. You'll see additional examples of symbolic constants in later programming projects.

Part III
Organizing the Tour: Structured Programming

The 5th Wave
By Rich Tennant

"I JUST HOPE THIS WILL PUT TO AN END ALL THE MOPING AND WHINING ABOUT NEEDING A MONITOR FOR HIS COMPUTER."

In This Part . . .

You've already begun to see the advantages of organizing programs into small blocks of code, known as SUB and FUNCTION procedures. To accomplish a particular task, a program makes a call to the procedure designed to carry out the task. If something goes wrong with a program, procedural organization simplifies the job of finding out where the problem is.

In the following chapters, you further explore the details of SUB and FUNCTION procedures. You also look at a selection of the built-in functions that QBasic supplies for general-purpose tasks.

To illustrate these topics, Part III presents a pair of programs you can use to develop a database of your favorite restaurants — the best eateries you've discovered around town or around the world. *Bon appetit!*

Chapter 8
SUBs or FUNCTIONs: It's Your Call

● ●

In This Chapter

▶ Organizing a program into procedures

▶ Creating SUB procedures

▶ Calling a SUB procedure

▶ Creating FUNCTION procedures

▶ Calling a FUNCTION procedure

● ●

*B*ecause the programs you've worked with up to now have been organized in procedures, you've already learned quite a bit about QBasic's SUB and FUNCTION structures. A SUB procedure is designed to perform a specific, carefully defined task. The task is repeated each time the program calls the procedure. By contrast, the primary job of a FUNCTION procedure is to calculate and return an item of information. The calculation is repeated whenever the program calls the function.

Every procedure has a name, which you make up when you create the procedure. The name of a procedure is defined in the SUB or FUNCTION statement at the beginning of the structure. A good procedure name indicates something essential about what the procedure is designed to do.

A *call* is a statement or expression that refers to a procedure by name and results in a performance of the procedure. A procedure can be called from either the main module or any other procedure in the same program. When a procedure completes its task, control of the program returns to the location where the procedure was originally called.

A call to a SUB procedure is a statement by itself. For example, suppose you've written a SUB procedure named DoSomething. A call to DoSomething looks like this:

```
DoSomething
```

By contrast, a call to a FUNCTION procedure always appears as part of a statement designed to use the value that the function returns. For example, a call to a function named GiveData might appear at the right side of an assignment statement:

```
x = GiveData
```

or in an output statement:

```
PRINT GiveData
```

The more you learn about SUB and FUNCTION procedures, the more skillfully you can use them as the building blocks of a program. In this chapter, you review the structural elements of procedures and focus on their use. In particular, you learn how to send information to a procedure and how to design a procedure to make use of information it receives.

To explore SUB and FUNCTION procedures in detail, you'll work with a project named the Restaurant Database program in this chapter.

You can use this program to develop and save a collection of your own personal restaurant reviews for locations anywhere in the world. Then, when you go back to a city, you can easily find that quiet cafe, your favorite restaurant, a fashionable bistro, or the local dive — whatever you're in the mood for. You can keep notes on food quality, price, and suitable ambiance for business meetings. (Closer to home, you can use the database to record information about favorite eateries in your neighborhood.) A related program presented in Chapter 9 helps you get information from this database whenever you need it.

Restaurant Ratings

Each time you run the Restaurant Database program, it conducts an input dialog to accept new restaurant records into the database. The database is saved in the root directory of your hard disk under the name \RESTLIST.DB. For each restaurant, you enter five items of information:

- The city where the restaurant is located
- The name of the restaurant
- A rating for the quality of the food (*, **, ***, or ****)

▶ A rating for the price of meals at the restaurant ($, $$, $$$, or $$$$)

▶ Any additional comments about the restaurant

When you've completed the information for a given restaurant, the program asks you to confirm that you want to save the record. Then you can continue entering additional records, or you can end the program.

For a sample run of the program, imagine you're in the middle of your first business trip to several large cities in West Africa and you've been busy entertaining clients at lunch and dinner in restaurants that people have recommended. You want to keep notes on these restaurants for use during future trips to the same cities. So at the end of each day, you turn on your laptop computer and run the Restaurant Database program to keep contemporaneous notes on your culinary experiences. Here's how the dialog might appear (your input is shown in boldface type):

```
International Restaurant Database
------------- ---------- --------

Record # 11

City? Dakar
Name? Restaurant de la Place
Quality (1 to 4)? ****
Prices (1 to 4)? $$$
Comments? Mostly French food, but also a few excellent local dishes.

Save this record? Y
Another record? Y
```

The program displays a title and tells you the current record number in the database. Then it begins the input dialog. You enter the city and the name of the restaurant. In response to the Quality and Prices prompts, you simply type a digit from 1 to 4. The program translates your input into the equivalent number of stars (*) or dollar signs ($). For example, you've given this restaurant your highest quality rating (four stars), and you've identified it as fairly expensive, with a price rating of three dollar signs. Finally, you can enter a one-line comment about the restaurant. Then you press the Y key to save the record to the database and press Y again to enter another restaurant record.

The program run ends when you finally press N in response to Another record? Each time you run the program, it appends new records to the end of the database.

Code It

Here is the complete listing of the program:

```
' Restaurant Database (RESTINPT.BAS)
' Accepts input for an international
' restaurant database.

DECLARE FUNCTION YesOrNo$ (question AS STRING)
DECLARE FUNCTION GetRating$ (prompt AS STRING, symbol AS STRING)
DECLARE FUNCTION GetRecordNum% ()
DECLARE SUB DoInput (recordNum AS INTEGER)

' Define the record type.
TYPE RestaurantType
  City AS STRING * 20
  RName AS STRING * 25
  Rating AS STRING * 1
  Prices AS STRING * 1
  Comments AS STRING * 65
END TYPE

' Declare the global Restaurant variable.
DIM SHARED Restaurant AS RestaurantType

' Open the database file and begin the input dialog.
OPEN "\RESTLIST.DB" FOR RANDOM AS #1 LEN = LEN(Restaurant)
DoInput GetRecordNum%

END   ' RESTINPT.BAS



SUB DoInput (recordNum AS INTEGER)

  ' Conduct the input dialog.
  DO
    CLS
    PRINT "International Restaurant Database"
    PRINT "------------- --------- --------"
    PRINT

    ' Display the current record number.
    PRINT "Record #"; recordNum
    PRINT

    ' Get input for each of the fields.
    LINE INPUT "City? "; Restaurant.City
    LINE INPUT "Name? "; Restaurant.RName
    Restaurant.Rating = GetRating$("Quality (1 to 4)? ", "*")
    Restaurant.Prices = GetRating$("Prices (1 to 4)?  ", "$")
    LINE INPUT "Comments? "; Restaurant.Comments

    PRINT
```

```
      ' Save the record if the user confirms.
      IF YesOrNo$("Save this record? ") = "Y" THEN
        PUT #1, recordNum, Restaurant
        recordNum = recordNum + 1
      END IF

   ' Continue the input until the user is done.
   LOOP UNTIL YesOrNo$("Another record?    ") = "N"

END SUB   ' DoInput



FUNCTION GetRating$ (prompt AS STRING, symbol AS STRING)

   ' Display an input prompt and
   ' get a rating from 1 to 4.
   PRINT prompt;

   ' Wait for appropriate input.
   DO
     answer$ = INKEY$
   LOOP UNTIL LEN(answer$) = 1 AND INSTR("1234", answer$) <> 0

   ' Display a string of rating symbols.
   PRINT STRING$(VAL(answer$), symbol)

   ' Return the input.
   GetRating$ = answer$

END FUNCTION   ' GetRating$



FUNCTION GetRecordNum%

   ' Calculate the record number for
   ' the next record in the database.
   GetRecordNum% = LOF(1) / LEN(Restaurant) + 1

END FUNCTION   ' GetRecordNum%



FUNCTION YesOrNo$ (question AS STRING)

   ' Display a question and wait
   ' for the user to type Y or N.

   PRINT question;
   DO
     answer$ = UCASE$(INKEY$)
   LOOP UNTIL answer$ = "Y" OR answer$ = "N"
   PRINT answer$

   YesOrNo$ = answer$

END FUNCTION   ' YesOrNo$
```

The program consists of a short main module followed by four procedures —
one SUB and three FUNCTIONs — as follows:

✔ DoInput is the SUB procedure. It repeats the input dialog for as many
restaurant records as you want to enter into the database. When you
confirm each record, the procedure saves the information to the database
file. DoInput is called once from the program's main module.

✔ The GetRating$ and YesOrNo$ functions conduct special parts of the input
dialog. GetRating$ receives your input for the quality and price ratings.
YesOrNo$ reads your responses to the `Save this record?` and `Another
record?` prompts. Both of these FUNCTION procedures return strings
representing your input, and both are called multiple times by the DoInput
procedure.

✔ The GetRecordNum% function calculates the number of records in the
restaurant database. It is called once from the program's main module and
returns an integer representing the size of the database.

You look at each of these procedures in detail as you study SUB and FUNCTION
procedures in this chapter.

By the way, the restaurant database is stored on disk in a format known as a
random access file. This format allows QBasic programs to gain efficient access
to any record in the file. The programming techniques for random access files
are very different from the text file procedures you've seen in previous programs. You'll explore techniques for handling both kinds of files in Chapters 18,
19, and 20.

Adding Procedures

There are two ways to create a procedure in a program listing:

✔ Pull down the Edit menu in the QBasic menu bar, and choose the New SUB
or New FUNCTION command. In the resulting dialog box, type the name
you want to assign to the new procedure, and click OK.

✔ Anywhere in the current program listing, type SUB or FUNCTION, followed
by the name of the new procedure. Then press Enter.

Either way, the QBasic editor displays the new procedure by itself in the View
window, and adds an END SUB or END FUNCTION statement as the final line of
the structure.

Be careful not to use a QBasic keyword as a SUB name or a FUNCTION name. (*Keywords* are the names of QBasic statements and built-in functions and any other words reserved as part of the language.) If you try to do so, QBasic displays an `Expected: identifier` **error message.** ▪

Immediately after the procedure name in the SUB or FUNCTION statement, you can type an optional list of parameters, enclosed in parentheses. A *parameter* is a variable representing a data item to be passed to the procedure at the time of a call.

Three of the four procedures in the Restaurant Database program contain parameter lists. So now's a good time to tackle them.

Creating Super SUBs

Here is the general format of a SUB procedure:

```
SUB ProcedureName (parameter1, parameter2, ...)

  ' The code of the procedure...

END SUB
```

The parameter list consists of variable names and their type declarations, enclosed in parentheses and separated by commas because we don't want them to mingle with the others. QBasic allows a procedure to have as many as 60 parameters, but in practice, most procedures contain fewer than 10. Procedures with 1, 2, or 3 parameters are probably the most common.

Like any variable, a parameter belongs to a specified type. You can define the type of a parameter by using one of QBasic's special *type characters* at the end of the variable name, as follows:

$	String parameter
%	Integer parameter
&	Long-integer parameter
!	Single-precision parameter
#	Double-precision parameter
no special character	Single-precision parameter

Alternatively, you can use an AS clause, just as in a DIM statement. The AS clause uses one of the following keywords to identify the parameter type: STRING, INTEGER, LONG, SINGLE, or DOUBLE.

For example, suppose you are writing a procedure named ShowInfo to display information about an employee. You have designed the procedure to receive two items of information from a call: a string containing the employee's name and an integer representing the employee's number. You can write the SUB statement for this procedure in two ways:

```
SUB ShowInfo (empName$, empNum%)
```

or

```
SUB ShowInfo (empName AS STRING, empNum AS INTEGER)
```

In the procedure's code, you use these two parameters just as you would any other variable. Their distinct feature is that they represent data that has been passed to the procedure from the caller.

Parameters can provide special items of information that affect the way the procedure works. For example, the DoInput procedure in the Restaurant Database program takes one integer parameter:

```
SUB DoInput (recordNum AS INTEGER)
```

The recordNum parameter indicates the current record number in the restaurant database. One of the procedure's first actions is to display this number on the screen above the input dialog:

```
PRINT "Record #"; recordNum
```

After the user enters and confirms a new restaurant record, the DoInput procedure uses recordNum again to specify the position where the record should be stored in the database.

Calling All SUBs

A call to a SUB procedure must send the items of information that are defined in the procedure's parameter list. In a call statement, the data values sent to the procedure are known as *arguments*. Here is the general form of a SUB procedure call:

```
ProcedureName argument1, argument2, ...
```

The argument list must match the parameter list in both number and type. In other words, the number of arguments in a call must be the same as the number of parameters in the corresponding SUB statement. Furthermore, the data type of each argument must match the data type of the corresponding parameter.

For example, suppose you are writing a call to the ShowInfo procedure, which you've defined as follows:

```
SUB ShowInfo (empName AS STRING, empNum AS INTEGER)
```

A call to ShowInfo must send a string and an integer, in that order. You can express the two required arguments in any way that results in data values of the appropriate types. The arguments might appear as literal values:

```
ShowInfo "Jane Dalton", 12345
```

or as variables:

```
ShowInfo curEmployee$, curEmpNum%
```

or even as expressions:

```
ShowInfo firstName$ + lastName$, prevNum% + 1
```

Again, the only requirement is that each argument match the type of the corresponding parameter.

In the example of the DoInput procedure in the Restaurant Database program, recall that the procedure has one integer parameter, as follows:

```
SUB DoInput (recordNum AS INTEGER)
```

The call to this procedure takes place in the program's main module, and sends an integer argument to the procedure as required:

```
DoInput GetRecordNum%
```

GetRecordNum% is a call to one of the program's three FUNCTION procedures. So this one statement actually performs two different procedure calls. First the call to GetRecordNum% returns the current record number in the open database file. Then the call to DoInput initiates the input dialog, supplying the value of GetRecordNum% as an argument.

Creating FUNCTION Procedures

Like a SUB procedure, a function may include a list of parameters, as follows:

```
FUNCTION FunctionName (parameter1, parameter2, ...)

  ' The code of the procedure ...

  FunctionName = returnValue

END FUNCTION
```

But a FUNCTION procedure has several important features that distinguish it from a SUB procedure:

- The first line of the procedure is a FUNCTION statement. The last line is END FUNCTION.

- The name of the function ends in a special type character ($, %, &, !, or #), indicating the type of value the function is defined to return. A function name that does not end in a special character returns a single-precision value by default. (You may not use an AS clause to define the return value of a function.)

- Somewhere in the function's code — usually near the end — is an assignment statement that defines the function's return value, as follows:

    ```
    FunctionName = returnValue
    ```

    At the left side of this assignment is the name of the function itself; at the right side is an expression that gives the return value.

Often a function uses its parameters in a sequence of calculations that produces an end result. Consider the following short example, which has three numeric parameters:

```
FUNCTION HotelBill (perNight, numNights%, exchRate)

    ' Calculate the charges in dollars for a hotel stay.

    totalBill = perNight * numNights%
    totalInDollars = totalBill / exchRate

    HotelBill = totalInDollars

END FUNCTION    ' HotelBill
```

This function computes the bill for a hotel stay, given the charge per night (perNight), the number of nights (numNights%), and the currency-to-dollar exchange rate (exchRate). The first two assignment statements in the function perform the calculations, and the final assignment defines the function's return value.

Calling FUNCTIONs

As you know, a function call is always part of a statement, never a statement by itself. Here's one general form of a function call, where the call appears on the right side of an assignment statement:

```
varName = FunctionName(argument1, argument2, ...)
```

Unlike the argument list in a SUB procedure call, the arguments sent to a function are enclosed in parentheses after the function's name. The number of arguments in the list must be the same as the number of parameters in the FUNCTION statement. The arguments may appear as literal values, variables, or expressions, as long as each argument matches the data type of the corresponding parameter.

Here is how you might call the HotelBill function:

```
ParisBill = HotelBill(550, 3, 5.7)
```

Given these three arguments, the call to HotelBill calculates the charge for a three-night stay in a hotel where the nightly rate is 550 francs with an exchange rate of 5.7 francs to the dollar. The statement assigns the result to a variable named `ParisBill`.

The Restaurant Database program contains three interesting examples of FUNCTION procedures. The GetRating$ procedure takes two arguments, both strings, as follows:

```
FUNCTION GetRating$ (prompt AS STRING, symbol AS STRING)
```

This function displays an input prompt on the screen (represented by the `prompt` parameter) and then waits for the user to type a digit from 1 to 4 as a rating for the quality or price of a restaurant. On the screen, the function displays a string of symbols (represented by the `symbol` parameter) to depict the rating. The function returns a single character from `"1"` to `"4"`; this string value is stored as a rating in the restaurant database.

The DoInput procedure calls GetRating$ twice, as follows, to conduct the input dialogs for the quality and price ratings:

```
Restaurant.Rating = GetRating$("Quality (1 to 4)? ", "*")
Restaurant.Prices = GetRating$("Prices (1 to 4)?  ", "$")
```

As you can see, each call to the procedure sends an appropriate input prompt and a symbol (* or $) to depict the rating.

Similarly, the YesOrNo$ function gets responses to the two yes-or-no questions that are part of the program's input dialog. YesOrNo$ has one string parameter, `question`, which represents the input prompt:

```
FUNCTION YesOrNo$ (question AS STRING)
```

The function returns a one-character string (`Y` or `N`) as the user's answer.

Finally, the GetRecordNum% has no parameters:

```
FUNCTION GetRecordNum%
```

It returns an integer value representing the current record number in the database. As you've seen, the main module calls this function as part of the call to the DoInput procedure, as follows:

```
DoInput GetRecordNum%
```

In Chapter 9, you examine additional procedures and learn more about procedure calls and arguments.

Chapter 9

How to Manage Arguments and Influence People

In This Chapter

▶ Passing arguments by reference

▶ Passing arguments by value

▶ Passing arguments as variables

▶ Protecting arguments from unwanted changes

---

*I*n this chapter you explore another important characteristic of procedure calls. Sometimes, a procedure changes the value of an argument that is passed to it. This may or may not be a good thing:

✔ Sometimes a changed argument value serves as an important exchange of data from the procedure to the caller. This two-way communication between procedures can be a valuable part of a program's design.

✔ Other times a caller needs to preserve the original values of its arguments. In this case you need a way to make sure that arguments are protected from any changes that may result from the procedure call.

Either way, you need to learn exactly when this phenomenon takes place so you'll be prepared to deal with it appropriately.

What Are You Arguing About?

You have to watch out for changes in arguments whenever *both* of the following conditions are true:

✔ An argument is expressed as a *variable name* in the procedure call. For example, in the following call, the numVal% variable is sent as an argument to the procedure named SampleProc:

```
SampleProc numVal%
```

> ✔ The procedure makes changes in the value of the corresponding parameter variable. For example, the SampleProc procedure receives the argument in the `inNum%` parameter, and then changes the value of `inNum%`:
>
> ```
> SUB SampleProc (inNum%)
>   inNum% = inNum% + 1
>   ' ...
> END SUB
> ```

Under these combined conditions, the change in the parameter is "passed back" to the argument in the procedure call. In the example, the value of the `numVal%` argument is increased by 1 when the SampleProc procedure returns control of the program to the caller.

In this situation, the argument variable is said to be passed *by reference* to the procedure. Behind the scenes, the caller and the procedure both have access to the same value in the computer's memory, even though they refer to the value by different names. If the procedure changes the value, the caller receives the change.

If you want to prevent changes in an argument, you must instead pass the argument *by value*. QBasic then makes a copy of the argument for use in the procedure. The procedure can then make changes in the copy without affecting the original value of the argument itself.

To illustrate the difference between passing arguments by reference and by value, this chapter presents a project named the Show Restaurants program. Show Restaurants displays records from the database that you created with the Restaurant Database program in Chapter 8. Specifically, the Show Restaurants program opens the restaurant database (RESTLIST.DB, stored in the root directory of your hard disk) and displays the records from any city you request.

Run It

When you first run the Show Restaurants program, a prompt appears on the screen asking you for the name of the city where you want to search for restaurants. You type the city and press Enter. In response, the program finds and displays all the restaurants recorded for the city you've requested.

For example, in the following output the program displays information about restaurants you tried during your business trip to West Africa:

```
What city? Dakar

Restaurant Senegalais     ***     $$
   --> High quality French and Senegalese food.
```

```
Cafe Casamancais        ***     $$$
   --> Tourist crowd, but good local food.

Restaurant de la Place  ****    $$$
   --> Mostly French food, but also a few excellent local dishes.


Press spacebar to continue ...
```

For each restaurant in the target city, the program displays the name of the restaurant, the quality and price ratings, and your comments about the restaurant.

If the database contains no restaurants for the city you request, a message appears on the screen. For example:

```
What city? London

No restaurants found for London.

Press spacebar to continue ...
```

After each city request, the program repeats the dialog, so you can look at the restaurants for as many cities as you want. To end the program, you press Enter in response to the What city? prompt.

Code it

Here is the listing of the Show Restaurants program:

```
' Show Restaurants (SHOWREST.BAS)
' Given a target city, displays restaurant
' descriptions from the RESTLIST.DB database.

DECLARE SUB DoDialog ()
DECLARE SUB Pause ()
DECLARE SUB PrintRecord (Rest AS ANY)
DECLARE SUB SearchCity (InCity AS STRING, numFound AS INTEGER)

' Define the record type.
TYPE RestaurantType
   City AS STRING * 20
   RName AS STRING * 25
   Rating AS STRING * 1
   Prices AS STRING * 1
   Comments AS STRING * 65
END TYPE

' Declare the global Restaurant variable.
DIM SHARED Restaurant AS RestaurantType
```

```
' Open the database file and begin the input dialog.
OPEN "\RESTLIST.DB" FOR RANDOM AS #1 LEN = LEN(Restaurant)
DoDialog

END   ' SHOWREST.BAS

SUB DoDialog

  ' Conduct the repeating dialog to
  ' list restaurants in selected cities.
  DO
    CLS
    num% = 0

    ' Get the user's city choice.
    LINE INPUT "What city? "; getCity$
    PRINT

    ' Search for and display restaurants in the city.
    SearchCity (getCity$), num%

    ' Display message if no restaurants are found.
    IF RTRIM$(getCity$) <> "" THEN
      IF num% = 0 THEN
        PRINT "No restaurants found for "; getCity$; "."
      END IF
      Pause
    END IF

  ' Stop dialog when user presses Enter
  ' in response to What city? prompt.
  LOOP UNTIL RTRIM$(getCity$) = ""

END SUB   ' DoDialog

SUB Pause

  ' Hold information on the screen
  ' until the user presses the spacebar.
  PRINT
  PRINT "Press spacebar to continue ...";
  DO
    s$ = INKEY$
  LOOP UNTIL s$ = " "

END SUB   ' Pause

SUB PrintRecord (Rest AS RestaurantType)

  ' Display the fields of a restaurant.
  PRINT Rest.RName;

  ' Display * or $ symbol for
  ' Rating and Prices fields.
  PRINT STRING$(VAL(Rest.Rating), "*");
  PRINT SPACE$(8 - VAL(Rest.Rating));
  PRINT STRING$(VAL(Rest.Prices), "$")
```

```
' Display comments on a new line.
PRINT "   --> "; Rest.Comments
PRINT

END SUB   ' PrintRecord

SUB SearchCity (inCity AS STRING, numFound AS INTEGER)

  ' Search through the whole database
  ' for a selected city.
  SEEK #1, 1

  ' Convert inCity name to uppercase for
  ' successful comparison with City field.
  inCity = UCASE$(inCity)

  ' Loop through the database.
  DO WHILE NOT EOF(1)
    GET #1, , Restaurant
    IF inCity = RTRIM$(UCASE$(Restaurant.City)) THEN

      ' Display any matching records.
      PrintRecord Restaurant
      numFound = numFound + 1
    END IF
  LOOP

END SUB   ' SearchCity
```

Along with the main module, the program contains four procedures. DoDialog conducts the input dialog. It elicits a city request and then calls the SearchCity procedure to search for restaurants in the target city. SearchCity in turn calls the PrintRecord procedure to display each restaurant record that matches the city request. To keep the information on the screen until you are ready to continue, DoDialog calls a small procedure named Pause, which displays the `Press spacebar to continue...` message.

Choose your arguments carefully

Your main interest in this program is the call to the SearchCity procedure, which takes place in the DoDialog procedure. The call appears as follows:

```
SearchCity (getCity$), num%
```

The SearchCity procedure is designed to take two arguments: `getCity$` represents the name of the target city that the user has requested, and `num%` is the number of restaurants found in this city. Before making the call to SearchCity, the DoDialog procedure initializes `num%` to zero:

```
num% = 0
```

If num% remains at zero after the call to SearchCity, no restaurants have been found for the target city, so the DoDialog procedure displays an appropriate message:

```
IF num% = 0 THEN
  PRINT "No restaurants found in "; getCity$; "."
END IF
```

In other words, DoDialog expects to receive from SearchCity any changes in the value of num%.

The SearchCity procedure receives its two arguments in the parameter variables inCity and numFound:

```
SUB SearchCity (inCity AS STRING, numFound AS INTEGER)
```

During its search through the restaurant database, SearchCity makes changes to both of these variables. First, it converts the value of inCity to all uppercase letters, using a built-in QBasic function named UCASE$ as follows:

```
inCity = UCASE$(inCity)
```

It also converts each City field to all uppercase as it reads the restaurant records from the database. These two conversions ensure reliable comparisons between inCity and each record's City field.

Each time SearchCity finds a record that matches the target inCity, the procedure increases the value of numFound by 1:

```
numFound = numFound + 1
```

By the time SearchCity reaches the end of the database, numFound therefore contains a count of the restaurant records that have been found for the target city, inCity.

Please Pass the Variables

As you've learned, an argument that appears as a variable name in a call statement is normally passed by reference. Depending on the context, this can be an advantage or a disadvantage. It's an advantage if the caller needs to receive information back from the procedure. But it's a disadvantage if the caller needs to protect its argument variable from changes.

The call to the SearchCity procedure illustrates both situations. The DoDialog procedure needs to know whether SearchCity has found any records for the target city. It reads this information in the value of the num% argument after the call to SearchCity. If num% is still zero, DoDialog displays a No restaurants found... message; if num% is not zero, no message needs to be displayed.

By contrast, DoDialog needs to protect the getCity$ argument from changes that take place in the SearchCity procedure. SearchCity converts the name of the target city to all uppercase letters, and this change would be carried back to DoDialog in an argument passed by reference. DoDialog, in turn, would display No restaurants found... messages, such as the following:

```
No restaurants found for LONDON.
```

The name of the city in this message should instead appear just as the user originally entered it from the keyboard:

```
No restaurants found for London.
```

The conversion to all uppercase letters could make the user wonder whether the search was carried out correctly.

To avoid any changes in the city name, the DoDialog procedure must therefore send the getCity$ argument by value rather than by reference. Doing so is easy; you simply enclose the argument in parentheses in the call statement. In the call to SearchCity, you can see that the getCity$ argument is sent by value and the num% argument is sent by reference, as follows:

```
SearchCity (getCity$), num%
```

When the SearchCity procedure is finished, the value of getCity$ remains exactly the same as it was before the call, but num% contains any new value that the procedure has assigned to the corresponding parameter variable.

In short, whenever you pass an argument as a variable, you create the potential for *two-way* communication between the called procedure and the caller. The caller can receive information back from the procedure, a feature that proves useful in some programs. But in some situations, you may want to suppress this two-way communication. To protect the argument from changes, you simply enclose the variable name in parentheses in the call statement.

In Chapter 8 and this chapter, you've learned how to create your own SUB and FUNCTION procedures in a QBasic program. Chapter 10 introduces you to a selection of functions that QBasic supplies; these are known as built-in functions.

Exposing Built-In Functions

*Q*Basic has a library of several dozen built-in functions designed to provide information, perform calculations, or carry out special operations on the data you supply in arguments. This large collection of tools simplifies your job as a programmer; instead of having to invent each procedure in a program, you can often call on a built-in function to do a particular task for you.

In this chapter, you begin learning what's available in the function library and how these tools work. You explore three basic categories of built-in functions — string functions, date and time functions, and numeric functions — and you review examples from programs you've worked with in previous chapters.

Built Right In

The result of a function is known as its *return* value. A call to a built-in function looks similar to a call to a FUNCTION procedure you've written yourself. The same rules apply:

✔ A function call always appears as part of a statement, never as a statement by itself. For example, an assignment statement can store a function's return value in a variable, and a PRINT statement can display the value on the screen.

✔ If a function requires arguments, you supply them within parentheses after the function's name, using commas to separate each argument.

✔ If a function requires no arguments, a call consists simply of the function's name without any parentheses.

✔ Each argument you supply must belong to the data type that the function expects to receive, but you can express arguments in any variety of formats: as literal values, as variables, as expressions, or even as other function calls.

In the QBasic editor, you can enter the name of a built-in function in any combination of uppercase and lowercase letters. The editor automatically converts the name to all uppercase letters when you complete the line of code. Watch for this conversion as you enter code into the View window. If you should inadvertently try to use a QBasic keyword as the name of a variable or procedure you're creating, the case conversion immediately alerts you to your error. ■

When to Have an Argument

Sometimes the arguments required by a built-in function are difficult to remember. To use a function successfully, you have to know the number and type of arguments it requires, and the order in which they must appear in the argument list. If any of these details are wrong, the function won't work or it won't produce the results you're expecting.

Then there's an additional wrinkle: Some functions have *optional* arguments, that is, arguments you can omit if you want to. In this case, you need to understand the function's default behavior if you omit an optional argument.

Consider the example of MID$, one of the built-in string functions you study later in this chapter. The MID$ function returns a *substring*, which is a sequence of characters from a source string. MID$ takes three arguments: one string and two integers. The first argument is the string from which the function returns a substring; the second argument indicates the starting position of the substring; and the third gives the number of characters in the substring. The syntax for MID$ is

```
MID$(s$, start, n)
```

In this function, the *n* argument is optional. If you omit it, MID$ returns a substring consisting of all the characters from *start* to the end of *s$*.

Unless you use MID$ frequently, you may easily forget one or more of these pertinent details. Fortunately, QBasic's online Help window is always ready to give you instant information about any function you want to use. If you're about to include a function in a line of code, the easiest way to get information is to type the function's name and then immediately press F1. For example, here's how you can display information about the MID$ function:

1. Begin typing the statement in which you'll be using the function.

2. Type MID$ at the appropriate place in the statement.

3. With the cursor still positioned next to MID$, press F1.

The Help window immediately appears on the screen. The information in the window includes a description of the function's return value, a clear depiction of the function's syntax, an explanation of each argument, and cross-references to any related built-in functions. Many Help topics also include sample code illustrating the function you're using.

When you've read the information you need, just press the Escape key to return to the View window. Then you can complete the line of code you've begun.

Alternatively, you can position the mouse pointer over a built-in function name in the View window and click the right mouse button to get information about the function. Help in QBasic is always just a keystroke or a mouse click away; don't forget to take advantage of it. ■

You can categorize built-in functions loosely by the types of values they return or sometimes by the types of values they work with. (But the categories aren't always clear-cut. A string function might return a numeric value that represents an item of information about a string argument.) In the upcoming sections, you look at a selection of functions that work with strings, functions that supply date and time values, and functions that work with numeric data.

Stringing Yourself Along

Among the most useful of all QBasic's built-in tools are the string functions. They're designed for several general purposes:

- ✔ To return information about a string

- ✔ To supply a substring from an existing string, or to search for a substring within a string

- ✔ To produce a modification of an existing string, with changes in the string's alphabetic case or the number of spaces

- ✔ To build a new string from information you supply

- ✔ To convert between string and numeric data types

You'll see examples of functions in all these categories.

Measuring a string

The LEN function returns an integer representing the number of characters in a string. The function takes one string argument:

```
LEN(s$)
```

The return value is the length of *s$* in characters.

LEN returns a value from 0 up to the maximum length of a string in QBasic. Officially, a string can be as long as 32,767 characters in QBasic, but your program may stop with an `Out of string space` error message if you attempt to create a string that approaches that length. A string of length 0 is known as an *empty* string. As a literal value, an empty string is represented by two quotation marks with nothing between them (`" "`). ▦

You'll find a useful example of the LEN function in the Currency Exchange program, presented in Chapter 1. The program's ShowCurrency procedure displays the current exchange rates for the country that the user selects. The first item of information that appears on the screen is the name of the country, which the procedure underlines with a string of hyphens. For example, suppose the user selects Switzerland from the list of available countries. The program displays the country name as follows:

```
Switzerland:
------------
```

Because there is a colon (:) at the end of the country name, the number of hyphens in the underlining must be equal to the length of the country name plus one. The procedure uses the LEN function to calculate this length:

```
PRINT country(choice); ":"
PRINT STRING$(LEN(country(choice)) + 1, "-")
```

The first of these two PRINT statements displays the country name, and the second displays a string of hyphens as underlining. The expression `LEN(country(choice)) + 1` calculates the required number of hyphens, and the STRING$ function (which you examine later in this chapter) returns the actual underlining string. Notice that the LEN expression appears as the first argument of the STRING$ function.

Bringing in the second string

A *substring* is a sequence of characters copied from a source string. The substring can consist of a single character or the entire length of the original string. QBasic has three functions that return substrings from a string you supply as an argument:

▶ LEFT$ returns a sequence of characters from the beginning of a string.

▶ RIGHT$ returns a sequence of characters from the end of a string.

▶ MID$ returns a sequence from any position within the source string.

These functions do not make any change in the original string; they simply produce a copy of a substring taken from the original.

Left, right . . .

The LEFT$ and RIGHT$ functions each take two arguments: the source string and the number of characters to be copied from the string, as follows:

```
LEFT$(s$, n)
RIGHT$(s$, n)
```

LEFT$ returns the first *n* characters of *s$*, and RIGHT$ returns the final *n* characters.

An example of the LEFT$ function appears in the Mailing Labels program, presented in Chapter 2. Before printing a page of labels, the program gives the user an opportunity to confirm or cancel the operation:

```
Print the labels?
```

To go ahead with the printing, the user types *yes*, *YES*, *y*, or *Y* (or any other response that begins with *Y*, for that matter) and then presses Enter.

The following lines from the program's CreateLabels procedure are in charge of displaying the prompt, accepting the keyboard input, and deciding what to do next:

```
INPUT "Print the labels"; yesNo$
IF UCASE$(LEFT$(yesNo$, 1)) = "Y" THEN PrintLabels
```

The INPUT statement stores the user's response in the string variable yesNo$. The next statement uses the LEFT$ function to copy the first character of yesNo$ and the UCASE$ function to convert this character to uppercase. (You'll examine UCASE$ later in this chapter.) If the character is *Y*, the program calls the PrintLabels procedure to go ahead with the printing. If it's anything else, the call to PrintLabels is skipped.

. . . and center

As you've seen, the MID$ function takes three arguments:

```
MID$(s$, start, n)
```

The function returns a count of *n* characters from the source string, *s$*, beginning from the position identified as *start*. In the following example, MID$ is used in a FOR loop to copy the characters of a string in a vertical arrangement down the center column of the screen:

```
language$ = "Microsoft QBasic"
CLS
FOR i% = 1 TO LEN(language$)
   PRINT TAB(40); MID$(language$, i%, 1)
NEXT I%
```

The loop moves character-by-character from the beginning to the end of the string `language$`. For each iteration of the loop, a call to MID$ returns a single character from the string, and the PRINT statement displays the character on the screen. Here's the result:

```
                                        M
                                        i
                                        c
                                        r
                                        o
                                        s
                                        o
                                        f
                                        t

                                        Q
                                        B
                                        a
                                        s
                                        i
                                        c
```

INSTRumental strings

INSTR searches for a substring within a source string. If the substring is found, INSTR returns an integer representing the position of the substring in the source string; otherwise, INSTR returns a value of zero.

INSTR takes two string arguments and an optional numeric argument:

```
INSTR(n, s1$, s2$)
```

The function searches for the *s2$* substring in the *s1$* source string. If you include the numeric argument *n*, INSTR begins searching at the *n*th character in *s1$*; otherwise, it searches from the first character in *s1$*. If *s2$* is found, INSTR returns an integer representing the position of *s2$* in *s1$*. Otherwise, if *s2$* is not found, INSTR returns a value of zero.

When a program is expecting the user to enter one of several possible input values, INSTR is an efficient way of making sure that the input is valid. In a program that uses this technique, *s1$* should be the complete set of valid input responses, and *s2$* is the user's actual response. If INSTR finds *s2$* in *s1$*, the input is valid; if not, the user should be prompted to respond again.

You can see an example of this technique in the Restaurant Database program (Chapter 8). The GetRating function displays an input prompt on the screen and then waits for the user to press one of four number keys: 1, 2, 3, or 4. Here is how it's accomplished:

```
PRINT prompt;

DO
    answer$ = INKEY$
LOOP UNTIL LEN(answer$) = 1 AND INSTR("1234", answer$) <> 0
```

A loop makes repeated calls to the INKEY$ function; when the user presses a key, the value of the key is assigned to the string variable answer$. The procedure then uses INSTR to find out whether answer$ is a valid input choice, that is, whether the user has pressed one of the four digit keys:

```
INSTR("1234", answer$) <> 0
```

If INSTR returns a value other than zero, the input is valid; otherwise, the loop continues to wait for a valid input response.

Changes in the string section

Some built-in functions are designed to return a string that is a modification of an existing string:

- ✔ The LTRIM$ and RTRIM$ functions eliminate spaces from the beginning or end of a string.
- ✔ The UCASE$ and LCASE$ functions convert the letters in a string to uppercase or lowercase.

These functions often prove useful when you need to standardize the format of an input string. For example, suppose your program needs to compare a user's input string with an existing value. But you can't be sure whether the user will type a response in uppercase, lowercase, or some combination of both and whether the response will include extraneous spaces before or after the nonspace information. As you'll see in upcoming examples, you can use combinations of the LTRIM$, RTRIM$, UCASE$, and LCASE$ functions to make the input string conform to a predictable format.

Each of these functions works with the value of a string argument. As usual, you can supply the value as a literal string, an expression, or a string variable. In no case does the function change the value of the original string you supply. If you supply the string argument as a variable, you can be sure that the variable will still contain its original value after the call to the function. ∎

Taking the air out of a string

LTRIM$ and RTRIM$ each take a single string argument, as follows:

```
LTRIM$(s$)
RTRIM$(s$)
```

LTRIM$ (left trim) returns a string in which leading spaces have been removed. RTRIM$ (right trim) returns a string without trailing spaces. If you want to remove spaces from both the beginning and the end of a string, you can use the two functions together, like this:

```
LTRIM$(RTRIM$(s$))
```

Neither of these functions has any effect on spaces embedded in the string. They remove only those spaces located before the first or after the last nonspace character.

In programs that accept important input values from the keyboard, you need to allow for the possibility that a fidgety user will tap on the spacebar before or after typing an item of information. A few extra spaces may look perfectly harmless on the input screen, but they can thwart any successful comparison between the input and an existing string in your program. Here's where LTRIM$ and RTRIM$ come in.

For example, the Travel Expense Log program (Chapter 5) asks the user for information about expenses, and stores the information on disk in an expense file. As you may recall, the first input item is the date of a given expense. The user has the option of entering an actual date or simply pressing the Enter key to record the current date, as shown in the following:

```
Expense Log
------- ---

Date (Enter for today):
```

If the input string is empty after this prompt, the program displays today's date on the screen and records it as the date of the expense. But what happens if the user absentmindedly presses the spacebar one or more times before pressing Enter? From the user's point of view, this still seems like a blank entry. But from the program's point of view, the input string is no longer empty; it consists of one or more space characters.

Anticipating heavy-handed users, the program uses LTRIM$ to eliminate any spaces from an otherwise blank input response. The following passage is from the GetExpenseRec procedure:

```
INPUT ; "Date (Enter for today): ", expDate$
IF LTRIM$(expDate$) = "" THEN
   PRINT DATE$
   expDate$ = DATE$
```

The user's input is stored in the string variable `expDate$`. If the user's input is either blank or a string of spaces — that is, if `LTRIM$(expDate$)` is an empty string — the program records today's date as the `expDate$` value.

The RTRIM$ function is useful in programs that read information from random-access database files on disk. A random-access file is arranged so that a program can read records from the file in any order. A string value from a random access file always has a fixed length; if the actual information in the string is shorter than the fixed length, the string is "padded" with trailing spaces. For example, suppose an address database contains a 20-character field for the name of each city in the file. In a record containing the 13-character name `San Francisco` in the city field, the name of the city is followed by 7 spaces to fill in the 20-character field.

It's important to eliminate these trailing spaces before attempting to compare a fixed-length string with another string. For example, the Show Restaurants program (Chapter 9) reads restaurant profiles from a random-access file, and displays all the restaurants from a target city that the user requests. In the SearchCity procedure, the target city is represented by the string variable `InCity`, and the city field is `Restaurant.City`. Before comparing these two strings, the program uses RTRIM$ to eliminate the trailing spaces from the restaurant field as follows:

```
GET #1, , Restaurant
IF InCity = RTRIM$(UCASE$(Restaurant.City)) THEN
   PrintRecord Restaurant
```

You learn much more about random-access files and databases in Chapter 19.

The case of the wrong case

UCASE$ and LCASE$ each take a single string argument, as follows:

```
UCASE$(s$)
LCASE$(s$)
```

UCASE$ returns a string in which all alphabetic characters are converted to uppercase. LCASE$ converts alphabetic characters to lowercase. Neither function has any effect on nonalphabetic information such as digits, spaces, or punctuation marks.

An illustration of UCASE$ appears in the Travel Expense Log program (Chapter 5). The program contains a function named YesOrNo$ that displays an input prompt on the screen and then waits for the user to press the Y key or the N key in response. The program uses QBasic's built-in INKEY$ function to read the one-character input. But because there's no way to predict whether the input will be entered as an uppercase or lowercase letter, the program immediately converts the input to uppercase to simplify comparisons with other strings:

```
PRINT question$;
DO
   answer$ = UCASE$(INKEY$)
LOOP UNTIL answer$ = "Y" OR answer$ = "N"
```

Without this simple case conversion, the program would have to check for four possible input values: *Y*, *y*, *N*, or *n*.

Repeating strings . . . strings . . . strings . . .

QBasic has two functions that return strings of repeating characters:

- ✔ The SPACE$ function returns a string of spaces.
- ✔ The STRING$ function returns a string consisting of one repeating character.

Both functions take an integer argument that specifies the length of the resulting string. In the SPACE$ function, this is the only argument:

```
SPACE$(n)
```

The function returns a string of *n* spaces. For example, the following statement builds a string containing ten leading spaces:

```
s$ = SPACE$(10) + firstName$
```

Sometimes you may use an expression as the argument of the SPACE$ function to calculate a specific number of spaces for an output line. Here is an example from the Show Restaurants program (Chapter 9):

```
PRINT SPACE$(8 - VAL(Rest.Rating));
```

The STRING$ function takes a second argument in which you specify the character that will make up the resulting string. You can supply this argument as a string or a number:

```
STRING$(n, s$)
STRING$(n, c)
```

In the first format, QBasic uses the first character in *s$* as the repeating character. In the second format, *c* is a numeric code from 0 to 255, representing one of the characters or symbols available for use in QBasic programs. (The complete character set is defined in the ASCII code, which you examine later in this chapter.)

STRING$ is useful for displaying lines and other shapes on the output screen. It gives you a way to highlight important information or divide the output visually into neat blocks of data. You've seen several examples of this use; here is one from the Exchange Rate program (Chapter 2):

```
PRINT STRING$(55, "-")
```

This statement displays a line of 55 hyphens across the screen to separate different portions of the output table. The program uses the statement three times, as you can see in the resulting output:

```
- - - - - - - - - - - - - - - - - - - - - - - - - - - - - - - - - - - - - - - - - - -
Country        Currency      In Dollars    $ In Currency
- - - - - - - - - - - - - - - - - - - - - - - - - - - - - - - - - - - - - - - - - - -
England        Pound          1.5075          $0.66
France         Franc          0.1748          $5.72
Germany        Mark           0.6089          $1.64
Holland        Guilder        0.5386          $1.86
Switzerland    Franc          0.6983          $1.43
- - - - - - - - - - - - - - - - - - - - - - - - - - - - - - - - - - - - - - - - - - -
```

The converts

The most technical string functions are those that convert between data types — producing strings from certain types of numeric values, or numbers from strings. For this topic, you need to know a little about how QBasic stores information in the computer's memory.

A string is stored as a sequence of characters, where each individual character is represented by an ASCII code number from 0 to 255. The ASCII code is simply a table that assigns a number to each of the 256 characters available for use in QBasic and other DOS programs. Portions of the code are devoted to specific kinds of characters. For example:

- The uppercase letters *A* to *Z* have the code numbers 65 to 90.

- The lowercase letters *a* to z are coded as 97 to 122.

- The digits 0 to 9 appear as codes 48 to 57.

- Punctuation marks are represented by code numbers 33 to 47.

- Foreign language characters have codes 128 to 165.

- A special set of graphics characters, which you can use to draw geometric shapes on the text output screen, are coded as 176 to 223.

Exploring ASCII

QBasic supplies two functions related to the ASCII code: CHR$ and ASC. The first of these, CHR$, takes as its argument a code number from 0 to 255, and returns the equivalent character. For example, the following statement displays the Greek letter π, which has the ASCII code 227:

```
PRINT CHR$(227)
```

The ASC function takes a character as its argument, and returns the equivalent ASCII code number. For example, this short program uses ASC to display the ASCII code numbers for characters you type from the keyboard:

```
DO
  s$ = INKEY$
  IF LEN(s$) = 1 THEN PRINT s$; " = "; ASC(s$)
LOOP UNTIL s$ = " "
```

The program continues displaying ASCII equivalents until you press the spacebar.

You can look at the entire ASCII code by choosing the Contents command from QBasic's Help menu and then selecting the ASCII Character Codes topic in the Quick Reference group. The first half of the code contains the characters you're likely to use most often; the second half, known as the extended ASCII code, contains special symbols, characters, and graphic shapes. ■

Digits in a string are represented in memory by their ASCII code equivalents, just like any other characters. By contrast, QBasic stores actual integer and floating-point values (belonging to the numeric data types you learned about in Chapter 7) in formats designed to provide optimum precision, range, and efficiency in calculations.

In some special circumstances, you may need to convert a string of digits to a numeric type value, or a number to a string of digits. QBasic provides two special built-in functions for these purposes:

- ✔ The STR$ function returns the string representation of a number.
- ✔ The VAL function returns the numeric equivalent of a string of digits.

Each of these functions takes a single argument. The STR$ function takes a numeric argument:

```
STR$(n)
```

STR$ returns a string of digits (along with an optional decimal point and plus or minus sign), equivalent to the way *n* would be displayed on the screen by the PRINT statement. For example, the following statement uses STR$ to convert a numeric value to a string that can then be combined with other string values:

```
s$ = employee$ + ", age " + STR$(age)
```

Conversely, the VAL function takes a string argument:

```
VAL(s$)
```

If *s$* contains digital characters (along with an optional decimal point and plus or minus sign), VAL returns the numeric equivalent. If not — for example, if the string contains alphabetic characters — VAL returns a value of zero.

The Restaurant Database program (Chapter 8) contains an illustration of the VAL function. For each restaurant profile that the user enters into the database, the program elicits two subjective ratings: one for the quality of the food and another for the price. To specify either of these ratings, the user simply presses 1, 2, 3, or 4. The program, in turn, displays an equivalent number of rating symbols — asterisks (*) for the quality rating or dollar signs ($) for the price rating. For example, here is how the input dialog might look as the user enters these data items:

```
International Restaurant Database
-------------- ---------- --------

Record # 14

City? Northeast Harbor, ME
Name? The Lobster Trap
Quality (1 to 4)? ****
Prices (1 to 4)?  $$$
```

To produce this display, the program has to convert the user's input into a string of symbols. Because the program uses the INKEY$ function to receive the input, the user's keystroke response is stored initially as a string, in the variable answer$:

```
answer$ = INKEY$
```

The program uses the VAL function to convert the value of answer$ to a number. The result of the conversion appears as the first argument of the STRING$ function, specifying the number of symbols that will appear on the screen, as follows:

```
PRINT STRING$(VAL(answer$), symbol)
```

If You've Got the Time

QBasic has two functions that read information from your computer's internal clock and calendar:

- ✔ TIME$ reads the system clock and returns a string in the form *hh:mm:ss*, providing the current time in 24-hour format.
- ✔ DATE$ reads the system calendar and returns a date string in the form *mm:dd:yyyy*.

Neither function takes arguments.

The following short program illustrates both TIME$ and DATE$. It displays the current date and time at the upper-right corner of your screen. While the program is running, the time changes every second:

```
' CLOCK.BAS

CLS
DO
  LOCATE 1, 60
  PRINT DATE$; "  "; TIME$
LOOP UNTIL INKEY$ = " "

END  ' CLOCK.BAS
```

The program produces a display such as the following:

```
12-21-1994  03:34:53
```

To stop the program, you simply press the spacebar.

Changing times

QBasic also supplies DATE$ and TIME$ *statements*, which you can use to change the system date and time in a program:

```
DATE$ = dateString$
TIME$ = timeString$
```

The *dateString$* can appear in the format *mm-dd-yyyy*, *mm-dd-yy*, *mm/dd/yyyy*, or *mm/dd/yy*. The *timeString$* can appear as *hh*, *hh:mm*, or *hh:mm:ss*. These statements have the same effect as the DATE and TIME commands in DOS.

You've seen another example of the DATE$ function in the Travel Expense Log program (Chapter 5). In the dialog for a new expense record, the program automatically supplies the current date if the user presses Enter in response to the Date prompt:

```
Expense Log
------- ---

Date (Enter for today): 12-21-1994
```

To accomplish this, the program uses the DATE$ function in a PRINT statement and also assigns the current date to the expDate$ variable, as follows:

```
IF LTRIM$(expDate$) = "" THEN
   PRINT DATE$
   expDate$ = DATE$
```

The value of expDate$ is later written to the data file on disk as the first field of the expense record.

Count Me In

QBasic supplies several categories of numeric functions. Some of these you may use frequently; others appear only in technical and mathematical applications:

- The integer and rounding functions provide various ways to convert a floating-point value to an integer. These include CINT, FIX, and INT.

- The RND function returns random numbers for use in game programs or simulations.

- The trigonometric and exponential functions supply special mathematical values. These functions are ATN, COS, SIN, TAN, EXP, LOG, and SQR.

- The ABS function gives the absolute value of a numeric argument, and SGN indicates the sign of its argument.

- Two functions return strings representing numeric base conversions. HEX$ provides a hexadecimal string, and OCT$ returns an octal string.

Part IV

Where to Go Next: Decisions in QBasic

"I STARTED DESIGNING DATABASE SOFTWARE SYSTEMS AFTER SEEING HOW EASY IT WAS TO DESIGN OFFICE FURNITURE."

In This Part . . .

*T*he computer makes decisions reliably and consistently, based on information and conditions you supply. QBasic gives you a variety of tools related to decision making. You can use the IF statement or the SELECT CASE structure to present the conditions for a complex decision and to lay out alternative courses of action in a program. QBasic's logical and relational operators enable you to express conditions accurately.

To illustrate decisions, the chapters in Part IV present a pair of programs designed to help you plan the transportation details of a business trip. What's the best way to get from point A to point B? A plane, a train, a bus, a car...or a *camel*?

Chapter 11
Go West, Young Man. No, East!

. . . .

In This Chapter

▶ Planning decisions

▶ Using the IF statement

▶ Writing conditional expressions

▶ Understanding relational operators

▶ Understanding logical operators

▶ Order of precedence for relational and logical operators

▶ Defining and using logical constants

▶ Designing multiline decision structures

. . . .

Decisions make a computer seem "smart." By writing decision statements in a program, you give the computer the power to choose between options in your code and to react appropriately to situations that occur during a run. When a program responds correctly to a request made from the keyboard or provides relevant information based on a condition, the user develops the uncanny notion that there's some kind of independent intelligence inside the computer box.

Like many illusions, this one requires a deliberate effort to create. Your skillfully written decision statements give the impression that the computer "understands" what the user wants and "knows" how to respond in an apt manner.

In this chapter you learn to use the versatile IF statement to express decisions in QBasic programs. IF allows a program to choose between alternative actions presented in your code. At the heart of every IF decision is a *condition* — an expression your program evaluates as true or false. If the condition is true, the program follows one course of action; if false, another.

To illustrate IF statements and conditional expressions, this chapter presents a programming project named the Transportation Planner. The program is designed to help you record information about the various modes of transportation you might use on a multistop business trip or vacation. When you anticipate using planes, trains, buses, or cars, you can use the Transportation Planner to keep track of travel reservations and schedules. You can then use a companion program named Transportation List (presented in Chapter 12) to review your travel records.

Transporting Yourself to Another Time and Place

When you run the Transportation Planner, the program begins by displaying a short menu of options. Selecting an option from this menu is the first step in creating each new record in your transportation file:

```
Transportation Planner
-------------- -------

Travel by:
  A)ir
  T)rain
  B)us
  R)ented Car

  Q)uit

  ---->
```

To choose a mode of transportation, you simply press the appropriate letter: A for airplane travel, T for a train trip, B for a bus ride, or R for a rented car. In response to your choice of a Travel by option, the program clears the screen and begins the input dialog for a new travel record. For each record, you enter several items of information:

The name of the airline, train line, bus line, or car rental agency

The place where your trip begins

The destination of the trip

The date of departure

The time of departure

The ticket status (reserved or not)

The payment status (paid or not paid)

For example, here's how the input dialog might appear for an airline reservation:

```
Travel by Air
-------------
Airline:         AirEuro
Departure from:  San Francisco
Destination:     Paris
Date:            12/17/93
Time:            8:35 am

Reserved? Y
Paid?     Y

Save this record? Y
```

In response to the first five prompts, you type an item of information and press Enter to complete the entry. For the last three questions, you simply press Y or N at the keyboard. The `Save this record?` prompt gives you the chance to examine the information you've typed and decide whether to save the record. After you answer this final question, the program's *Travel by* menu reappears on the screen.

The input dialog is a little different for a car rental record than for other records. Two of the usual input items do not apply: When you rent a car, there's no fixed departure time for your trip, and you don't complete the payment until you return the car. The program therefore skips the `Time:` and `Paid?` prompts if you choose `Rented Car` as the mode of transportation. Here's an example:

```
Travel by Rented Car
--------------------
Rental Agency:  CarEuro
Departure from: Caen
Destination:    various
Date:           1/19/94

Reserved? Y

Save this record? Y
```

In the program listing, you'll see several key decision statements related to this alternate record structure.

When you press Y in response to the `Save this record?` prompt, the program writes your travel record to a file named TRANPLAN.DB, which is located in the root directory of your hard disk. You can save any number of records during each run of the program. After entering the final record for a given run, you press Q to quit the program.

You can run the Transportation Planner program more than once as you continue to make plans for a trip. The Transportation List program, presented in the next chapter, opens the TRANPLAN.DB file and prints the travel records it contains.

Code It

Here is the listing of the Transportation Planner program:

```
' Transportation Planner (TRANPLAN.BAS)
' Helps you plan transportation for
' a business trip.

DECLARE FUNCTION TrueFalse% (prompt AS STRING)
DECLARE SUB TravelPlan (which AS INTEGER)
DECLARE FUNCTION GetAnswer% (prompt$, validChars$)
DECLARE SUB TransportMenu ()

' Define the record type.
TYPE TransportType
  Mode AS INTEGER
  Company AS STRING * 10
  From AS STRING * 15
  Dest AS STRING * 15
  DepartDate AS STRING * 10
  DepartTime AS STRING * 5
  Reserved AS INTEGER
  Paid AS INTEGER
END TYPE

' The record variable and counter are global.
DIM SHARED TransRec AS TransportType
DIM SHARED numRecs AS INTEGER

' Define logical constants.
CONST False = 0
CONST True = NOT False

' Open the database and count its records.
OPEN "\TRANPLAN.DB" FOR RANDOM AS #1 LEN = LEN(TransRec)
numRecs = LOF(1) / LEN(TransRec)

' Display the menu and start the input dialog.
TransportMenu

END  ' TRANPLAN.BAS


FUNCTION GetAnswer% (prompt$, validChars$)

  ' Get a character of input from
  ' the user at the keyboard.
```

```
    PRINT prompt$;
    DO
      inChar$ = UCASE$(INKEY$)

      ' Examine the input.
      charPos% = INSTR(validChars$, inChar$)
      IF (LEN(inChar$) = 1) AND (charPos% <> 0) THEN
        okChar% = True
      ELSE
        okChar% = False
      END IF

    ' Stop looping when a valid character is received.
    LOOP UNTIL okChar%

    ' Display the input character, but return the
    ' integer representing its position in validChars.
    PRINT inChar$
    GetAnswer% = charPos%

END FUNCTION   ' GetAnswer%



SUB TransportMenu

  ' Display the transportation menu on
  ' the screen, and get the user's choice.

  DO
    CLS
    PRINT "Transportation Planner"
    PRINT "-------------- -------"
    PRINT
    PRINT "Travel by:"
    PRINT "  A)ir"
    PRINT "  T)rain"
    PRINT "  B)us"
    PRINT "  R)ented Car"
    PRINT
    PRINT "  Q)uit"
    PRINT
    choice% = GetAnswer%("  ----> ", "ATBRQ")

    IF choice% < 5 THEN TravelPlan choice%

  LOOP UNTIL choice% = 5

END SUB   ' TransportMenu



SUB TravelPlan (which AS INTEGER)

  ' Read one travel record and
  ' save it in the database.

  CLS
```

(continued)

```
' Create a title and the first input prompt.
title$ = "Travel by "
IF which = 1 THEN
  title$ = title$ + "Air"
  coPrompt$ = "Airline"
ELSEIF which = 2 THEN
  title$ = title$ + "Train"
  coPrompt$ = "Line"
ELSEIF which = 3 THEN
  title$ = title$ + "Bus"
  coPrompt$ = "Company"
ELSE
  title$ = title$ + "Rented Car"
  coPrompt$ = "Rental Agency"
END IF

PRINT title$
PRINT STRING$(LEN(title$), "-")

TransRec.Mode = which

' Get the Company, From, Dest, and DapartDate fields.
PRINT coPrompt$; ":"; SPACE$(15 - LEN(coPrompt$));
LINE INPUT TransRec.Company
LINE INPUT "Departure from: ", TransRec.From
LINE INPUT "Destination:    ", TransRec.Dest
LINE INPUT "Date:           ", TransRec.DepartDate

' No DepartTime field for a car rental record.
IF which <> 4 THEN
  LINE INPUT "Time:           ", TransRec.DepartTime
ELSE
  TransRec.DepartTime = ""
END IF
PRINT

' Get the Reserved and Paid fields
TransRec.Reserved = TrueFalse%("Reserved? ")

' No Paid field for a car rental record.
IF which <> 4 THEN TransRec.Paid = TrueFalse%("Paid?     ")
PRINT

' Save the record if the user confirms.
IF TrueFalse%("Save this record? ") THEN
  numRecs = numRecs + 1
  PUT #1, numRecs, TransRec
END IF

END SUB   ' TravelPlan
```

```
FUNCTION TrueFalse% (prompt AS STRING)

  ' Get a yes/no or true/false answer.

  temp% = GetAnswer%(prompt, "YN")
  IF temp% = 1 THEN
    TrueFalse% = True
  ELSE
    TrueFalse% = False
  END IF

END FUNCTION  ' TrueFalse%
```

The program listing includes a main module followed by four procedures —
two FUNCTION procedures and two SUB procedures. Here's what the procedures do:

- ✔ The TransportMenu procedure displays the program's menu on the
  screen and accepts the user's menu choices. TransportMenu then calls the
  TravelPlan procedure to respond to a menu choice.

- ✔ The TravelPlan procedure conducts the input dialog for each new travel
  record.

- ✔ The GetAnswer% function is an input tool that accepts single-letter
  responses from the keyboard. The TransportMenu procedure uses this
  function to accept the user's menu choices.

- ✔ The TrueFalse% function is a more specialized input routine that accepts
  yes-or-no answers. The TravelPlan procedure uses this function to accept
  Y or N responses to the last three questions of the input dialog.

Glancing through the program listing for the first time, you'll find several IF
statements, varying in length and complexity. These decisions allow the
program to respond appropriately to the data and instructions the user enters
from the keyboard:

- ✔ A decision in the TransportMenu procedure governs the program's
  response to a menu choice.

- ✔ Decision statements in the TravelPlan procedure ensure an appropriate
  input dialog for a selected travel mode. One IF statement is in charge of
  building appropriate input prompts, and others provide only the questions
  that apply to a given travel record.

- ✔ IF statements in the GetAnswer% and TrueFalse% functions validate and
  interpret the single-character answers entered from the keyboard.

You focus on these decisions as you continue through this chapter.

Making IFfy Statements

Depending on the complexity of the decision, you can use IF as either a one-line statement or a multiline block structure. Both formats use the QBasic keywords IF, THEN, and ELSE:

- ✓ IF introduces the condition on which the decision is based.
- ✓ THEN identifies the action that is performed if the condition is true.
- ✓ ELSE specifies the alternate action that is performed if the condition is false.

A block structure uses some additional keywords:

- ✓ ELSEIF introduces another condition that the program evaluates if no previous condition has turned out to be true. (The optional ELSEIF clause may be included multiple times in a single decision structure.)
- ✓ END IF marks the end of the decision structure.

In the sections ahead you'll examine the details of the IF statement in both its one-line and multiline forms.

A one-liner

The one-line IF statement is the simpler of the two formats. It presents a condition and a choice of actions on a single line:

```
IF condition THEN action1 ELSE action2
```

In this statement, *condition* is an expression that QBasic evaluates as true or false, and *action1* and *action2* are statements — assignments, PRINT or INPUT statements, procedure calls, or any of the other QBasic statements you've learned to use. If *condition* is true, the program performs *action1* and skips *action2*; conversely, if *condition* is false, the program skips *action1* and performs *action2*.

For a first example, imagine you're writing a program that gives the user the option of displaying information on the screen or sending it to the printer. The following INPUT statement gets the user's choice between the two output destinations:

```
INPUT "S)creen or P)rinter"; c$
```

The user's response is stored in the string variable c$. Suppose the program's next task is to decide between two procedure calls: a call to the ShowInfo procedure displays the information on the screen, or a call to the PrintInfo procedure sends the information to the printer. Here is the decision statement:

```
IF UCASE$(LEFT$(c$, 1)) = "S" THEN ShowInfo ELSE PrintInfo
```

In other words, if the first letter of the user's input is *S* or *s*, this statement makes the call to ShowInfo, the action specified in the THEN clause; otherwise, PrintInfo is called, the action of the ELSE clause. Notice the condition in this statement — the expression between the keywords IF and THEN:

```
UCASE$(LEFT$(c$, 1)) = "S"
```

This expression is an *equality*; it is true if the expression on the left side of the equal sign has the same value as the literal string on the right. You'll see other kinds of conditions as you continue through this chapter.

The ELSE clause is optional in the IF statement. If you leave it out, the one-line IF statement becomes simply:

```
IF condition THEN action
```

In this case, the *action* is performed if the *condition* is true. If the *condition* is false, this IF statement results in no action. An example of this simple decision statement appears in the TransportMenu procedure of the Transportation Planner program. The procedure displays the program's menu on the screen and calls the GetAnswer% function to read the user's menu choice and convert it to an integer from 1 to 5. This value is stored in the integer variable named choice%. If choice% is a value from 1 to 4, the program next makes a call to the TravelPlan procedure to conduct the input dialog for a new travel record:

```
IF choice% < 5 THEN TravelPlan choice%
```

This time the conditional expression is an *inequality*; the < symbol stands for *less than*. Paraphrased, this statement says, "If the variable choice% contains a value less than 5, make a call to the TravelPlan procedure and send choice% as an argument to the procedure." If choice% is not less than 5 — that is, if the user has chosen the Quit option — the program makes no call to the TravelPlan procedure.

Before looking at multiline IF structures, take a look at the various forms of conditional expressions you can include in a QBasic program.

Conditional expressions

You've already learned to create arithmetic expressions in QBasic, using operations such as multiplication (*), division (/), addition (+), and subtraction (-). An arithmetic expression produces a value belonging to one of QBasic's numeric data types. A *conditional* expression results in a *logical* value that QBasic reads as true or false.

As you begin formulating conditional expressions, you'll inevitably begin to think of the values *true* and *false* as though they belong to a separate data type — the *logical* type, as opposed to the string or numeric types. But QBasic has no explicit way to designate true and false as a distinct data type. Inside the computer's memory, QBasic secretly represents logical values as numbers. A value of false is stored as 0, and a value of true is stored as -1. Knowing this secret can occasionally prove useful, as you'll learn later in this chapter. Meanwhile, it's perfectly natural to think of true and false as a unique data type. ▪

You've already seen some examples of conditions. The following expression is true if the first letter of the string variable c$ is S or s:

```
UCASE$(LEFT$(c$, 1)) = "S"
```

The expression is false if c$ begins with any other letter. Likewise, the following expression is true if the integer variable choice% contains a value less than 5:

```
choice% < 5
```

It is false if choice% is greater than or equal to 5.

As these two examples begin to illustrate, conditional expressions are built with different kinds of operations than those used in arithmetic expressions. Specifically, you can include two sets of operations in conditional expressions:

- ✔ Relational operations perform comparisons between two values. The equal to (=) and less than (<) operations are examples.

- ✔ Logical operations combine values of true and false to produce logical results. The most commonly used QBasic logical operations are AND, OR, and NOT.

Don't let these operations confuse you. You use the same logical concepts in everyday language. For example, suppose you go into a store to buy a pair of shoes. When you tell the sales clerk that you want size 6 in brown or black, you're expressing the conditions for your purchase. The shoes you buy have to be a certain size *and* they have to be in one of the two colors that you've selected. In a QBasic program, you could express these conditions as follows:

```
shoeSize% = 6 AND (shoeColor$ = "brown" OR shoeColor$ = "black")
```

Understanding the logic of conditional expressions is not hard; the only difficulty is in learning to use the operators.

TIP

Note the distinction between the terms *operator* and *operation*. An *operator* is a symbol or keyword that represents an operation. For example, the + symbol is the operator that represents addition; likewise, < represents the relational operation *less than*. Furthermore, an *operand* is a value that is the object of an operation. In the expressions a + b and a < b, for example, the values a and b are operands. ▪

Next, you examine QBasic's relational and logical operations in detail.

Relational operations

There are six relational operations, represented by the following symbols:

<	Less than
<=	Less than or equal to
>	Greater than
>=	Greater than or equal to
=	Equal to
<>	Not equal to

You use these operators to compare two values in a conditional expression. The expression is true if the comparison is accurate, or false if it is inaccurate. For example, suppose a equals 1, b equals 2, and c equals 3. The following comparisons are all true:

```
a < c
c >= a + b
c - a = b
```

And the following are all false:

```
a > c
b = a * 3
c <= b
```

In an expression that contains both arithmetic and relational operations, QBasic always performs the arithmetic first and the comparison second. For example, in the expression c >= a + b, QBasic first finds the value of a+b and then compares the sum with the value of c. (You learn more about the order of operations later in this chapter.)

You can find several interesting examples of relational operators in the Transportation Planner program. You've already seen how the program processes the user's menu choices:

```
IF choice% < 5 THEN TravelPlan choice%
```

When the user selects one of the transportation modes in the program's menu, the integer variable `choice%` has a value of 1, 2, 3, or 4 (that is, a value less than 5). In this case, the program calls the TravelPlan procedure to continue the input dialog. But if the user choose the `Quit` option, `choice%` has a value of 5, and no further procedure calls are made.

An example of the *not equal to* operation appears in the TravelPlan procedure. If the user has chosen the fourth menu option, for a rented car, the program omits some of the usual input prompts. For example, the `Paid?` prompt doesn't apply to a car rental. The following statement displays `Paid?` on the screen only for menu choices other than 4:

```
IF which <> 4 THEN TransRec.Paid = TrueFalse%("Paid?    ")
```

In the TravelPlan procedure, the integer variable `which` represents the user's menu choice. If `which` is not equal to 4, the procedure calls the TrueFalse% function to elicit a yes-or-no response to the `Paid?` prompt. If `which` is 4, this call is skipped. By the way, the TrueFalse% function is designed to return an integer value that represents true or false.

Additional examples of relational operations appear throughout this chapter.

Logical operators

QBasic's six logical operations are represented by the keywords NOT, AND, OR, XOR, EQV, and IMP.

Logical operators are sometimes known as *Boolean operators*, in honor of the 19th-century English mathematician and logician George Boole. Likewise, true and false are sometimes referred to as Boolean values. ■

Five of the logical operators — AND, OR, XOR, EQV, and IMP — work with pairs of operands; you use them to combine two logical values in an expression. By contrast, NOT is a unary operator; it works on a single value. Each of these operators produces a logical result. In the following descriptions, assume that the operands `v1` and `v2` both represent values of true or false:

  ✔ NOT produces the reverse value of its operand:

```
NOT v1
```

If `v1` is true, NOT `v1` results in a value of false; if `v1` is false, NOT `v1` is true.

✔ AND results in a value of true only if both its operands are true:

```
v1 AND v2
```

If both v1 and v2 are true, the AND operation results in a value of true. If either value is false or if both are false, AND results in false.

✔ OR results in a value of true if either of its operands or both its operands are true:

```
v1 OR v2
```

If v1 is true, or v2 is true, or both are true, the OR operation results in true. Only if v1 and v2 are both false does OR result in false.

✔ XOR is true only if its two operands have different values:

```
v1 XOR v2
```

If one of the operands is true and the other is false, XOR results in true. If both v1 and v2 are true or if both are false, XOR is false.

✔ EQV is true if its two operands are the same:

```
v1 EQV v2
```

IF both v1 and v2 are true or both are false, EQV results in true. If one of the operands is true and the other is false, EQV is false.

✔ IMP is false if its first operand is true and the second is false. Otherwise, IMP is true:

```
v1 IMP v2
```

If v1 is true and v2 is false, IMP is false. For all other combinations of values, IMP is true.

The simplest and most commonly used of QBasic's six logical operators are AND and OR. In particular, you can use them to evaluate input that the user enters from the keyboard.

For example, suppose you're writing a program that offers the user three numbered options in a short menu. Your program responds to options 1 and 2 by calling a procedure named Do1Or2 and processes option 3 by calling Do3. The program begins by displaying the menu on the screen and eliciting the user's menu choice. The response is stored in the integer variable opt%. Then the following IF statement decides between a call to Do1Or2 or Do3:

```
IF opt% = 1 OR opt% = 2 THEN Do1Or2 ELSE Do3
```

The condition of this statement contains an OR operator. The condition is true if the variable opt% contains a value of 1 or 2; in this case, the program calls the Do1Or2 procedure. Otherwise, if opt% contains another value (specifically, 3), the program calls Do3.

Sometimes you need to ensure that two conditions are both true before your
program proceeds with an action. In this case, you use the AND operator to test
the conditions. An example appears in the GetAnswer$ function of the Trans-
portation Planner program. The procedure calls QBasic's INKEY$ function to
read a one-key response to a prompt that has been displayed on the screen,
and then uses the INSTR function to look for the response in a string of valid
characters:

```
inChar$ = UCASE$(INKEY$)
charPos% = INSTR(validChars$, inChar$)
```

The user's response is valid if two conditions are true. The input string,
inChar$, should consist of exactly one character, and the character must be
found in validChars$, the string of valid characters. The following IF state-
ment uses the AND operator to check for both of these conditions:

```
IF (LEN(inChar$) = 1) AND (charPos% <> 0) THEN
```

Recall that the INSTR function returns a value of 0 if the target string, inChar$
in this case, is not found in the source string, validChars$. In this IF statement,
the condition is true only if LEN(inChar$) is 1 and charPos% is not 0. If either
of these expressions is false, the condition is also false, and the GetAnswer%
function continues waiting for valid input from the keyboard.

As you saw earlier, some conditional expressions may use a combination of two
or more logical operators. In the shoe store example, an OR operation expresses the condition for the shoe color, and an AND condition expresses the
combination of size and color requirements:

```
shoeSize% = 6 AND (shoeColor$ = "brown" OR shoeColor$ = "black")
```

When you write an expression that contains a combination of two or more
operations, you always have to be concerned about the order in which QBasic
will evaluate the operations. Back in Chapter 7, you learned the specific order in
which arithmetic operations are performed, and you learned also to use
parentheses to *override* the default order of operations. Similar rules apply to
the relational and logical operations, as discussed in the next section.

Who goes first?

In an expression that contains a combination of arithmetic, relational, and logical
operations, QBasic performs the operations in the following order, by default:

- ✔ First, all the arithmetic operations are performed, following the usual
  order of arithmetic precedence.
- ✔ Second, all the relational operations are performed from left to right.
- ✔ Third, all the logical operations are performed in this order: NOT, AND,
  OR, XOR, EQV, IMP.

Thanks to this preset order, many expressions you write are automatically evaluated in the way you would expect. For example, in the following expressions, QBasic performs the arithmetic operations before the relational ones:

```
c >= a + b
c - a = b
b = a * 3
```

And in this expression, the relational operations are evaluated before the logical operation:

```
x >= 5 AND x < 32
```

But sometimes the default order of operations gives the wrong answer for a particular application. For example, suppose you were to write the conditional expression for your shoe size and color preference as follows:

```
shoeSize% = 6 AND shoeColor$ = "brown" OR shoeColor$ = "black"
```

Because QBasic evaluates the AND before the OR operation, this expression could result in a value of true for a shoe description that does not match your requirements. For example, the expression is true if `shoeSize%` equals 8 and `shoeColor$` is "black"; in this case, the AND operation is false but the subsequent OR operation is true.

You can use parentheses to override QBasic's default order of precedence. Simply place parentheses around the operation that you want QBasic to evaluate first. For example:

```
shoeSize% = 6 AND (shoeColor$ = "brown" OR shoeColor$ = "black")
```

In this form, the expression yields the correct result. A `shoeSize%` value of 8 and a `shoeColor$` value of black results in a false value.

Conditional expressions can become very complex, especially if you are combining operations of several types. Sometimes you may decide to use parentheses simply to make an expression more readable. For example, in the following expression, the parentheses are not necessary because they do not change the default order in which QBasic would evaluate the operations. But they may result in an expression that is easier for you to understand:

```
IF (x = 5) AND (y <= 17) THEN DoCalc
```

Use parentheses in this way when you want to clarify a complex expression in your code.

Each open parenthesis in an expression must be matched by a close parenthesis; otherwise, the QBasic editor will reject your statement. ▪

True and False as symbolic constants

In some programming languages, True and False are predefined identifiers that you can use to represent logical constants in a program. This is not the case in QBasic, but you can easily define these two names as *symbolic constants* in any program. To do so, you use the CONST statement, which you first learned about in Chapter 7.

CONST defines a symbolic constant — a name for a value that remains unchanged throughout a program. Symbolic constants defined in a program's main module are available for use in all the program's procedures and functions. For this reason, the main module is the ideal place to define the constants True and False. ■

Keep in mind what you've learned about the numeric equivalent of logical values: QBasic stores false as a value of 0 and true as -1. Accordingly, the Transportation Planner program defines True and False as follows:

```
CONST False = 0
CONST True = NOT False
```

In this passage, False is defined by the literal value 0, but True is defined by the expression NOT False. Alternatively, you could define True as follows:

```
CONST True = -1
```

But the expression NOT False means that you don't have to remember the actual value that QBasic uses internally to represent the value of True. (It also helps you write code that is easier to translate into other programming environments, where True may be represented differently.)

After these constants are defined, you can use them to assign logical values to variables. For example, take a look at the TrueFalse% function in the Transportation Planner program:

```
FUNCTION TrueFalse% (prompt AS STRING)

  temp% = GetAnswer%(prompt, "YN")
  IF temp% = 1 THEN
    TrueFalse% = True
  ELSE
    TrueFalse% = False
  END IF

END FUNCTION    ' TrueFalse%
```

This FUNCTION procedure calls the GetAnswer% function to elicit a response of Y or N from the user. GetAnswer% returns a value of 1 for Y or 2 for N. The program assigns this value to temp% and then uses an IF structure to determine whether TrueFalse% should return a value of true or false. If temp% is 1, TrueFalse% returns the value of the True constant; if 2, TrueFalse% returns False.

The program subsequently stores true or false as the values of the `Reserved` and `Paid` fields of a transportation record. For example, here is the statement that elicits yes-or-no input for the `Reserved` field and stores it as a true or false value:

```
TransRec.Reserved = TrueFalse%("Reserved? ")
```

As you can see, the use of `True` and `False` as symbolic constants makes your code easier to write and to understand.

If then — or else

The one-line decision statement is fine for decisions that choose between two simple actions. But sometimes you want to design a decision that chooses between two or more *blocks* of code, where a block consists of several QBasic statements in sequence. In this case, you write your decision as a multiline structure.

One simple form of the decision structure can be represented as follows:

```
IF condition THEN

   ' Block of code to be performed
   ' if the condition is true.

ELSE

   ' Block of code to be performed
   ' if the condition is false.

END IF
```

In this form, the keywords of the decision structure serve to define distinct blocks of code. The statements located between the IF line and the ELSE line make up the block that is performed if the condition is true, and the statements between ELSE and END IF make up the block that the decision selects if the condition is false. Each block may contain any number of statements.

For example, the following passage contains a decision that conducts one of two input dialogs, depending on the user's age:

```
INPUT "How old are you"; age%
IF age% < 17 THEN
   INPUT "Where do you go to school"; school$
   INPUT "What grade are you in"; grade$
   INPUT "When will you graduate"; gradYear$
ELSE
   INPUT "What level of schooling have you completed"; level$
   INPUT "What is your current employment"; emp$
   INPUT "Do you expect to continue your education"; cont$
END IF
```

Each dialog consists of three INPUT statements. If the user reports an age that is less than 17, the first three INPUT statements are performed; if the user is 17 or over, the second three are performed.

Notice the use of indentation to set off the individual blocks of code in a decision structure. This optional typographical effect can help you see at a glance how the decision is designed. In the programs in this book, two-space indentations are used for blocks of code in decision structures and loops. ■

The ELSE clause is optional in a decision structure. In the following example from the Transportation Planner program, only one block of code is in the decision structure:

```
IF TrueFalse%("Save this record? ") THEN
  numRecs = numRecs + 1
  PUT #1, numRecs, TransRec
END IF
```

The condition for this decision is expressed as a call to the TrueFalse% function. If the function returns a value of true, the block of statements between IF and END IF is performed; if false, the decision results in no further action.

You can use a multiline decision structure even when the blocks of code contain only one statement each. You might decide to do so simply to avoid a long and complex one-line IF statement. For example, the following decision from the TravelPlan procedure determines whether or not the program should elicit a DepartTime field for the current transportation record:

```
IF which <> 4 THEN
    LINE INPUT "Time:              ", TransRec.DepartTime
  ELSE
    TransRec.DepartTime = ""
END IF
```

If the user's menu choice (which) is anything other than 4, the Time: prompt appears on the screen as part of the input dialog. But if the user chooses the fourth menu option, R)ented Car, the DepartTime field is recorded as an empty string.

A common mistake is to omit the END IF statement that marks the end of a decision structure. Anytime you organize a decision into multiple lines and blocks of code, you must complete the structure with an END IF line. Otherwise, QBasic will have no way of knowing where the decision stops. ■

Using the ELSEIF clause

Finally, the ELSEIF clause gives you the opportunity to write decisions that are based on multiple conditions. A decision structure may contain any number of ELSEIF clauses, each with its own condition and corresponding block of code, as follows:

```
IF condition1 THEN

    ' Block of code to be performed
    ' if condition1 is true.

ELSEIF condition2 THEN

    ' Block of code to be performed
    ' if condition2 is true.

ELSEIF condition3 THEN

    ' Block of code to be performed
    ' if condition3 is true.

ELSE

    ' Block of code to be performed
    ' if none of the conditions is true.

END IF
```

In this structure, QBasic evaluates each condition in sequence: first the condition in the IF statement at the top of the decision, and then each of the ELSEIF conditions in turn. If any condition is true, the corresponding block of code is performed, and then the remainder of the decision structure is skipped. But if none of the conditions is true and if the structure contains an ELSE clause, QBasic performs the block located between ELSE and END IF.

The Transportation Planner program uses such a decision structure to plan certain parts of the input dialog in response to the user's choice of a transportation mode:

```
title$ = "Travel by "
IF which = 1 THEN
    title$ = title$ + "Air"
    coPrompt$ = "Airline"
ELSEIF which = 2 THEN
    title$ = title$ + "Train"
    coPrompt$ = "Line"
ELSEIF which = 3 THEN
    title$ = title$ + "Bus"
    coPrompt$ = "Company"
ELSE
    title$ = title$ + "Rented Car"
    coPrompt$ = "Rental Agency"
END IF
```

Depending on the menu choice (which), the program plans one of four titles and prompts for the upcoming input dialog. As you can see, the code uses ELSEIF and ELSE clauses to designate the code that should be selected for each possible menu choice.

Sometimes you can simplify a complex decision structure by using a different statement that QBasic supplies for decisions: SELECT CASE. You learn about this statement in the next chapter.

Chapter 12

London, Paris, Venice, or Rome?

. . . .

In This Chapter

▶ Selecting alternatives

▶ Using the SELECT CASE structure

▶ Understanding CASE expressions

▶ Understanding nested decisions

. . . .

*1*n this chapter you continue to explore the variety of ways you can express decisions in QBasic programs. You focus on two specific topics: the SELECT CASE decision structure and nested decisions.

Like the IF structure, SELECT CASE allows you to divide a decision into blocks of code representing different options that the decision can choose among. The SELECT CASE decision bases its choice on a match between a test expression and individual CASE expressions located at the top of each block of code. QBasic programmers frequently use SELECT CASE for processing menu choices or for working with predictable categories of input data.

A nested decision is an IF or SELECT CASE statement that appears inside the code of another decision structure. Nesting can significantly increase the complexity of decisions in a QBasic program.

To illustrate the SELECT CASE statement and nesting, this chapter presents a project named the Transportation List program, a companion to the Transportation Planner program you examined in Chapter 11. The Transportation List program opens the TRANPLAN.DB database, in which you've recorded the travel reservations and schedules for an upcoming business trip or vacation. Then the program prints a list of all the records in the database, from beginning to end. In so doing, it illustrates a variety of approaches to decision making.

Where Am I Going?

Before running the Transportation List program, make sure you've created a TRANPLAN.DB database by running the Transportation Planner program (TRANPLAN.BAS) one or more times. The Transportation List program looks for the database in the root directory of your hard disk. Then turn on your printer, load TRANLIST.BAS into the QBasic editor, and press F5. The program reads all the travel records you've recorded and sends them to the printer. Here's an example of the output:

```
Transportation
---------------

Airline: AirEuro
            Departure: San Francisco    Destination: Paris
            Date: 1/17/94               Time: 8:35
            Reserved: Yes               Paid: Yes

Train Line: SNCF
            Departure: Paris            Destination: Caen
            Date: 1/19/94               Time: 10:20
            Reserved: Yes               Paid: No

Car Rental Agency: CarEuro
            Departure: Caen             Destination: various
            Date: 1/19/94
            Reserved: Yes

Train Line: SNCF
            Departure: Caen             Destination: Paris
            Date: 1/22/94               Time: 9:30
            Reserved: Yes               Paid: No

Airline: AirEuro
            Departure: Paris            Destination: Rome
            Date: 1/23/94               Time: 1:45
            Reserved: Yes               Paid: Yes
```

As you see, the program prints as many as seven fields of information for each travel record: the travel company, the place of departure, the destination, the date and time of the trip, and the reservation and payment status. For a car rental record, the departure time and payment status fields do not apply.

After you've printed the complete set of travel records for a given trip, you can save the current TRANPLAN.DB database by renaming it. For example, you might save it under a name like TRAN1-94.BAK, indicating the date of the trip described in the database. Then the next time you run the Transportation Planner program, it will start a new database for another trip. The TRANLIST.BAS program always prints the database currently named TRANPLAN.DB.

Code It

Here is the listing of the Transportation List program:

```
' Transportion List (TRANLIST.BAS)
' Lists the transportation plans
' for an upcoming business trip.
' (Reads the TRANPLAN.DB database.)

DECLARE SUB ShowAir ()
DECLARE SUB ShowTrain ()
DECLARE SUB ShowBus ()
DECLARE SUB ShowRental ()
DECLARE SUB ShowFields ()
DECLARE SUB ReadRecord (rec AS INTEGER)

' Define the record type.
TYPE TransportType
  Mode AS INTEGER
  Company AS STRING * 10
  From AS STRING * 15
  Dest AS STRING * 15
  DepartDate AS STRING * 10
  DepartTime AS STRING * 5
  Reserved AS INTEGER
  Paid AS INTEGER
END TYPE

' The record variable is global.
DIM SHARED TransRec AS TransportType
DIM numRecs AS INTEGER

' Open the database and calculate the number of records.
OPEN "\TRANPLAN.DB" FOR RANDOM AS #1 LEN = LEN(TransRec)
numRecs = LOF(1) / LEN(TransRec)

CLS
LPRINT "Transportation"
LPRINT "--------------"
LPRINT

' Read and display each record.
FOR i% = 1 TO numRecs
  ReadRecord i%
NEXT i%

END   ' TRANLIST.BAS



SUB ReadRecord (rec AS INTEGER)

  ' Read one record from the transportation
  ' database and call the appropriate
  ' procedure to display the information.
```

(continued)

```
GET #1, rec, TransRec
SELECT CASE TransRec.Mode
  CASE 1
    ShowAir
  CASE 2
    ShowTrain
  CASE 3
    ShowBus
  CASE 4
    ShowRental

  CASE ELSE
    PRINT "Can't display record"; rec
END SELECT
LPRINT

END SUB   ' ReadRecord


SUB ShowAir

  ' Display an air transportation record.

  LPRINT "Airline: "; TransRec.Company
  ShowFields

END SUB   ' ShowAir


SUB ShowBus

  ' Display a bus trip record.

  LPRINT "Bus Company: "; TransRec.Company
  ShowFields

END SUB   ' ShowBus


SUB ShowFields

  ' Display the place of departure, the destination,
  ' the date and time, and the reservation status.

  LPRINT , "Departure: "; TransRec.From;
  LPRINT "  Destination: "; TransRec.Dest
  LPRINT , "Date: "; TransRec.DepartDate,

  ' Time field not available for car rental.
  IF TransRec.Mode <> 4 THEN
    LPRINT "Time: "; TransRec.DepartTime
  ELSE
    LPRINT
  END IF
```

```
          LPRINT , "Reserved: ";
          IF TransRec.Reserved THEN
            LPRINT "Yes", ,
          ELSE
            LPRINT "No", ,
          END IF

          ' Paid field not available for car rental.
          IF TransRec.Mode <> 4 THEN
            LPRINT "Paid: ";
            IF TransRec.Paid THEN
              LPRINT "Yes"
            ELSE
              LPRINT "No"
            END IF
          ELSE
            LPRINT
          END IF

      END SUB  ' ShowFields



      SUB ShowRental

        ' Display a car rental record.

        LPRINT "Car Rental Agency: "; TransRec.Company
        ShowFields

      END SUB  ' ShowRental



      SUB ShowTrain

        ' Display a train record.

        LPRINT "Train Line: "; TransRec.Company
        ShowFields

      END SUB  ' ShowTrain
```

The program consists of a main module followed by six relatively short procedures. The main module opens the travel database and determines the number of records it contains. Then it makes one call to a procedure named ReadRecord for each record in the database. The program continues as follows:

✔ The ReadRecord procedure reads one travel record from the database, storing it in a globally defined data structure that will be available to all the program's procedures. The first field in each record is an integer from 1 to 4 that indicates the mode of transportation: air, rail, bus, or rented car. Accordingly, ReadRecord uses a SELECT CASE statement to determine which of four procedures to call next: ShowAir, ShowTrain, ShowBus, or ShowRental.

✔ Each of these four procedures prints the name of the transportation company and then calls the ShowFields procedure to print the remainder of the current record.

✔ The ShowFields procedure organizes the output according to the transportation mode of the current record. Then the process begins over again for the next record in the database.

Several of these procedures contain interesting examples of decision structures.

A Select Case

A SELECT decision chooses at most one block of code to perform, among the multiple blocks you include in the structure. Each block of code is marked off by a CASE clause. The decision works by comparing the value of a test expression with expressions that appear at the top of each CASE block. When a match is found, the decision performs the corresponding block of code.

Here is one way to represent the general format of the SELECT CASE structure:

```
SELECT CASE testExpression

CASE expression1

   ' Block of code to be performed
   ' if a match is found between
   ' testExpression and expression1

CASE expression2

   ' Block of code to be performed
   ' if a match is found between
   ' testExpression and expression2

CASE expression3

   ' Block of code to be performed
   ' if a match is found between
   ' testExpression and expression3

' Any number of additional CASE
' blocks may be included.

CASE ELSE

   ' Block of code to be performed
   ' if no match is found between
   ' testExpression and any of the
   ' previous CASE expressions.

END SELECT
```

This is how the SELECT CASE decision proceeds:

1. The decision begins by comparing the value of *testExpression* with *expression1* in the first CASE clause.

2. If there is a match between the two expressions, QBasic performs the first block of code — that is, the statements between the first and second CASE clauses.

3. If there is no match, the program goes to the next CASE expression. If a match is found, the corresponding block of code is performed. Then the action of the decision is complete; no further CASE expressions are compared.

4. If the decision reaches the final CASE clause — identified as CASE ELSE — without finding a match in any of the previous CASE clauses, the CASE ELSE block is performed. (But note that the CASE ELSE clause is optional. If it is not present in a SELECT structure, the decision results in no action if no match is found between *testExpression* and a CASE expression.)

The Transportation List program contains a simple example of a SELECT structure, located in the ReadRecord procedure. The procedure begins by reading one travel record from the database, and storing the record in the variable TransRec. The transportation mode — an integer from 1 to 4 — is represented by the name TransRec.Mode. (You learn more about this special *record.field* notation in Chapter 16.) Given this value, the following SELECT structure chooses one of four procedures to call for printing the current record:

```
SELECT CASE TransRec.Mode
   CASE 1
      ShowAir
   CASE 2
      ShowTrain
   CASE 3
      ShowBus
   CASE 4
      ShowRental

   CASE ELSE
      PRINT "Can't display record"; rec
END SELECT
```

If the Mode field is 1, the program calls the ShowAir procedure; if 2, ShowTrain; if 3, ShowBus; and if 4, ShowRental.

In the unlikely event that TransRec.Mode is some value other than 1, 2, 3, or 4, the program has no way of handling the record. Accordingly, a CASE ELSE clause provides the code to be performed in this event; the program displays a brief error message on the screen.

In this example, the CASE expressions all consist of single numbers. Although this is not an unusual way to use the SELECT decision, the structure is actually more versatile, and allows you to write CASE expressions in a variety of ways.

CASE Expressions 101

The CASE clause can contain a *list* or *range* of values, in any of the following formats:

- ✔ A list, where each value is separated from the next by a comma, as follows:

  ```
  CASE expression1, expression2, ...
  ```

  A match occurs when *testExpression* equals any of the values in the list.

- ✔ A range of values, expressed with the TO keyword:

  ```
  CASE expression1 TO expression2
  ```

  A match occurs when *testExpression* equals any value in the range.

- ✔ A relational expression, introduced by the keyword IS and employing one of QBasic's six relational operators (<, <=, >, >=, =, or <>):

  ```
  CASE IS relationalOperation expression
  ```

  A match occurs if the value of *testExpression* is correctly described by the relation.

The following short program illustrates all of these possibilities. It's designed to suggest appropriate gifts for children in several age groups:

```
PRINT "Ideal Birthday Presents"
INPUT "What is the child's age"; age%

SELECT CASE age%

  CASE 1, 2

    PRINT "Stuffed animals."
    PRINT "Clothes."

  CASE 3 TO 5

    PRINT "Books."
    PRINT "Puzzles."
    PRINT "Large rubber balls."

  CASE 6, 7

    PRINT "Electronic games."

  CASE IS >= 8

    PRINT "Clothes."
    PRINT "Sports equipment."
    PRINT "Computer software."

END SELECT
```

The four CASE blocks in this decision describe four age groups: ages 1 and 2; ages 3 to 5; ages 6 and 7; and ages 8 and over. The corresponding blocks of code display gift suggestions on the screen.

TIP

SELECT CASE versus IF: And the winner is . . .

In many programs, you can reasonably use either the SELECT CASE structure or a multiline IF structure. The choice is a matter of preference. For example, the Transportation Planner program in Chapter 11 contains the following long IF structure:

```
IF which = 1 THEN
   title$ = title$ + "Air"
   coPrompt$ = "Airline"
ELSEIF which = 2 THEN
   title$ = title$ + "Train"
   coPrompt$ = "Line"
ELSEIF which = 3 THEN
   title$ = title$ + "Bus"
   coPrompt$ = "Company"
ELSE
   title$ = title$ + "Rented Car"
   coPrompt$ = "Rental Agency"
END IF
```

This decision could have been designed as a SELECT statement:

```
SELECT CASE which
   CASE 1
      title$ = title$ + "Air"
      coPrompt$ = "Airline"
   CASE 2
      title$ = title$ + "Train"
      coPrompt$ = "Line"
   CASE 3
      title$ = title$ + "Bus"
      coPrompt$ = "Company"
   CASE ELSE
      title$ = title$ + "Rented Car"
      coPrompt$ = "Rental Agency"
END SELECT
```

During a program run, these two structures result in the same decisions.

Nesting Instincts

Sometimes one decision leads to another. When this happens in a program, you may find yourself organizing your code in a series of *nested* decisions. This simply means that an "inner" decision is contained in one of the blocks of code belonging to an "outer" decision. If the outer decision selects that particular block, the program will have yet another decision structure to perform.

The ShowFields procedure of the Transportation List program has a simple example. It takes place where the program is ready to print the Paid field of the current travel record:

```
IF TransRec.Mode <> 4 THEN
  LPRINT "Paid: ";
  IF TransRec.Paid THEN
    LPRINT "Yes"
  ELSE
    LPRINT "No"
  END IF
ELSE
  LPRINT
END IF
```

The Paid field is available for only the first three travel modes — air, rail, or bus, represented by the integers 1, 2, and 3. If the mode is 4, the program skips the Paid field:

```
IF TransRec.Mode <> 4 THEN
```

But if the current travel record has an appropriate mode, the program next has to decide whether to display *Yes* or *No* as the value of the Paid field. This is the job of the nested decision:

```
IF TransRec.Paid Then
  LPRINT "Yes"
ELSE
  LPRINT "No"
END IF
```

 Notice the use of indentation for the levels of nesting in this passage. Because each nested structure is indented further than the outer structure, you can easily visualize the levels of nesting. ▪

Nesting can occur at multiple levels in QBasic decision structures. Decisions can also be nested in a loop structure, which is the topic of the next two chapters.

Part V

Destinations Revisited: Loops in QBasic

The 5th Wave — By Rich Tennant

PC DESCENDING A STAIRCASE

"THE ARTIST WAS ALSO A PROGRAMMER AND EVIDENTLY PRODUCED SEVERAL VARIATIONS ON THIS THEME."

1 In This Part . . .

In Part V you learn how to make the computer repeat itself in useful ways. QBasic provides two main loop structures for controlling repetition: The DO loop is based on a conditional expression, and the FOR loop is based on a variable that counts the repetitions. These are among the most powerful and important statements in the language.

To illustrate loops, Part V presents a pair of programs you can use to record your impressions of the business meetings you attend. Who said what to whom — and what did it really mean? You can keep track of all this information — and retrieve it again when you need it — using the two Meetings programs.

Chapter 13

Just DO It!

*Y*our computer has unlimited capacity for repetition. Whatever the task — processing hundreds of database records, performing scores of calculations, or printing dozens of copies of nearly identical documents — the computer completes each repetition reliably and efficiently. As you create your own QBasic programs, you'll often want to take advantage of the computer's penchant for repetition. To make the computer repeat a task, you organize a block of code in a special structure known as a *loop*.

A loop has two basic components:

✔ The block of code that you want the computer to perform repeatedly

✔ An instruction that controls the duration of the looping — and tells the computer when to stop

But this isn't quite the whole story. In the design of a loop, your typical goal is to provide the computer with distinct information to work with during each *iteration* of the loop. The code remains the same, but the data changes. This is what makes repetition truly powerful: Each time around the loop, the computer can process the *next* record in a database, perform a calculation on a *different* set of data, or conduct a *new* input or output operation.

QBasic provides two kinds of loops, known by the keywords DO and FOR. In this chapter you learn how to use DO loops, and in Chapter 14 you concentrate on FOR loops. To study loops in action, you'll work with yet another new pair of QBasic projects, called the Business Meetings program and the Meetings List program:

> ✔ The Business Meetings program, presented in this chapter, is designed to help you record information about important meetings with clients, colleagues, sales people, suppliers, consultants, or other people you meet during business trips. For each record, you enter the names of the people you've met with, and the date, place, time, and subject of the meeting. You can include several lines of notes about the meeting. The program saves all this information in a database file on disk.
>
> ✔ The Meetings List program (presented in Chapter 14) opens this database file and prints your meeting records neatly onto paper. However many meetings you've recorded in the file, the program sends each of them one-by-one to the printer.

As you examine the code of these two programs, you'll find several interesting examples of DO loops and FOR loops.

Getting Down to Business

When you first run the Business Meetings program, it displays a title on the screen and immediately begins prompting you for information about a recent business meeting. It asks you for six specific data items, and gives you the opportunity to enter up to five lines of notes. Here's a sample of the input dialog:

```
Description of Business Meeting
----------- -- -------- -------

Meeting Date? 1/12/94
        With? Susan Altman
       Place? Paris
        Time? 10:30
       Until? 12:00
     Subject? Business potential

Notes:
Line 1 -> Susan has been exploring potential markets for our
Line 2 -> software products in France. She's found several large
Line 3 -> companies that would be interested in our database.
Line 4 -> if we come up with a good French version. Susan
Line 5 -> plans a presentation at the home office next month.

Save this record? Y
Another record? Y
```

You press Enter to complete each data entry and each line of notes. If you want to include fewer than five note lines, you simply press Enter in response to a Line prompt; the program stops prompting you for additional notes. For example, here's how the dialog might appear if you enter only three lines of notes:

```
Description of Business Meeting
----------- -- -------- -------

Meeting Date? 1/12/94
        With? Jacques Denis
       Place? Paris
        Time? 14:30
       Until? 17:00
     Subject? Database translation

Notes:
Line 1 -> M. Denis is interested in working on the French
Line 2 -> translation of our database system. He has experience
Line 3 -> but he's expensive. Look for other candidates first.
Line 4 ->

Save this record? Y
Another record? Y
```

At the end of each record, the program asks you to confirm your entry before saving. If you press Y in response to the `Save this record?` prompt, the program adds your record to the database. (If you press N, the record is abandoned.) The meetings database is saved in the root directory of your hard disk, under the name MEETINGS.DB.

Finally, the program asks you whether you want to continue entering records. During a given run of the program, you can enter a single record or many records. To continue the program, you press Y in response to the `Another record?` prompt. To stop the program, press N. Each time you run the program, your new record entries are appended to the end of the MEETINGS.DB file.

Code It

Here is the complete listing of the Business Meetings program:

```
' Business Meetings (MEETINGS.BAS)
' Saves information and notes about
' meetings conducted during business trips.

DECLARE SUB MeetingInput ()
DECLARE FUNCTION YesNo$ (question$)
DECLARE SUB GetMeetingInfo ()

' The meeting record type.
TYPE MeetingRec
  MeetDate AS STRING * 10
  MetWith AS STRING * 45
  MeetPlace AS STRING * 15
  TimeFrom AS STRING * 5
  TimeTo AS STRING * 5
  Subject AS STRING * 20
  Notes AS STRING * 400
END TYPE
```

(continued)

```
' The global Meeting record variable
' and the global record counter, curRec.
DIM SHARED Meeting AS MeetingRec
DIM SHARED curRec AS INTEGER

' Open the meetings database as a random-access file.
OPEN "\MEETINGS.DB" FOR RANDOM AS #1 LEN = LEN(Meeting)
curRec = LOF(1) / LEN(Meeting)

' Begin the input dialog.
GetMeetingInfo

END   ' MEETINGS.BAS



SUB GetMeetingInfo

  ' Accept records one at a time until
  ' user has no more records to enter.

  DO

    CLS
    MeetingInput  ' Conduct the input dialog.

    ' Save the record if the user confirms.
    IF YesNo$("Save this record? ") = "Y" THEN
      curRec = curRec + 1
      PUT #1, curRec, Meeting
    END IF

  LOOP UNTIL YesNo$("Another record? ") = "N"

END SUB   ' GetMeetingInfo



SUB MeetingInput

  ' Conduct input dialog for a
  ' business meeting record.

  PRINT "Description of Business Meeting"
  PRINT "----------- -- -------- -------"
  PRINT
  LINE INPUT "Meeting Date? "; Meeting.MeetDate
  LINE INPUT "        With? "; Meeting.MetWith
  LINE INPUT "       Place? "; Meeting.MeetPlace
  LINE INPUT "        Time? "; Meeting.TimeFrom
  LINE INPUT "       Until? "; Meeting.TimeTo
  LINE INPUT "     Subject? "; Meeting.Subject

  ' Initialize variable for notes.
  temp$ = ""
  ln% = 0

  PRINT
  PRINT "Notes:"
```

```
' Accept up to five lines of notes.
DO

   ln% = ln% + 1
   PRINT "Line"; ln%; "-> ";
   LINE INPUT inLine$

   ' If line is not blank, add to note text.
   IF LTRIM$(inLine$) <> "" THEN
     temp$ = temp$ + inLine$ + CHR$(13)
   END IF

LOOP WHILE ln% < 5 AND LTRIM$(inLine$) <> ""

   ' Save the Notes field.
   Meeting.Notes = temp$

   PRINT

END SUB   ' MeetingInput



FUNCTION YesNo$ (question$)

   ' Display a question and wait
   ' for the user to type Y or N.

   PRINT question$;

   DO
      answer$ = UCASE$(INKEY$)
   LOOP UNTIL answer$ = "Y" OR answer$ = "N"

   PRINT answer$

   YesNo$ = answer$

END FUNCTION   ' YesNo$
```

The program contains a main module followed by three procedures. Each of the procedures has an interesting example of a DO loop. As you might guess, all the loops are involved with specific input tasks:

✔ The GetMeetingInfo procedure controls the duration of the input dialog. It repeats the dialog as long as the user wants to continue entering new records.

✔ The MeetingInput procedure is in charge of the details of the input. It displays the prompts on the screen and receives the input from the keyboard. A DO loop in this procedure controls the input of notes. As long as the user continues entering text in response to the Line prompts, the procedure prompts repeatedly for additional lines of notes, up to a maximum of five lines.

✔ The YesNo$ function accepts a response of Y or N from the keyboard. To reject irrelevant input, the procedure uses a DO loop that continues reading the keyboard until the user presses one of the two valid keys.

As you'll see in these examples, DO loops use conditional expressions to control the duration of the looping. In this program, the conditions are based on the user's actions. Does the user want to enter another record? Is the user still entering text in response to the Line prompts? Has the user pressed an appropriate key from the keyboard? Answers to these questions — translated into the true or false values of specific conditional expressions — determine whether or not the looping continues.

DO Loops If That's What You Do Best

The first requirement of a loop structure is to identify the block of code that will be performed repeatedly during the looping. You meet this requirement in a DO loop by writing specific statements at the beginning and the end of the loop:

- ✔ A DO statement always marks the top of the loop.
- ✔ A LOOP statement always marks the bottom.

The statements located between DO and LOOP make up the body of the loop — that is, the code that will be performed once for each iteration.

The conditional expression that controls the duration of the looping can appear either in the DO statement at the top of the loop or in the LOOP statement at the bottom. Furthermore, the condition can appear in either of two clauses, introduced by the keywords WHILE or UNTIL. The two most commonly used DO loop formats have a WHILE clause in the DO statement at the top of the loop or an UNTIL clause in the LOOP statement at the bottom. Here is a loop with the condition at the top:

```
DO WHILE condition

   ' The block of statements that the
   ' computer will perform repeatedly
   ' as long as the condition is true.

LOOP
```

And here is a loop with the condition located at the bottom:

```
DO

   ' The block of statements that the
   ' computer will perform repeatedly
   ' until the condition is true.

LOOP UNTIL condition
```

In both cases, *condition* is an expression that results in a value of true or false.

Staying in the loop

The DO WHILE and LOOP UNTIL formats are based on traditional programming practices, but you're free to switch them around. DO UNTIL and LOOP WHILE work just as well, as you'll see later in this chapter.

The placement of the condition at the top or the bottom of a loop can be an important factor in the loop's behavior. With the expression located at the top of the loop, QBasic evaluates the condition *before* the first iteration; if the condition has the "wrong" value, QBasic immediately skips the entire loop without performing a single iteration. By contrast, if the expression is located at the bottom of the loop, QBasic always performs the block of code at least one time. *After* the first iteration, QBasic evaluates the condition and determines whether to continue the looping.

QBasic evaluates the condition once for each iteration of the loop. A change in the condition's value ultimately causes the loop to stop:

- ✔ In a WHILE clause, the looping continues as long as the condition is true. Looping stops when the condition becomes false.

- ✔ In an UNTIL clause, the looping continues as long as the condition is false. Looping stops when the condition becomes true.

Just as in decision statements, you can use a variety of operations to build conditions. The relational operations (represented by $<$, $<=$, $>$, $>=$, $=$, $<>$) and the logical operations (represented by NOT, AND, OR, XOR, EQV, and IMP) are available for use in DO loops. Turn back to Chapter 11 for a review of these operations.

You control the duration of a DO loop by your choice of a WHILE clause or an UNTIL clause, as discussed in the upcoming sections.

WHILE it lasts

When you want the repetition to continue as long as a condition remains true, use a WHILE clause in your DO loop. With the WHILE clause in the DO statement at the top of the loop, QBasic evaluates the condition before the first iteration.

For example, a program that reads information from a file on disk typically needs a way to determine when it has read the last item of information from the file. For this purpose, QBasic provides a function named EOF, which stands for *end of file*. The EOF function returns a value of false as long is there is still more information to be read from a particular open file. But when the program reaches the end of the file, EOF returns true. The EOF function is therefore the ideal condition to use in a DO loop that reads a file. Consider this loop from the Travel Expense Table program (presented back in Chapter 6):

```
DO WHILE NOT EOF(1)
   ShowExpenseRec
LOOP
```

Each iteration of this loop makes a call to the ShowExpenseRec procedure, which in turn reads a line of text from the EXPLOG.TXT file and displays the information on the screen. At the beginning of each iteration, the program makes a call to the EOF function. If the expression NOT EOF(1) is true — meaning that the program has not yet reached the end of the file — the looping continues. When the value of the conditional expression switches to false, the looping stops. (You learn more about reading files and using the EOF function in Chapters 18 and 19.)

In this first example, the condition that controls the duration of the looping appears in the DO statement at the top of the loop. If the file happens to be empty, the expression NOT EOF(1) returns a value of false at the outset. In this event, no call is made to the ShowExpenseRec procedure; QBasic skips the loop without performing any iterations.

By contrast, the Business Meetings program contains a loop in which the WHILE clause is at the end:

```
DO

   ln% = ln% + 1
   PRINT "Line"; ln%; "-> ";
   LINE INPUT inLine$

   ' If line is not blank, add to note text.
   IF LTRIM$(inLine$) <> "" THEN
     temp$ = temp$ + inLine$ + CHR$(13)
   END IF

LOOP WHILE ln% < 5 AND LTRIM$(inLine$) <> ""
```

This loop prompts the user to enter lines of notes for the current meeting record. As many as five lines of text can be entered from the keyboard, but the user has the option of including fewer lines. Each new line of input is stored in the string variable inLine$, and the program uses the integer variable ln% to count the number of lines that have been entered. This variable is increased by 1 at the beginning of each iteration:

```
ln% = ln% + 1
```

Gone with the WEND

To maintain compatibility with older versions of the language, QBasic supports another kind of WHILE loop, in the following format:

```
WHILE condition

    ' The block of statements that the
    ' computer will perform repeatedly
    ' as long as the condition is true.

WEND
```

This loop continues while *condition* is true. Its behavior is the same as the DO WHILE loop:

```
DO WHILE condition

    ' The block of statements that the
    ' computer will perform repeatedly
    ' as long as the condition is true.

LOOP
```

You may occasionally see programs that contain the WHILE WEND loop, but you should avoid using it. The DO loop is much more versatile and has become the standard conditional loop structure in QBasic programming.

The looping ends either when `ln%` reaches a value of 5 or when the user enters a blank line in response to the `Line` prompt. The WHILE clause uses an AND operation to express this compound condition:

```
    WHILE ln% < 5 AND LTRIM$(inLine$) <> ""
```

When either of these relational expressions produces a false value — that is, when `ln%` reaches 5 or when `inLine$` is blank — the looping stops.

Because the WHILE condition is at the bottom of this loop, the program always prompts for at least one line of notes. The user can stop the looping at any time by pressing Enter in response to the `Line` prompt, but the program always provides the option.

UNTIL then...

An UNTIL clause stops the looping when a condition becomes true. As long as the value of the condition is false, the iterations continue. The Business Meetings program contains two interesting examples. First, the loop that controls the duration of the input dialog is located in the GetMeetingInfo procedure:

```
DO

   CLS
   MeetingInput   ' Conduct the input dialog.

   ' Save the record if the user confirms.
   IF YesNo$("Save this record? ") = "Y" THEN
      curRec = curRec + 1
      PUT #1, curRec, Meeting
   END IF

LOOP UNTIL YesNo$("Another record? ") = "N"
```

Each iteration of this loop makes a call to the MeetingInput procedure to elicit one new meeting record. An IF decision nested inside the loop then asks the user to confirm that the record should be saved in the meetings database. Finally, the UNTIL clause at the bottom of the loop makes a call to a function named YesNo$. This function displays the Another Record? prompt on the screen and waits for the user to press the Y or N key. Accordingly, the function returns a string value of "Y" or "N." As long as the value is "Y" the UNTIL condition remains false, and the input dialog continues. But when the user presses N, the function returns "N" and the UNTIL condition becomes false. When this value terminates the DO loop, the input dialog is complete.

The YesNo$ function itself contains the other example of the UNTIL clause. The function uses the QBasic INKEY$ function to read input from the keyboard one character at a time. Each letter that the user presses is converted to uppercase and then stored in the string variable answer$:

```
DO
   answer$ = UCASE$(INKEY$)
LOOP UNTIL answer$ = "Y" OR answer$ = "N"
```

If the user inadvertently presses a key other than Y or N, the following expression results in a value of false:

```
answer$ = "Y" OR answer$ = "N"
```

In other words, the looping continues until the user presses either Y or N. When one of the two valid input characters has been received, the UNTIL condition becomes true, and the looping stops. The YesNo$ function then displays the value of answer$ on the screen and returns this string to the caller, as follows:

```
PRINT answer$

YesNo$ = answer$
```

Hit the Break!

An *infinite loop* is a repetition structure that has no logical stopping point. You can create an infinite loop on purpose by writing a DO loop that contains no WHILE or UNTIL clause. For example, try entering the following loop in the QBasic editor:

```
DO
   PRINT "No end in sight...   ";
LOOP
```

Press F5 to run the program, and the screen quickly fills with unending repetitions of the same output message, as shown in Figure 13-1.

Figure 13-1:
Output from
an infinite
loop.

```
No end in sight...  No end in sight...  No end in sight...  No end in sight...
No end in sight...  No end in sight...  No end in sight...  No end in sight...
No end in sight...  No end in sight...  No end in sight...  No end in sight...
No end in sight...  No end in sight...  No end in sight...  No end in sight...
No end in sight...  No end in sight...  No end in sight...  No end in sight...
No end in sight...  No end in sight...  No end in sight...  No end in sight...
No end in sight...  No end in sight...  No end in sight...  No end in sight...
No end in sight...  No end in sight...
```

To stop the looping, hold down the Ctrl key and press the Break key. This keyboard combination stops a program that is out of control.

Sometimes programmers create infinite loops accidentally, by writing WHILE or UNTIL conditions that fail to trigger the end of the looping. Specifically, an infinite loop occurs in either of the following situations:

- The loop contains a WHILE condition that is always true; no event in the program switches the condition to false.

- The loop contains an UNTIL condition that is always false; no event in the program switches the condition to true.

Watch out for these two programming errors, and always be prepared to press Ctrl-Break if you inadvertently create an infinite loop.

Chapter 14

What Goes Around, Comes Around

As you learned in Chapter 13, a DO loop is based on a condition; the looping stops when the value of the condition changes from true to false or from false to true. By contrast, a FOR loop contains a numeric *counter variable* that controls the duration of the looping. Your program completes one iteration for each change in the value of this counter variable. When the counter moves beyond a specified range, the looping stops.

FOR loops are useful in a variety of programming contexts. You should consider using a FOR loop whenever you can

✔ Specify in advance the exact number of iterations that the loop should go through.

✔ Define a variable that represents the correct number of iterations. (The value of this variable can be determined during the program run, so that each performance of a loop may result in a different number of iterations.)

✔ Write an expression that calculates the appropriate number of iterations. (Again, the number of iterations may vary from one run to the next.)

As in a DO structure, the FOR loop identifies a block of code that will be performed repeatedly during the looping. Two parts of a FOR loop serve as markers for the beginning and the end of the code:

✔ The FOR statement always marks the beginning of the loop. This statement also defines the counter variable and specifies the range of values it will go through during the looping.

✔ The NEXT statement marks the end of the loop.

The statements between FOR and NEXT are performed once for each iteration of the loop.

In many FOR loops, the counter variable itself becomes a useful data item in the performance of the loop. You can display this counter on the screen, perform calculations with it, or use it as an index to access other information. The more you learn about using FOR loops, the more important this counter variable can become in the design of your program.

In this chapter you master the structure of the FOR loop and examine several examples. Along the way, you work with a short project named the Meetings List program, which is designed to print the database records you created with the Business Meetings program in Chapter 13. The Meetings List program uses a FOR loop to move record-by-record through the meetings database.

Making a List and Checking It Twice

Before you run the Meetings List program, make sure the MEETINGS.DB file is stored in the root directory of your hard disk. This file is created the first time you run the Business Meetings program. Each additional time you run the program, you have the opportunity to append new meeting records to the file.

To print the records in the database, open the Meetings List program (MEETLIST.BAS), turn on your printer, and press F5 to run the program. The program opens the database, reads its records one at a time, and sends each record to the printer. Here's a sample of the output:

```
Business Meetings
-------- --------


Date:    1/12/94
With:    Susan Altman
Place:   Paris
Time:    10:30
Until:   12:00
Subject: Business potential

Notes:
------
Susan has been exploring potential markets for our
software products in France. She's found several large
companies that would be interested in our database,
if we come up with a good French version. Susan
plans a presentation at the home office next month.
```

```
Date:     1/12/94
With:     Jacques Denis
Place:    Paris
Time:     14:30
Until:    17:00
Subject: Database translation

Notes:
------
M. Denis is interested in working on the French
translation of our database system. He has experience
but he's expensive. Look for other candidates first.


Date:     1/13/94
With:     Francois Renaud, Susan Altman
Place:    Paris
Time:     12:30
Until:    14:30
Subject: Database application

Notes:
------
We discussed in detail how our database system could
streamline operations in M. Renaud's small manufacturing
business. He seemed enthusiastic, and we agreed to
provide him with additional details and a demonstration
program next month.
```

As you can see, the program prints all the fields of each record — the date of a meeting, the people who were present, and the place, time, and subject of the meeting. Finally, the program prints the lines of notes you've included in the meeting record.

Code It

The Meetings List consists of a main module followed by a single procedure. Here is the program listing:

```
' Meetings List (MEETLIST.BAS)
' Prints information and notes about
' meetings conducted during business trips.
' (Reads \MEETINGS.DB, created by MEETINGS.BAS.)

DECLARE SUB PrintMeetings ()
```

(continued)

```
' The meeting record type.
TYPE MeetingRec
  MeetDate AS STRING * 10
  MetWith AS STRING * 45
  MeetPlace AS STRING * 15
  TimeFrom AS STRING * 5
  TimeTo AS STRING * 5
  Subject AS STRING * 20
  Notes AS STRING * 400
END TYPE

' The global Meeting record variable
' and the global record counter, curRec.
DIM SHARED Meeting AS MeetingRec
DIM SHARED curRec AS INTEGER

' Open the meetings database as a random-access file.
OPEN "\MEETINGS.DB" FOR RANDOM AS #1 LEN = LEN(Meeting)
curRec = LOF(1) / LEN(Meeting)

PrintMeetings   ' Print the meeting records.

END   ' MEETLIST.BAS

SUB PrintMeetings

  ' Print the meeting records.

  LPRINT "Business Meetings"
  LPRINT "-------- --------"
  LPRINT

  FOR i% = 1 TO curRec
    GET #1, , Meeting
    LPRINT "Date:     "; Meeting.MeetDate
    LPRINT "With:     "; Meeting.MetWith
    LPRINT "Place:    "; Meeting.MeetPlace
    LPRINT "Time:     "; Meeting.TimeFrom
    LPRINT "Until:    "; Meeting.TimeTo
    LPRINT "Subject: "; Meeting.Subject
    LPRINT
    LPRINT "Notes:"
    LPRINT "------"
    LPRINT RTRIM$(Meeting.Notes)
    LPRINT
  NEXT i%

END SUB   ' PrintMeetings
```

The main module opens the meetings database and calculates the number of
records the database contains. The record count is stored in the global integer
variable curRec. Next the program makes a call to the procedure named
PrintMeetings. This procedure uses a FOR loop to read and print each meeting
record, from the beginning to the end of the database. You take a close look at
this loop later in this chapter.

Don't Get Thrown FOR a Loop

In its simplest form, the FOR loop uses an integer counter that increases by 1 for each iteration. In this case, the loop's syntax can be represented as follows:

```
FOR counter% = v1 TO v2

  ' The block of statements that the
  ' computer will perform repeatedly
  ' as counter% increases from v1 to v2.

NEXT counter%
```

In this format, *counter%* is the name of a variable, and *v1* and *v2* specify the range of values that *counter%* will represent during the looping. You can write *v1* and *v2* as literal numeric values such as 1 and 10, variables such as first% and last%, or expressions such as a% * 5 and a% * 5 + 20.

Here are the steps QBasic goes through to perform a FOR loop:

1. Assign the value of *v1* to *counter%*.

2. Compare the new value of *counter%* with *v2*:

   If *counter%* is less than or equal to *v2*, perform all the statements located between FOR and NEXT once.

   If *counter%* is greater than *v2*, stop the looping and jump down to the statement located after NEXT.

3. If the looping hasn't yet stopped, increase the value of *counter%* by 1 and continue again as described in step 2.

Consider a simple example. The following program conducts an input dialog for annual income amounts over a ten-year period, and then displays the total income for the ten years:

```
CLS
PRINT "Enter your annual income"
PRINT "for the last ten years:"
PRINT

total = 0
FOR years% = 1985 TO 1994
  PRINT years%;
  INPUT ": ", income
  total = total + income
NEXT years%

PRINT
PRINT "Your total income for period is ";
PRINT USING "$$#,####"; total
```

In the program's FOR loop, the counter variable is named years%. Its value increases from 1985 to 1994 during the iterations of the loop. For each iteration, the loop displays the year and waits for the user to input an income amount. After each input, the program adds the current income amount to the accumulated total. Here's an example of the dialog and the resulting output:

```
Enter your annual income
for the last ten years:

 1985 : 29500
 1986 : 31500
 1987 : 33000
 1988 : 35000
 1989 : 37500
 1990 : 40000
 1991 : 43000
 1992 : 47000
 1993 : 51500
 1994 : 55000

Your total income for period is  $403,000
```

Notice how the value of the counter variable years% is used during the looping. The first statement in the loop displays the variable's value on the screen as part of the input prompt for the year's income.

Because the starting and ending values are expressed as literal numbers in this loop, the program performs a fixed number of iterations during each run. By contrast, a FOR loop in the Meetings List program uses a variable to express the range of the counter. The following loop, from the PrintMeetings procedure, reads and prints all the records from the meetings database:

```
FOR i% = 1 TO curRec
  GET #1, , Meeting
  LPRINT "Date:     "; Meeting.MeetDate
  LPRINT "With:     "; Meeting.MetWith
  LPRINT "Place:    "; Meeting.MeetPlace
  LPRINT "Time:     "; Meeting.TimeFrom
  LPRINT "Until:    "; Meeting.TimeTo
  LPRINT "Subject:  "; Meeting.Subject
  LPRINT
  LPRINT "Notes:"
  LPRINT "------"
  LPRINT RTRIM$(Meeting.Notes)
  LPRINT
NEXT i%
```

Here the duration of the looping is determined by the value of the variable curRec. The main module opens the meetings database, calculates the number of records stored in the file, and assigns the value to the global variable curRec. To read and print the entire file, the loop increments the counter variable i%

from 1 to `curRec`. For each iteration of the loop, a GET statement reads the next record from the database file, and a sequence of LPRINT statements send the fields of the record to the printer. (You'll learn more about the GET statement in Chapter 19.) When `i%` reaches the value of `curRec`, the entire file has been read and printed, and the looping stops.

In this case, the duration of the looping is completely dependent on the number of records the program finds in the meetings database. Whether there are three records or thirty or three hundred, the number of iterations is equal to the record count.

In the two FOR loop examples you've seen so far, one of the counter variables is named `years%` and the other is named `i%`. Programmers are fond of using one-letter variable names as counters in FOR loops — especially the names `i%`, `j%`, and `k%`. As a general rule, a meaningful variable name such as `years%` is better than an arbitrary one-letter name. Meaningful variable names make your code clearer and easier to read. But in FOR loops, programmers often opt for brevity over meaning. So get used to seeing `i%`, `j%`, and `k%` as the counter variables in FOR loops; there's nothing particularly significant about these names, but they're used a lot all the same. ■

STEP by STEP

Sometimes you'll want to increase the counter variable by a value other than 1 for each iteration of a FOR loop. In this case, you can use the STEP clause in the FOR statement to indicate the increment amount. Here is a general format for the FOR loop with a STEP clause:

```
FOR counter% = v1 TO v2 STEP incr

   ' The block of statements that the
   ' computer will perform repeatedly.

NEXT counter%
```

As a result of the STEP clause, QBasic increases the value of *counter%* by *incr* instead of 1 after each iteration. You can express the increment amount as a literal value, a variable, or an expression.

For example, the following program conducts an input dialog that asks for a person's job titles over a period of twenty years, at five-year intervals:

```
DIM jobs$(1970 TO 1990)

CLS
PRINT "Job Changes"
PRINT
PRINT "Enter the kind of work you've done"
PRINT "during each of the following years."
PRINT
```

```
FOR years% = 1970 TO 1990 STEP 5
  PRINT years%;
  INPUT ": ", jobs$(years%)
NEXT years%
```

Thanks to the STEP clause in this loop, the years% counter goes up in increments of 5, from 1970 to 1990. Again, the value of years% is used as the input prompt in the resulting input dialog:

```
Job Changes

Enter the kind of work you've done
during each of the following years.

  1970 : Student
  1975 : Teacher
  1980 : Editor
  1985 : Programmer
  1990 : Writer
```

Interestingly enough, the STEP clause also allows you to *decrease* the value of the counter variable as the iterations progress. If this is what you want to do, you write the FOR statement as follows:

```
FOR counter% = v2 TO v1 STEP decr
```

where *v2* is greater than *v1* and the STEP clause provides a decrement amount, that is, a negative value. For example, the following loop displays years in descending order, in five-year decrements:

```
PRINT "Jobs:"

FOR years% = 1990 TO 1970 STEP -5
  PRINT years%; jobs$(years%)
NEXT years%
```

During the looping, the years% counter takes on values from 1990 to 1970 in steps of –5. Here is an example of the resulting output:

```
Jobs:
  1990 Writer
  1985 Programmer
  1980 Editor
  1975 Teacher
  1970 Student
```

Under the following two sets of circumstances, a FOR loop results in no iterations:

✔ The starting value you specify for the counter variable is greater than the ending value, and the STEP value is positive

✔ The starting value is less than the ending value, and the STEP value is negative

For example, the following loops result in no iterations:

```
FOR i% = 1 TO 10 STEP -1
   PRINT i%
NEXT i%


 FOR i% = 10 TO 1 STEP 2
   PRINT i%
NEXT i%
```

(Do you see why?) ▪

Noninteger counters

All the FOR loop examples you've seen up to this point have had integer-type counter variables. Although the use of integer counters is common in FOR loops, you are free to use counters belonging to any QBasic numeric data type — including integer, long integer, single-precision, or double-precision variables. Using a noninteger counter allows you to increase or decrease the variable by fractional values as the iterations proceed.

For example, consider the following currency exchange program:

```
dollarToFranc = 5
dollarToCFA = 500

CLS
PRINT "US Dollars", "French Francs", "   West African CFA"
PRINT "----------", "-------------", "   ----------------"

FOR dollars = .25 TO 5 STEP .25
   PRINT USING "$$#.##"; dollars;
   PRINT , USING "  ##.## FF"; dollars * dollarToFranc;
   PRINT , USING "    #### CFA"; dollars * dollarToCFA
NEXT dollars
```

The counter in this program's FOR loop is a single-precision variable named dollars. The loop increases the value of dollars from 0.25 to 5.0 in increments of 0.25. For each iteration of the loop, the program displays the value of dollars, and the calculated exchange rates in French francs and West African CFA. Here is the resulting currency exchange table:

US Dollars	French Francs	West African CFA
$0.25	1.25 FF	125 CFA
$0.50	2.50 FF	250 CFA
$0.75	3.75 FF	375 CFA
$1.00	5.00 FF	500 CFA
$1.25	6.25 FF	625 CFA
$1.50	7.50 FF	750 CFA
$1.75	8.75 FF	875 CFA
$2.00	10.00 FF	1000 CFA
$2.25	11.25 FF	1125 CFA
$2.50	12.50 FF	1250 CFA
$2.75	13.75 FF	1375 CFA
$3.00	15.00 FF	1500 CFA
$3.25	16.25 FF	1625 CFA
$3.50	17.50 FF	1750 CFA
$3.75	18.75 FF	1875 CFA
$4.00	20.00 FF	2000 CFA
$4.25	21.25 FF	2125 CFA
$4.50	22.50 FF	2250 CFA
$4.75	23.75 FF	2375 CFA
$5.00	25.00 FF	2500 CFA

In this application, you can see the advantage of a noninteger counter variable; it allows you to work with the precise fractional values that you want to display in the table.

You can also decrease a noninteger counter variable by a fractional amount. For example:

```
FOR dollars = 5 TO .25 STEP -.25
```

This FOR statement decreases dollars by .25 for each iteration of the loop. ∎

DO Nest Your FOR Loops

You've seen how to use nesting in IF structures to produce complex decisions in a QBasic program. DO loops and FOR loops can likewise be nested, resulting in powerful patterns of repetition. When one loop is nested inside another, the inner loop goes through its entire cycle of iterations once for each iteration of the outer loop. When carefully planned, nested loops allow you to accomplish a lot of work in a compact amount of code.

Consider this classic example, which simply displays a multiplication table on the screen:

```
FOR i% = 1 TO 10
  FOR j% = 1 TO 10
    PRINT USING "  ###"; i% * j%;
  NEXT j%
  PRINT
NEXT i%
```

The outer loop uses a counter named i%, and the inner loop uses j%. For each iteration of the outer loop, the inner loop displays a row of ten numbers on the screen; each number is calculated as the product of i% and j%. As the outer loop goes through its own ten iterations, the program produces ten rows of values, resulting in a table of 100 numbers. Here is the output:

```
 1   2   3   4   5   6   7   8   9   10
 2   4   6   8  10  12  14  16  18   20
 3   6   9  12  15  18  21  24  27   30
 4   8  12  16  20  24  28  32  36   40
 5  10  15  20  25  30  35  40  45   50
 6  12  18  24  30  36  42  48  54   60
 7  14  21  28  35  42  49  56  63   70
 8  16  24  32  40  48  56  64  72   80
 9  18  27  36  45  54  63  72  81   90
10  20  30  40  50  60  70  80  90  100
```

Although this output is not very useful, the program itself is an instructive one to study as a first example of nested loops. The table gives you an opportunity to visualize the action: Each iteration of the outer loop results in multiple iterations of the inner loop. In the code itself, notice that each loop has its own distinct counter variable and its own NEXT statement to mark the end of the loop. Also note the use of indentation to make the nesting easier to understand.

Mixing up counter variables is probably the most common source of errors in a program that uses nested loops. As you develop nested structures, look carefully at the counters in each FOR statement and corresponding NEXT statement. Make sure the counters match. Also double-check the use of counters in the code inside the loops. A misused counter variable can cause obvious problems in your output, but can be a subtle bug to locate in the code. For an example of this kind of bug, turn back to Chapter 3. ■

The Labels program from Chapter 3 has a great illustration of nested loops. As you recall, the program prints copies of a single mailing address onto a three-column sheet of gummed labels. Figure 14-1 is an example of the program's output.

```
J. T. Smith          J. T. Smith          J. T. Smith
Share-Nau Hotel      Share-Nau Hotel      Share-Nau Hotel
Kabul, Afghanistan   Kabul, Afghanistan   Kabul, Afghanistan


J. T. Smith          J. T. Smith          J. T. Smith
Share-Nau Hotel      Share-Nau Hotel      Share-Nau Hotel
Kabul, Afghanistan   Kabul, Afghanistan   Kabul, Afghanistan


J. T. Smith          J. T. Smith          J. T. Smith
Share-Nau Hotel      Share-Nau Hotel      Share-Nau Hotel
Kabul, Afghanistan   Kabul, Afghanistan   Kabul, Afghanistan
```

Figure 14-1:
Output from
the Labels
program.

The code that produces these labels consists of a complex arrangement of nested loops:

```
FOR i% = 1 TO 10        ' Rows of labels.
   FOR j% = 1 TO n%      ' Lines of text in a label.
     FOR k% = 1 TO 3     ' Columns of labels.
        nextTab% = 2 + (k% - 1) * 27
        LPRINT TAB(nextTab%); Label(j%);
     NEXT k%
     LPRINT
   NEXT j%

   ' Leave blank lines between labels.
   FOR blank% = 1 TO 6 - n%
     LPRINT
   NEXT blank%
NEXT i%
```

The three loops in the first part of this passage use the counter variables i%, j%, and k%. The outermost loop arranges to print ten rows of mailing labels on a page. The middle loop controls the number of lines in each label, and the innermost loop prints three copies of each address line at appropriate horizontal positions — to produce columns of labels. At the end of the code, another nested loop is in charge of producing the correct number of blank lines between each row of labels.

As you see, nested loops require careful planning and precise implementation. But the results can be extraordinarily powerful. You'll learn more about nested loops in the next chapter, as you turn to the topic of arrays.

Part VI
Memories:
Arrays and Records

In This Part . . .

QBasic gives you two important ways to organize quantities of interrelated information in a program. An *array* is a subscripted variable that represents a list or table of data belonging to a consistent type. By contrast, a *record variable* represents fields that may belong to different data types. In Part VI you learn to use both of these data structures. You also examine the important difference between a static array and a dynamic array — a distinction that determines whether or not a program can adjust to data requirements that are not known until run time.

To illustrate these concepts, Part VI presents three programs. First, two different versions of a Travel Expense Summary program give you the opportunity to explore the use of arrays and records. Then, an International Sales program shows you the advantages of a data structure whose size can change during run time.

Chapter 15

Creating Dazzling Arrays

. . . .

In This Chapter

▶ Planning the use of arrays

▶ Declaring one-dimensional arrays

▶ Defining the type and scope of an array

▶ Using FOR loops to work with arrays

▶ Defining a custom range of subscripts for an array

▶ Creating static and dynamic arrays

▶ Creating and using multidimensional arrays

▶ Sorting the data in an array

. . . .

*A*n *array* is a list, a table, or other multidimensional arrangement of data items, all represented by a single variable name. In programs that work with large amounts of interrelated information, arrays are an indispensable way of organizing data. This chapter shows you how to declare and use arrays in a QBasic program.

The DIM statement declares an array and defines its characteristics. As you learned in Chapter 7, you can use DIM also to declare *simple* variables — names that represent single data items at a time. An array has some features in common with a simple variable; both represent values belonging to a consistent data type, and both have a designated *scope* that determines where they are available for use in your program.

But an array has some additional characteristics. Most importantly, every array has a specific number of *dimensions*, which determine how the array's data items are organized. Arrays containing one, two, or three dimensions are probably the most commonly used data structures in QBasic programs. To visualize the meaning of dimension in this context, think of the typical ways you might see information arranged on paper:

> ✔ A one-dimensional array represents a list of data.

> ✔ A two-dimensional array represents a table of data, arranged in rows and columns.

☐ ✔ A three-dimensional array represents several data tables, each with the same number of rows and columns.

You can also define arrays that contain more than three dimensions, but applications for such structures are rare.

To explore arrays in this chapter, you'll work with a new project named the Travel Expense Summary program (EXPSUMM1.BAS). This program conducts an input dialog in which you enter your travel expenses in specific categories. When the input is complete, the program prints a sorted expense table that summarizes the data you've entered. The program stores your expense data in several arrays, of various data types and dimensions. As you examine and run this project, you'll get a clear idea of the power and convenience of arrays in QBasic programming.

Mo' Money, Mo' Money, Mo' Money

When you return from a business trip in which you've gone to several cities, the Travel Expense Summary program is a useful tool for gathering and organizing your travel expense information. The program arranges your expense data by the various cities you visited during the trip. When you first run the program, it asks you for the number of cities. Then you enter information for each city: the city's name, the date when you arrived, and your total expenditures for hotels, food, and "other." The input dialog guides you through the number of cities you specified at the beginning of the program run.

For example, here's a dialog for a business trip that included four cities:

```
How many cities? 4


City # 1
--------
City? Paris
Date? 1/17/94
Hotel expense? 593.18
Food expense?  695.56
Other expense? 325.19

City # 2
--------
City? Caen
Date? 1/20/94
Hotel expense? 375.35
Food expense?  435.41
Other expense? 182.62
```

```
City # 3
--------
City? Strasbourg
Date? 1/24/94
Hotel expense?  482.62
Food expense?   745.93
Other expense?  225.81

City # 4
--------
City? Chartres
Date? 1/28/94
Hotel expense?  225.98
Food expense?   382.88
Other expense?  150.55
```

When this part of the dialog is complete, the program asks you how you want the data arranged in the printed output. You can choose to alphabetize the table by cities or to arrange it in descending order of expense totals:

```
Sort by C)ities or by T)otals?
```

To specify your sorting instructions, type Cities or Totals (or just C or T). Make sure your printer is on and ready to print, and then press Enter to start the output. The program immediately begins printing your expense table. Depending on the sorting option you chose, the rows of the table appear either in alphabetical order by city name:

```
TRAVEL EXPENSE SUMMARY
---------------------------------------------------------------
City         Date         Hotel      Food      Other      Totals
---------------------------------------------------------------
Caen         1/20/94    $375.35    $435.41    $182.62      $993.38
Chartres     1/28/94    $225.98    $382.88    $150.55      $759.41
Paris        1/17/94    $593.18    $695.56    $325.19    $1,613.93
Strasbourg   1/24/94    $482.62    $745.93    $225.81    $1,454.36
---------------------------------------------------------------
TOTAL                                                    $4,821.08
```

or in numeric order by expense totals:

```
TRAVEL EXPENSE SUMMARY
---------------------------------------------------------------
City         Date         Hotel      Food      Other      Totals
---------------------------------------------------------------
Paris        1/17/94    $593.18    $695.56    $325.19    $1,613.93
Strasbourg   1/24/94    $482.62    $745.93    $225.81    $1,454.36
Caen         1/20/94    $375.35    $435.41    $182.62      $993.38
Chartres     1/28/94    $225.98    $382.88    $150.55      $759.41
---------------------------------------------------------------
TOTAL                                                    $4,821.08
```

Notice that the program calculates the total expense amount for each city, and the total for the entire trip. When the printed output is complete, the program run is over.

Code It

Here is the complete listing of the Travel Expense Summary program:

```
' Travel Expense Summary (EXPSUMM1.BAS)
' Gets expense information and prints
' a sorted summary table.

DECLARE SUB PrintInfo ()
DECLARE SUB SortInfo ()
DECLARE SUB SwapInfo (p1%, p2%)
DECLARE SUB GetInfo ()
DECLARE FUNCTION GetNumCities% ()

' The variable num represents the
' number of city records.
DIM SHARED num AS INTEGER
num = GetNumCities%

' After getting num, declare the
' four global arrays.
DIM SHARED cities$(num), dates$(num)
DIM SHARED expenses(num, 3), totals(num)

GetInfo     ' Conduct the input dialog.
SortInfo    ' Sort the data table.
PrintInfo   ' Print the data.

END   ' EXPSUMM1.BAS


SUB GetInfo

  ' Conduct the input dialog for
  ' travel expense information.

  FOR i% = 1 TO num
    PRINT "City #"; i%
    PRINT "--------"
    INPUT "City"; cities$(i%)
    INPUT "Date"; dates$(i%)
    INPUT "Hotel expense? ", expenses(i%, 1)
    INPUT "Food expense?  ", expenses(i%, 2)
    INPUT "Other expense? ", expenses(i%, 3)

    ' Compute the expense totals.
    totals(i%) = 0
    FOR j% = 1 TO 3
      totals(i%) = totals(i%) + expenses(i%, j%)
    NEXT j%
    PRINT
  NEXT i%

END SUB   ' GetInfo
```

```
FUNCTION GetNumCities%

  ' Find out how many cities there will be.

  CLS
  INPUT "How many cities"; inCities%
  GetNumCities% = inCities%
  PRINT
  PRINT

END FUNCTION  ' GetNumCities%



SUB PrintInfo

  ' Print the table.

  ' The title and the column heads.
  LPRINT
  LPRINT TAB(22); "TRAVEL EXPENSE SUMMARY"
  LPRINT STRING$(66, "-")
  LPRINT "City"; TAB(15); "Date"; TAB(30);
  LPRINT "Hotel"; TAB(40); "Food"; TAB(50);
  LPRINT "Other"; TAB(60); "Totals"
  LPRINT STRING$(66, "-")

  ' The data.
  FOR i% = 1 TO num
    LPRINT cities$(i%); TAB(15);
    LPRINT dates$(i%); TAB(25);

    ' The expense data and totals.
    FOR j% = 1 TO 3
      LPRINT USING "$$#,###.##"; expenses(i%, j%);
      LPRINT TAB(25 + j% * 10);
    NEXT j%
    LPRINT USING "  $$#,###.##"; totals(i%)

  NEXT i%

  ' The grand total.
  grandTot = 0
  FOR i% = 1 TO num
    grandTot = grandTot + totals(i%)
  NEXT i%
  LPRINT STRING$(66, "-")
  LPRINT "TOTAL"; TAB(55);
  LPRINT USING " $$##,###.##"; grandTot

END SUB  ' PrintInfo



SUB SortInfo

  ' Sort the expense information either by
  ' cities (alphabetically) or totals (numerically).
```

(continued)

```
' Get the user's sort preference.
PRINT
INPUT "Sort by C)ities or by T)otals"; sort$
CLS
sort$ = UCASE$(LEFT$(sort$, 1))

' Do a bubble sort.
FOR i% = 1 TO num - 1
  FOR j% = i% + 1 TO num

    ' Sort by cities...
    IF sort$ = "C" THEN
      IF cities$(i%) > cities$(j%) THEN
        SwapInfo i%, j%
      END IF

      ' ... or by totals.
    ELSE
      IF totals(i%) < totals(j%) THEN
        SwapInfo i%, j%
      END IF
    END IF
  NEXT j%
NEXT i%

END SUB  ' SortInfo



SUB SwapInfo (p1%, p2%)

  ' Exchange the order of
  ' rows in the expense table.

  SWAP cities$(p1%), cities$(p2%)
  SWAP dates$(p1%), dates$(p2%)

  ' Swap the rows of expenses and totals.
  FOR i% = 1 TO 3
    SWAP expenses(p1%, i%), expenses(p2%, i%)
  NEXT i%
  SWAP totals(p1%), totals(p2%)

END SUB   ' SwapInfo
```

The program organizes the input data in four arrays, named cities$, dates$, expenses, and totals. These arrays are declared in the main module and used throughout the program. Five procedures perform the program's input, sorting, and output operations:

- ✔ The GetNumCities% function displays the first input prompt on the screen, asking for the number of cities visited during the business trip.

- ✔ The GetInfo procedure conducts the entire input dialog for each of the cities in the trip, and calculates the total expense amount for each city.

- ✔ The SortInfo procedure sorts the information either by cities or by totals.

- ✔ The SwapInfo procedure exchanges individual rows of data during the sorting process.
- ✔ The PrintInfo procedure sends the sorted table to the printer.

You'll examine samples of code from each of these procedures as you continue to learn about arrays.

Well, I Declare!

You use the DIM statement to declare several characteristics of an array, including the name, scope, data type, and dimensions. Among these characteristics, *dimension* is the only concept that's new to you at this point in your work. In the sections ahead, you first look at one-dimensional arrays and then learn to declare multidimensional arrays.

Working in another dimension

In a program's main module, you can declare a one-dimensional global array as follows:

```
DIM SHARED arrayName(length) AS dataType
```

Here are the components of this declaration:

- ✔ *arrayName* is a name that conforms to QBasic's rules for variable names; it must begin with a letter and may contain a combination of letters and digits.
- ✔ SHARED means that the array is available globally; any procedure in the program can read or change the data stored in the array. (To define a local array, place a DIM statement inside a procedure and omit the SHARED keyword.)
- ✔ *length* specifies the number of data items the array can represent. The actual size is *length* + 1 because items are numbered from 0 to *length* in the array. (More on this point shortly.) You can supply the length as a literal numeric value, a variable, or an expression.
- ✔ *dataType* is a keyword representing one of QBasic's five data types: STRING, INTEGER, LONG, SINGLE, or DOUBLE. (Alternatively, *dataType* can be the name of a user-defined type, as you'll learn in Chapter 16.)

For example, the following DIM statement declares a one-dimensional string array named countries, and specifies its length as 7:

```
DIM countries(7) AS STRING
```

The AS clause is optional in the array declaration, just as it is in declarations for simple variables. You can instead use one of the special characters that represent variable types: $ for a string array, % for an integer array, & for a long-integer array, ! (or no special character) for a single-precision array, or # for a double-precision array. For example, you can declare a string array named countries$ as follows:

```
DIM countries$(7)
```

Whichever way you declare an array's type, keep in mind that all the data stored in the array must belong to this one type.

After you've declared an array, you can use QBasic statements to assign values to the elements of the array. You identify each element by specifying a subscript in parentheses immediately after the array name. For example, the countries$ array has eight elements, with subscripts ranging from 0 to 7:

```
countries$(0)
countries$(1)
countries$(2)
countries$(3)
countries$(4)
countries$(5)
countries$(6)
countries$(7)
```

Although the length of the countries$ array is specified as 7, the array actually contains *eight* elements, because the subscripts begin at 0. The array can therefore store a list of eight strings. You're free to use these array elements in any way that suits the data requirements of your program. For example, you might decide to store values only in countries$(1) to countries$(7), leaving countries$(0) unused.

An array's subscript is also known as the *index* into the array. The countries$ array has index values from 0 to 7. ■

Getting a handle on arrays

The FOR loop is an extremely convenient structure for handling arrays. As you've learned, a FOR loop uses a special counter variable to control the duration of the looping; this variable serves perfectly as the subscript for accessing the elements of an array. For example, the loop in the following code elicits input values for elements 1 to 7 of the countries$ array:

```
DIM countries$(7)

PRINT "Name the countries you've visited:"
FOR i% = 1 TO 7
  PRINT "   #"; i%;
  INPUT ": ", countries$(i%)
NEXT i%
```

During the looping, the counter variable i% goes through the integer values from 1 to 7. In the INPUT statement inside the loop, i% appears as the subscript of the countries$ array. As the looping proceeds, each input string is therefore assigned to a different element of the array, from countries$(1) to countries$(7). (The program doesn't use countries$(0).) The input dialog stores a list of seven strings in the countries$ array, as in this sample:

```
Name the countries you've visited:
   # 1 : Senegal
   # 2 : Gambia
   # 3 : Mali
   # 4 : Burkina Faso
   # 5 : Togo
   # 6 : Ghana
   # 7 : Ivory Coast
```

After the input dialog is complete, your program can use other statements to access the data stored in the array. For example, the FOR loop in the following code uses concatenation to create one long string from all the elements in the countries$ array:

```
message$ = "You've visited "
FOR i% = 1 TO 7

  message$ = message$ + countries$(i%)

  SELECT CASE i%
    CASE 1 TO 5
      message$ = message$ + ", "
    CASE 6
      message$ = message$ + ", and "
    CASE 7
      message$ = message$ + "."
  END SELECT

NEXT i%
PRINT message$
```

Here is the output from this passage of code:

```
You've visited Ivory Coast, Ghana, Togo, Burkina Faso, Mali, Gambia,
          and Senegal.
```

Gore and Clinton: static and dynamic

When you use a literal numeric value to declare the length of an array, QBasic creates a *static array* by default. For example, countries$ is a static array:

```
DIM countries$(7)
```

In this context, *static* means that QBasic allocates the memory space required for the array when you first start the program. The allocation remains unchanged throughout the program run.

Designer arrays

QBasic also allows you to establish a custom range of subscripts for an array. In the DIM statement that declares the array, you use the keyword TO to specify the range:

```
DIM arrayName(sub1 TO sub2)
```

In this format, the elements of the array range from *arrayName(sub1)* to *arrayName(sub2)*.

For example, the following program declares a single-precision array named income to store annual income amounts for the years from 1985 to 1994:

```
DIM income(1985 TO 1994)

CLS
PRINT "Enter your income for each year:"
FOR i% = 1985 TO 1994
  PRINT i%;
  INPUT ": ", income(i%)
NEXT i%
```

In the FOR loop that elicits input for the array, the counter variable i% takes on integer values from 1985 to 1994, the same as the range of subscripts defined for the income array. As the looping proceeds, the input is stored in income(1985) to income(1994).

A static array is fine when you know in advance how much data you want to store in the array. But sometimes the size requirements are determined interactively during a program run. In this case, you need to create a *dynamic array*. QBasic allocates memory space for a dynamic array during a run. The initial size of the array can therefore be based on information that's not available until the program begins. Furthermore, the size of the array can change one or more times during a run.

The easiest way to create a dynamic array is to use a variable to specify the size of the array. Several examples appear in the Travel Expense Summary program. As you recall, the program begins by prompting for the number of cities to be included in the expense table. This input is conducted by the GetNumCities% function. An assignment statement in the main module makes a call to GetNumCities% and stores the return value in the global integer variable num:

```
DIM SHARED num AS INTEGER
num = GetNumCities%
```

GetNumCities% displays the input prompt on the screen. The input value is stored in the integer variable inCities% and then returned as the value of GetNumCities%, as follows:

```
INPUT "How many cities"; inCities%
GetNumCities% = inCities%
```

Suppose you enter a value of 4 in response to this prompt, as follows:

```
How many cities? 4
```

Back in the main module, the value 4 is assigned to the variable num. The program then uses num to specify the sizes of several dynamic arrays. For example, the cities$ array is designed to store the names of the cities visited during the business trip, and the dates$ array stores the dates of the visits to these cities. These arrays are declared in a single DIM statement, as follows:

```
DIM cities$(num), dates$(num)
```

Because a variable is used to declare their sizes, these arrays are dynamic by default. The sizes of the arrays may be different each time the program is run.

You can use one DIM statement to declare two or more arrays, or you can declare each array individually in its own DIM statement. The result is the same. ▮

Throughout the Travel Expense Summary program, num represents the lengths of the arrays. For example, here is the beginning of the FOR loop that conducts the input dialog:

```
FOR i% = 1 TO num
  PRINT "City #"; i%
  PRINT "--------"
  INPUT "City"; cities$(i%)
  INPUT "Date"; dates$(i%)
```

As you can see, the program elicits a value for each of the elements of the cities$ and dates$ arrays, from 1 to num.

The Travel Expense Summary program declares two other dynamic arrays that you'll examine shortly.

3-D and beyond

To create an array of more than one dimension, you specify the length of each dimension in a DIM statement. The dimensions appear in parentheses just after the array name. Here is the general format for declaring a two-dimensional array:

```
DIM arrayName2(length1, length2)
```

And here is the format for a three-dimensional array:

```
DIM arrayName3(length1, length2, length3)
```

Alternatively, you can use the *sub1* TO *sub2* format to define custom subscript ranges for the dimensions of an array, as follows:

```
DIM arrayName2(sub1 TO sub2, sub3 TO sub4)
DIM arrayName3(sub1 TO sub2, sub3 TO sub4, sub5 TO sub6)
```

A too-dimensional array

In the following example, a DIM statement declares a two-dimensional single-precision array named expenses:

```
DIM expenses(4, 3)
```

Because the range of each dimension begins at 0, you can think of this array as a table containing five rows and four columns (or, conversely, five columns and four rows, depending on how you organize the data in the array). Here are the elements of the array:

```
expenses(0,0) expenses(0,1) expenses(0,2) expenses(0,3)
expenses(1,0) expenses(1,1) expenses(1,2) expenses(1,3)
expenses(2,0) expenses(2,1) expenses(2,2) expenses(2,3)
expenses(3,0) expenses(3,1) expenses(3,2) expenses(3,3)
expenses(4,0) expenses(4,1) expenses(4,2) expenses(4,3)
```

Again, if your program doesn't need the elements with subscripts of zero, you are free to leave them unused.

A pair of nested FOR loops presents the ideal structure for processing a two-dimensional array. For example, suppose your program has already assigned values to elements (1,1) to (4,3) of the expenses array. You can use the following FOR loop to display the values of these elements on the screen in table form:

```
FOR i% = 1 TO 4
  FOR j% = 1 TO 3
    PRINT USING "$$#,###.##"; expenses(i%, j%);
  NEXT j%
  PRINT
NEXT i%
```

As you can see in the notation expenses(i%, j%), the program uses the counter variable of the outer loop (i%) to access the first dimension of the array, and the counter of the inner loop (j%) to access the second dimension. This program displays the expenses data in a table containing three columns by four rows; for example:

```
$705.55    $533.42    $579.52
$289.56    $301.95    $774.74
 $14.02    $760.72    $814.49
$709.04     $45.35    $414.03
```

The Travel Expenses Summary program declares a two-dimensional array named expenses, but as a dynamic array. After eliciting a value for num, the program declares the group of four arrays that will represent the expense data:

```
DIM SHARED cities$(num), dates$(num)
DIM SHARED expenses(num, 3), totals(num)
```

As you've seen, the cities$ and dates$ arrays are designed to store the names of cities and the dates of the visits, respectively. The expenses array stores three expense figures for each city, where a given city is represented by num:

- ✔ expenses(num, 1) is the hotel expense category for city num

- ✔ expenses(num, 2) is the food expense category for city num

- ✔ expenses(num, 3) is the "other" expense category for city num

Finally, the totals array is designed to store the sum of the three expense figures for each city.

The program contains several nested arrays that process this combination of one- and two-dimensional arrays. First, the GetInfo procedure uses the following loops to conduct the input dialog and to calculate the total expense associated with each city:

```
FOR i% = 1 TO num
   PRINT "City #"; i%
   PRINT "--------"
   INPUT "City"; cities$(i%)
   INPUT "Date"; dates$(i%)
   INPUT "Hotel expense? ", expenses(i%, 1)
   INPUT "Food expense?  ", expenses(i%, 2)
   INPUT "Other expense? ", expenses(i%, 3)

   ' Compute the expense totals.
   totals(i%) = 0
   FOR j% = 1 TO 3
     totals(i%) = totals(i%) + expenses(i%, j%)
   NEXT j%
   PRINT
NEXT i%
```

The outer loop (FOR i% = 1 TO num) displays each input prompt on the screen and accepts the user's responses. The inner loop (FOR j% = 1 TO 3) uses the totals array to accumulate the total expense amount for each city.

Likewise, the PrintInfo procedure contains a pair of loops responsible for sending the expense table to the printer:

```
FOR i% = 1 TO num
   LPRINT cities$(i%); TAB(15);
   LPRINT dates$(i%); TAB(25);

   ' The expense data and totals.
   FOR j% = 1 TO 3
      LPRINT USING "$$#,###.##"; expenses(i%, j%);
      LPRINT TAB(25 + j% * 10);
   NEXT j%
   LPRINT USING "  $$#,###.##"; totals(i%)

NEXT i%
```

Here the outer loop organizes a row of output for each city in the expense data, and the inner loop prints the three expense figures for a given city.

All these loops are worth studying carefully as illustrations of the relationship between FOR loops and arrays. But perhaps the most interesting and complex of all the loops in the program are the ones that sort the data table.

Sorting assorted data

The program uses a technique known as the *bubble sort* to rearrange the rows of the expense table. Normally the bubble sort is simple and requires only a half-dozen lines of code to carry out. But in the Travel Expense Summary program, there are two complications:

✔ The program offers two different sorting *keys*. The table can be sorted alphabetically by city names or numerically by expense totals.

✔ The data table itself is stored not in a single data structure, but rather in four different arrays of different types and dimensions.

Because of these factors, the SortInfo and SwapInfo procedures are detailed and challenging. Here is a brief guide to the action they carry out:

1. The SortInfo procedure elicits the user's sorting instructions and stores the response (a "C" or a "T") in the string variable sort$:

```
INPUT "Sort by C)ities or by T)otals"; sort$
sort$ = UCASE$(LEFT$(sort$, 1))
```

2. A pair of loops controls the sorting process:

```
FOR i% = 1 TO num - 1
   FOR j% = i% + 1 TO num
```

3. Within the inner loop, an IF decision determines which sort the user has requested:

```
IF sort$ = "C" THEN
```

4. Depending on the choice, the program makes comparisons between elements in the cities$ array or the totals array, and swaps rows in the table whenever two elements are found to be out of order:

```
    IF cities$(i%) > cities$(j%) THEN
        SwapInfo i%, j%
    END IF

ELSE

    IF totals(i%) < totals(j%) THEN
        SwapInfo i%, j%
    END IF
```

5. The SwapInfo procedure, in turn, exchanges the positions of appropriate elements in the four arrays (cities$, dates$, expenses, and totals).

6. When the looping in the SortInfo procedure is complete, the expense table has been rearranged either alphabetically or numerically.

In Chapter 16 you'll see a second version of the Travel Expense Summary program, illustrating another important QBasic data structure known as the user-defined structure. Several of the program's tasks prove simpler when the data is reorganized in this alternate form.

Chapter 16

Data Structures You Can Build

*A*s you've seen, an array contains multiple data values, all belonging to one data type. In a string array, all the elements are strings; in a numeric array, all the values are numbers. By contrast, another important QBasic data structure — known as the *user-defined type* — allows you to create variables that represent multiple values of different types. In this chapter, you learn to work with this powerful data structure.

The user-defined type is ideal for use in database applications, as illustrated in several of the programs you've seen. A database is a collection of *records* in which information is organized in a consistent way. The individual data items in a record are known as *fields*. For example, if you think of your personal address book as a database, each separate address is a record. An individual record consists of fields such as the name, address, city, state, zip code, and phone number of one person in your book.

Because the user-defined type is so closely associated with database programs, QBasic programmers commonly use database terminology to describe the components of the data structure itself:

🗸 Most programmers refer to a user-defined type as a *record structure*.

🗸 In this context, the *elements* of a user-defined type are known as the *fields* of the record structure.

🗸 A variable belonging to a user-defined type is simply a *record variable*.

🗸 An array belonging to a user-defined type is an *array of records*.

This database terminology is used throughout this chapter to describe the components of QBasic's user-defined data type.

Creating a record variable is a two-step process in a QBasic program:

1. You first use a TYPE statement to define a record structure. The definition consists of a type name followed by a list of field names. Each field belongs to a specific data type.

2. You then use a DIM statement to declare a record variable or an array of records.

To illustrate this process, this chapter presents a second version of the Travel Expense Summary program you worked with in Chapter 15. In the first version (EXPSUMM1.BAS), a table of expense data is stored as a group of interrelated string and numeric arrays. In this new version (EXPSUMM2.BAS), the expense table is instead represented by an array of records. As you'll see, the use of this new data structure streamlines the program's procedures and generally makes the code easier to read and understand.

Expense It!

When you run the second version of the program, you'll see that it works the same as the first. The program begins by asking you to enter the number of cities you visited during your recent business trip:

```
How many cities? 3
```

In the ensuing input dialog, you enter five fields of information for each city: the name of the city, the date of the visit, and the expense totals for hotels, food, and "other." For review, here is a sample of the input dialog:

```
City # 1
--------
City? San Jose
Date? 1/31/94
Hotel expense? 374.80
Food expense?  529.53
Other expense? 129.15

City # 2
--------
City? Los Angeles
Date? 2/2/94
Hotel expense? 185.18
Food expense?  312.42
Other expense? 155.18
```

```
City # 3
---------
City? San Diego
Date? 2/3/94
Hotel expense? 123.94
Food expense?  245.18
Other expense? 255.67
```

When the dialog is complete, the program asks you whether you want to sort the output by city names or by expense totals:

```
Sort by C)ities or by T)otals? c
```

Depending on your response, the expense summary table is printed in alphabetical order or in descending order of expense totals. For example, here's the table in alphabetical order:

```
                    TRAVEL EXPENSE SUMMARY
-----------------------------------------------------------------
City           Date         Hotel      Food     Other      Totals
-----------------------------------------------------------------
Los Angeles    2/2/94     $185.18   $312.42   $155.18     $652.78
San Diego      2/3/94     $123.94   $245.18   $255.67     $624.79
San Jose       1/31/94    $374.80   $529.53   $129.15   $1,033.48
-----------------------------------------------------------------
TOTAL                                                    $2,311.05
```

Code It

Here is the listing of the Travel Expense Summary program, version 2:

```
' Travel Expense Summary, Version 2 (EXPSUMM2.BAS)
' Gets expense information and prints
' a sorted summary table.
' Uses an array of records.

DECLARE SUB PrintInfo ()
DECLARE SUB SortInfo ()
DECLARE SUB GetInfo ()
DECLARE FUNCTION GetNumCities% ()

' The expense record type.
TYPE ExpenseRecType
  City AS STRING * 12
  Date AS STRING * 10
  Hotel AS SINGLE
  Food AS SINGLE
  Other AS SINGLE
  Total AS SINGLE
END TYPE
```

(continued)

```
' The variable num represents the
' number of city records.
DIM SHARED num AS INTEGER
num = GetNumCities%

' After getting num, declare the
' array of records.
DIM SHARED ExpInfo(num) AS ExpenseRecType

GetInfo     ' Conduct the input dialog.
SortInfo    ' Sort the data table.
PrintInfo   ' Print the data.

END   ' EXPSUMM2.BAS



SUB GetInfo

  ' Conduct the input dialog for
  ' travel expense information.

  FOR i% = 1 TO num
    PRINT "City #"; i%
    PRINT "--------"
    INPUT "City"; ExpInfo(i%).City
    INPUT "Date"; ExpInfo(i%).Date

    INPUT "Hotel expense? ", ExpInfo(i%).Hotel
    INPUT "Food expense?  ", ExpInfo(i%).Food
    INPUT "Other expense? ", ExpInfo(i%).Other

    ' Compute total field.
    ExpInfo(i%).Total = ExpInfo(i%).Hotel + ExpInfo(i%).Food
    ExpInfo(i%).Total = ExpInfo(i%).Total + ExpInfo(i%).Other

    PRINT

  NEXT i%

END SUB   ' GetInfo



FUNCTION GetNumCities%

  ' Find out how many cities there will be.

  CLS
  INPUT "How many cities"; inCities%
  GetNumCities% = inCities%
  PRINT
  PRINT

END FUNCTION   ' GetNumCities%
```

```
SUB PrintInfo

  ' Print the table.

  ' The title and the column heads.
  LPRINT
  LPRINT TAB(22); "TRAVEL EXPENSE SUMMARY"
  LPRINT STRING$(66, "-")
  LPRINT "City"; TAB(15); "Date"; TAB(30);
  LPRINT "Hotel"; TAB(40); "Food"; TAB(50);
  LPRINT "Other"; TAB(60); "Totals"
  LPRINT STRING$(66, "-")

  ' The data.
  FOR i% = 1 TO num
    LPRINT ExpInfo(i%).City; TAB(15);
    LPRINT ExpInfo(i%).Date; TAB(25);

    ' The expense data and totals.
    LPRINT USING "$$#,###.##"; ExpInfo(i%).Hotel;
    LPRINT TAB(35); USING "$$#,###.##"; ExpInfo(i%).Food;
    LPRINT TAB(45); USING "$$#,###.##"; ExpInfo(i%).Other;
    LPRINT TAB(57); USING "$$#,###.##"; ExpInfo(i%).Total
  NEXT i%

  ' The grand total.
  grandTot = 0
  FOR i% = 1 TO num
    grandTot = grandTot + ExpInfo(i%).Total
  NEXT i%
  LPRINT STRING$(66, "-")
  LPRINT "TOTAL"; TAB(55);
  LPRINT USING " $$##,###.##"; grandTot

END SUB   ' PrintInfo


SUB SortInfo

  ' Sort the expense information either by
  ' cities (alphabetically) or by totals (numerically).

  ' Get the user's sort preference.
  PRINT
  INPUT "Sort by C)ities or by T)otals"; sort$
  CLS
  sort$ = UCASE$(LEFT$(sort$, 1))

  ' Do a bubble sort.
  FOR i% = 1 TO num - 1
    FOR j% = i% + 1 TO num

      ' Sort by cities...
      IF sort$ = "C" THEN
        IF ExpInfo(i%).City > ExpInfo(j%).City THEN
          SWAP ExpInfo(i%), ExpInfo(j%)
        END IF
```

(continued)

```
              ' ... or by totals.
              ELSE
                IF ExpInfo(i%).Total < ExpInfo(j%).Total THEN
                  SWAP ExpInfo(i%), ExpInfo(j%)
                END IF
              END IF
            NEXT j%
          NEXT i%

END SUB  ' SortInfo
```

The names of the procedures in the second version are the same as those in the first, but one procedure is omitted. The GetNumCities% function begins the input process by asking the user for the number of cities in the business trip. The GetInfo procedure then conducts the remainder of the input dialog, eliciting one complete record of information for each city. The SortInfo procedure sorts the expense records, either by city names or by expense totals. Because the table is now organized as an array of records, the sorting procedure is easier than in the first version; the extra SwapInfo procedure is no longer needed. Finally, the PrintInfo procedure sends the data table to the printer.

The expense record structure — named `ExpenseRecType` — is defined at the top of the program in the main module, where an array of records named `ExpInfo` is also declared. As you'll see, each procedure in the program illustrates various ways to use this structure.

LPs, 45s, and Other Record Structures

You write a TYPE statement to define a record structure in QBasic. You can then use the structure to declare record variables and arrays of records. The general form of the TYPE statement is as follows:

```
TYPE TypeName
   FieldName1 AS dataType
   FieldName2 AS dataType
   FieldName3 AS dataType

   ' ... additional field definitions

END TYPE
```

In this statement, *TypeName* is the name you devise for the record structure, and *FieldName1*, *FieldName2*, *FieldName3*, and so on are the names you give to the fields in the structure. You must also identify a data type for each field. The *dataType* may be any of QBasic's predefined types: STRING, INTEGER, LONG,

SINGLE, or DOUBLE. But STRING fields must be defined as *fixed-length* strings. You specify the length in characters of each string in the following format:

```
FieldName AS STRING * length
```

where *length* is an integer.

For example, here is the ExpenseRecType structure as defined in the second version of the Travel Expense Summary program:

```
TYPE ExpenseRecType
   City AS STRING * 12
   Date AS STRING * 10
   Hotel AS SINGLE
   Food AS SINGLE
   Other AS SINGLE
   Total AS SINGLE
END TYPE
```

The structure has six fields, named City, Date, Hotel, Food, Other, and Total. The two string fields, City and Date, have fixed lengths of 12 and 10 characters, respectively. The remaining four are single-precision fields. Hotel, Food, and Other are designated to represent the three expense categories for a given record, and Total represents the total expense amount.

In record time

Keep in mind that the TYPE statement defines a new data structure but does not create any new variables belonging to this data type. The next step in the development of your code is to declare the record variables and arrays of records that your program will use to represent data. You use the DIM statement for this purpose.

Here is the general form of the DIM statement for declaring a record variable:

```
DIM RecordVar AS TypeName
```

In this statement, *TypeName* is the name of a record structure you've defined in a previous TYPE statement. *RecordVar* can therefore represent one complete record belonging to this type. After the variable is declared, your program uses a special notation to identify the individual fields of the record variable. This notation is a combination of the record name and a field name, separated by a period:

```
RecordVar.FieldName1
RecordVar.FieldName2
RecordVar.FieldName3
```

You can use the *RecordVar.FieldName* notation in assignment statements, PRINT and INPUT statements, or any other kind of statement in which you normally include variable names.

The notation for an array of records is only slightly more detailed. Here is how you declare an array of records:

```
DIM RecordArray(length) AS TypeName
```

As you would expect, *length* indicates the number of records that the array can store. (Actually, the array can contain *length + 1* records, because the subscripts of the array begin at zero.) After this array is declared, your program uses the following notation to identify the fields of a single record in the array:

```
RecordArray(i%).FieldName1
RecordArray(i%).FieldName2
RecordArray(i%).FieldName3
```

where i% is a subscript for one of the elements of the array.

Working in the fields

Like the first version of the Travel Expense Summary program, the second version creates a dynamic array to represent the expense data entered from the keyboard. The number of cities, num, is determined interactively through a call to the GetNumCities% function. Then the following DIM statement declares a global array of records:

```
DIM SHARED ExpInfo(num) AS ExpenseRecType
```

Each element of the ExpInfo array can store one complete expense record, with all the fields defined in the ExpenseRecType statement. Here is how these fields are represented for record i%:

```
ExpInfo(i%).City
ExpInfo(i%).Date
ExpInfo(i%).Hotel
ExpInfo(i%).Food
ExpInfo(i%).Other
ExpInfo(i%).Total
```

The GetInfo procedure uses this notation to conduct the input dialog and store each field of a given ExpInfo record:

```
FOR i% = 1 TO num
    PRINT "City #"; i%
    PRINT "--------"
    INPUT "City"; ExpInfo(i%).City
```

```
INPUT "Date"; ExpInfo(i%).Date

INPUT "Hotel expense? ", ExpInfo(i%).Hotel
INPUT "Food expense?  ", ExpInfo(i%).Food
INPUT "Other expense? ", ExpInfo(i%).Other
```

The Total field is then calculated as the sum of the three individual expense categories:

```
ExpInfo(i%).Total = ExpInfo(i%).Hotel + ExpInfo(i%).Food
ExpInfo(i%).Total = ExpInfo(i%).Total + ExpInfo(i%).Other
```

Likewise, the PrintInfo procedure uses the same field notation to print the expense table, record by record:

```
FOR i% = 1 TO num
    LPRINT ExpInfo(i%).City; TAB(15);
    LPRINT ExpInfo(i%).Date; TAB(25);

    ' The expense data and totals.
    LPRINT USING "$$#,###.##"; ExpInfo(i%).Hotel;
    LPRINT TAB(35); USING "$$#,###.##"; ExpInfo(i%).Food;
    LPRINT TAB(45); USING "$$#,###.##"; ExpInfo(i%).Other;
    LPRINT TAB(57); USING "$$#,###.##"; ExpInfo(i%).Total
NEXT i%
```

By studying these passages carefully, you'll see exactly how a record variable represents data in a QBasic program. But the most elegant use of the record structure appears in the procedure that sorts the expense table, SortInfo.

Bubbling to the Surface

Like the first version of the program, the second version uses a bubble sort to rearrange the order of the expense records. The SortInfo procedure uses a pair of loops to go through the entire array of records and to make comparisons between the appropriate fields:

```
FOR i% = 1 TO num - 1
    FOR j% = i% + 1 TO num
```

If the user has chosen an alphabetical sort by city names, the program makes comparisons between pairs of `City` fields in the `ExpInfo` array:

```
IF sort$ = "C" THEN
  IF ExpInfo(i%).City > ExpInfo(j%).City THEN
```

Alternatively, if the user has chosen a numeric sort, the comparisons are between pairs of `Total` fields:

```
ELSE
  IF ExpInfo(i%).Total < ExpInfo(j%).Total THEN
```

Here is where the array of records becomes much more convenient than the separate arrays of strings and numbers in the first version. When the program has to exchange the order of any two records, it does so simply by referring to two entire records in the ExpInfo array:

```
SWAP ExpInfo(i%), ExpInfo(j%)
```

The program uses QBasic's SWAP statement to exchange the positions of the two records. Conveniently, there is no need to refer to the individual fields in these records. Two whole records are swapped at a time.

Chapter 17

Dynamic Arrays:
The Good News Is . . .

- -

In This Chapter

▶ Anticipating the need for a dynamic array

▶ Using REDIM to change the size of an array

▶ Understanding the consequences of REDIM

▶ Restoring data after a REDIM operation

- -

*I*n both versions of the Travel Expense Summary program (presented in Chapters 15 and 16), you have to indicate *in advance* how much data there is to enter. The program's first input prompt asks you for the number of cities included in a business trip:

```
How many cities?
```

Your response to this question determines not only the length of the input dialog, but also the size of the dynamic arrays that the program uses to store the input data.

In many programs, this initial request may seem reasonable — or at least only slightly inconvenient. For short sets of available data, you can easily count the number of records before you begin entering them into the program.

But in other applications, you may not be able to anticipate the extent of the input data. The data set may be large and unwieldy, or you may not even know how much data there will eventually be. In this case, a program should be prepared to adjust to the requirements of the data. The input dialog should continue until all the information is entered and stored successfully in the appropriate data structures. This means that the program may have to increase the size of a dynamic array repeatedly and systematically to accommodate the data.

QBasic allows dynamic arrays to be redimensioned any number of times during a program run. But this is a good-news and bad-news story. The good news is that QBasic's REDIM statement effectively resizes any dimension of an existing dynamic array. The bad news is that REDIM also erases all the existing data in the resized array. The elements of a numeric array become zero, and the elements of a string array become empty strings. This is one of those awkward "features" left over from early versions of BASIC. When you write a program that changes the size of an array during run time, you have to figure out a way to save the existing data while you make room for new data.

It's not too hard to think of a solution to this problem. Your program can

1. Copy data from the original array to another array designed to hold the data temporarily.

2. Use REDIM to change the size of the original array.

3. Copy the data back into the resized array from the temporary array.

These steps are not complicated, but they require some careful planning.

To illustrate the use of REDIM, this chapter presents a project called the International Sales Program. The program conducts an input dialog for a company's global sales data over a period of years. Because the input represents historical information, it can begin at any year that the user specifies and can continue for any number of years; the program imposes no limits on the extent of the data. When the input is complete, the program prepares a summary table of the data and sends the table to the printer. In the next section of this chapter, you look at a sample run of this program.

Run the Numbers

For each year of sales data, the program elicits annual sales figures in four geographical categories: American, European, Asian, and Other. The program does *not* begin by asking you for the number of years of sales data you plan to enter; it adjusts to any number of years you enter.

The first input specifies the dollar units in which you plan to enter the sales data. The input prompt appears as follows:

```
What dollar units?
e.g., thousands, millions
(Press Enter for dollars.)
->
```

For example, if you plan to round your sales entries to the nearest thousand dollars, you should enter thousands in response to this prompt. Then a sales entry of 1778 actually means $1,778,000. Alternatively, enter any other dollar unit that you want to use. If you plan to enter exact dollar amounts — not rounded to a larger unit — just press Enter in response to this prompt. (In the printed output, the program identifies the dollar unit just below the title.)

After this initial entry, the program begins the input dialog for the sales data. After each year's data, the program asks whether you want to enter another year. If you press Y, the dialog continues; if N, the program prepares the output table and sends it to the printer. Here is a sample of the input dialog for six years of sales data:

```
Year? 1988
American sales? 1778
European sales? 1121
    Asian sales? 876
    Other sales? 543

Another year? Y

Year? 1989
American sales? 1951
European sales? 1311
    Asian sales? 897
    Other sales? 579

Another year? Y

Year? 1990
American sales? 2151
European sales? 1535
    Asian sales? 1211
    Other sales? 879

Another year? Y

Year? 1991
American sales? 2512
European sales? 1798
    Asian sales? 1523
    Other sales? 1314

Another year? Y

Year? 1992
American sales? 2891
European sales? 2314
    Asian sales? 1822
    Other sales? 1781

Another year? Y

Year? 1993
American sales? 3512
European sales? 3121
    Asian sales? 2313
    Other sales? 2121

Another year? N
```

As soon as you press N in response to the Another year? prompt, the output to the printer begins. (Make sure your printer is ready to operate before you press N.) Figure 17-1 shows the output table for this sample set of input data.

Figure 17-1:
The sales
table from
the
International
Sales
program.

```
                      International Sales Summary
                        (in thousands of dollars)

     Year    American    European      Asian        Other       Total
     ----    --------    --------      -----        -----       -----
     1988     $1,778      $1,121       $876         $543        $4,318
     1989     $1,951      $1,311       $897         $579        $4,738
     1990     $2,151      $1,535      $1,211        $879        $5,776
     1991     $2,512      $1,798      $1,523       $1,314       $7,147
     1992     $2,891      $2,314      $1,822       $1,781       $8,808
     1993     $3,512      $3,121      $2,313       $2,121      $11,067

    TOTALS   $14,795     $11,200     $8,642       $7,217      $41,854
```

Notice that the program calculates two groups of totals for the table. At the end of each row of data you see the total international sales for a given year. At the bottom of each column you see the total regional sales for the entire period. The final calculation — at the lower-right corner of the table — is the grand total of all regional sales for the period.

In the upcoming sections, you find out how the program resizes an array of records for each new year of data.

Code It

Here is the entire listing of the program:

```
' International Sales Program (INTRSALE.BAS)
' Accepts international sales figures by
' region and prepares a summary table.

DECLARE SUB ExpandSalesArray ()
DECLARE SUB GetAnnualSales ()
DECLARE SUB GetUnits ()
DECLARE SUB ShowSalesSummary ()
DECLARE FUNCTION YesNo! (prompt$)

' The quarterly sales record type.
TYPE ISalesType
   Year AS INTEGER
   American AS DOUBLE
   European AS DOUBLE
   Asian AS DOUBLE
   Other AS DOUBLE
END TYPE

' The number of records and the units.
DIM SHARED n AS INTEGER, units AS STRING
n = 1
```

```
' The global array of sales records.
DIM SHARED ISales(n) AS ISalesType

' Conduct the input dialog.
CLS
GetUnits
DO
   GetAnnualSales
LOOP UNTIL NOT YesNo("Another year? ")

' Print the sales summary.
ShowSalesSummary

END   ' INTRSALE.BAS



SUB ExpandSalesArray

   ' Increase the length of the sales array
   ' by one additional record element.

   ' Declare a temporary array to hold the data.
   DIM TempSales(n) AS ISalesType

   ' Copy all the current records to the
   ' temporary array.
   FOR i% = 1 TO n
     TempSales(i%) = ISales(i%)
   NEXT i%

   ' Redimension the sales array.
   n = n + 1
   REDIM ISales(n)

   ' Copy the existing records back
   ' to the sales array.
   FOR i% = 1 TO n - 1
     ISales(i%) = TempSales(i%)
   NEXT i%

END SUB   ' ExpandSalesArray



SUB GetAnnualSales

   ' Conduct the input dialog
   ' for one annual sales record.

   INPUT "Year"; ISales(n).Year
   INPUT "American sales"; ISales(n).American
   INPUT "European sales"; ISales(n).European
   INPUT "   Asian sales"; ISales(n).Asian
   INPUT "   Other sales"; ISales(n).Other

END SUB   ' GetAnnualSales
```

(continued)

```
SUB GetUnits

  ' Ask the user to indicate
  ' the dollar units for the data.

  PRINT "What dollar units?"
  PRINT "e.g., thousands, millions"
  PRINT "(Press Enter for dollars.)"
  INPUT " -> ", units

  IF LTRIM$(units) = "" THEN
    units = "(in dollars)"
  ELSE
    units = "(in " + units + " of dollars)"
  END IF
  CLS

END SUB  ' GetUnits



SUB ShowSalesSummary

  ' Print the sales summary.

  ' The title.
  CLS
  LPRINT TAB(27); "International Sales Summary"
  t% = (80 - LEN(units)) / 2
  LPRINT TAB(t%); units
  LPRINT

  ' The column headings.
  LPRINT " Year"; TAB(15); "American"; "      European";
  LPRINT "        Asian"; "          Other";
  LPRINT "          Total"
  LPRINT " ----"; TAB(15); "--------"; "      --------";
  LPRINT "        -----"; "          -----";
  LPRINT "          -----"

  ' The sales data.
  template$ = "    $$#,######"
  amerTot = 0
  euroTot = 0
  asiaTot = 0
  otherTot = 0
  grandTot = 0
  FOR i% = 1 TO n
    LPRINT ISales(i%).Year; TAB(10);
    LPRINT USING template$; ISales(i%).American;
    LPRINT USING template$; ISales(i%).European;
    LPRINT USING template$; ISales(i%).Asian;
    LPRINT USING template$; ISales(i%).Other;
    tot = ISales(i%).American + ISales(i%).European
    tot = tot + ISales(i%).Asian + ISales(i%).Other
    LPRINT USING template$; tot
```

```
     ' Calculate the grand totals.
     amerTot = amerTot + ISales(i%).American
     euroTot = euroTot + ISales(i%).European
     asiaTot = asiaTot + ISales(i%).Asian
     otherTot = otherTot + ISales(i%).Other
     grandTot = grandTot + tot
  NEXT i%

  ' The total sales for all regions.
  LPRINT
  LPRINT "TOTALS"; TAB(10);
  LPRINT USING template$; amerTot;
  LPRINT USING template$; euroTot;
  LPRINT USING template$; asiaTot;
  LPRINT USING template$; otherTot;
  LPRINT USING template$; grandTot

END SUB   ' ShowSalesSummary



FUNCTION YesNo (prompt$)

  ' Get a yes-or-no response.

  PRINT
  PRINT prompt$;

  ' Wait for Y or N from the keyboard.
  DO
    ans$ = UCASE$(INKEY$)
  LOOP UNTIL LEN(ans$) = 1 AND INSTR("YN", ans$)
  PRINT ans$
  PRINT

  ' If the user wants to add a record,
  ' expand the sales array by one element.
  IF ans$ = "Y" THEN ExpandSalesArray

  ' Return a value of true or false.
  YesNo = (ans$ = "Y")

END FUNCTION   ' YesNo
```

In the main module, the program declares an array of records to store the input data. A TYPE statement defines the record structure named ISalesType, which contains fields for the year and for each of the four geographical sales categories:

```
TYPE ISalesType
   Year AS INTEGER
   American AS DOUBLE
   European AS DOUBLE
   Asian AS DOUBLE
   Other AS DOUBLE
END TYPE
```

Then a DIM statement declares `ISales` as a dynamic array of `ISalesType` records.

The program contains five procedures. GetUnits and GetAnnualSales conduct the input dialog, and ShowSalesSummary prints the data table at the end of a program run. The YesNo function displays the `Another year?` prompt on the screen after each year's input, and waits for a Y or N response. If you answer affirmatively, the YesNo function makes an important call to ExpandSalesArray, which uses REDIM to increase the size of the `ISales` array before the next input.

REDIM and Weep

Keep in mind that REDIM works only with dynamic arrays. As you know, the most common way to define a dynamic array is to use a variable to specify the length of the array in a DIM statement. For example, the following statement defines the `ISales` array:

```
DIM SHARED ISales(n) AS ISalesType
```

`ISales` is a one-dimensional dynamic array of records, global in scope. Its initial size is defined by the value of the global variable n at the beginning of the program.

The syntax of the REDIM statement is almost the same as DIM. Here is how the program changes the size of the `ISales` array:

```
n = n + 1
REDIM ISales(n)
```

The program increases the value of n by 1, and then uses n to specify the new length of the array in a REDIM statement.

To declare a global array, you can include the SHARED keyword in the REDIM statement. But if an array has already been declared as global in a previous DIM statement, you can omit SHARED without affecting the scope of the array.

QBasic imposes two important restrictions on the use of REDIM:

- If your program mistakenly uses REDIM to attempt a change in the length of a static array, QBasic displays the error message `Array already dimensioned` when you try to run the program.

- If you try to use REDIM to change the number of dimensions in an array, QBasic displays the error message `Wrong number of dimensions`. You can change the length of any dimension in an array, but you can't change the number of dimensions. For example, a one-dimensional array can't be changed to a two-dimensional array. ▪

The side effects of using REDIM

As you've learned, REDIM doesn't just change the dimensions of an array; it also erases all the data currently stored in the array. Here's a short program that demonstrates this important side effect:

```
' REDIM Test (REDMTEST.BAS)
' Demonstrates the effect of
' the REDIM statement.

DECLARE SUB AssignData ()
DECLARE SUB ShowBounds ()
DECLARE SUB ShowData ()

DIM SHARED n AS INTEGER
n = 15
DIM SHARED Test(n) AS INTEGER

AssignData

CLS
PRINT "Test data before REDIM:"
ShowData
ShowBounds

REDIM Test(n + 5) AS INTEGER

PRINT
PRINT "Test data after REDIM:"
ShowData
ShowBounds

END  ' REDMTEST.BAS



SUB AssignData

  ' Assign data to the
  ' Test array.

  FOR i% = 0 TO n
    Test(i%) = i%
  NEXT i%

END SUB  ' AssignData



SUB ShowBounds

  ' Show the lower and upper bounds
  ' of the Test array.
```

(continued)

```
      PRINT "First subscript is"; LBOUND(Test)
      PRINT "Last subscript is"; UBOUND(Test)

END SUB   ' ShowBounds


SUB ShowData

   ' Show the current contents
   ' of the Test array.

   FOR i% = 0 TO n
     PRINT Test(i%);
   NEXT i%
   PRINT

END SUB   ' ShowData
```

This program begins by declaring a one-dimensional numeric array named
Test. The length of Test is initially declared by the value of the variable n,
which is 15:

```
n = 15
DIM SHARED Test(n) AS INTEGER
```

After the declaration, a call to a procedure named AssignData stores values in
all the elements of the array, and then the ShowData and ShowBounds procedures display the array's data and subscript range on the screen.

Next the program uses a REDIM statement to increase the length of the Test array:

```
REDIM Test(n + 5) AS INTEGER
```

A second set of calls to ShowData and ShowBounds display the array's data and
subscript range again after the resizing. Here is the screen output you see when
you run this program:

```
Test data before REDIM:
 0  1  2  3  4  5  6  7  8  9  10  11  12  13  14  15
First subscript is 0
Last subscript is 15

Test data after REDIM:
 0  0  0  0  0  0  0  0  0  0  0  0  0  0  0  0
First subscript is 0
Last subscript is 20
```

This output clearly shows the effect of REDIM. Before the REDIM statement, the
Test array contains the values assigned to it in the AssignData procedure. After
REDIM, all the elements of the array contain values of zero. The previous data is lost.

You can try this experiment on a string array. After the REDIM statement, each element in the array becomes an empty string.

This demonstration program also illustrates two built-in QBasic functions that can prove useful with dynamic arrays: LBOUND and UBOUND. The LBOUND function returns the first available subscript for an array dimension, and UBOUND returns the last subscript. Here is how the program uses these functions to display the bounds of the Test array:

```
PRINT "First subscript is"; LBOUND(Test)
PRINT "Last subscript is"; UBOUND(Test)
```

Recovering from REDIM

Because of the REDIM statement's side effect, the International Sales program has to set up a temporary array to hold the current data set before each expansion of the ISales array. This step takes place in the ExpandSalesArray procedure. The procedure begins by declaring a local array of ISalesType records named TempSales:

```
DIM TempSales(n) AS ISalesType
```

TempSales has a length of n, the current number of sales records. After the array is declared, the procedure uses a FOR loop to copy all the existing records from ISales to TempSales:

```
FOR i% = 1 TO n
  TempSales(i%) = ISales(i%)
NEXT i%
```

Only then can the program safely change the size of the ISales array:

```
n = n + 1
REDIM ISales(n)
```

At this point, all the numeric fields are zero in the records of the ISales array. So the next step is to copy the sales records back to ISales from the TempSales array. Again, a simple FOR loop does the job:

```
FOR i% = 1 TO n - 1
  ISales(i%) = TempSales(i%)
NEXT i%
```

This process takes place just before each new record entry. Thanks to the ExpandSalesArray procedure, the user can enter any amount of annual sales data without committing to a fixed number of records in advance.

Part VII
Keeping Track:
Data File Programming

The 5th Wave   By Rich Tennant

Bill and Irwin discover The Land of Lost Files

MY GOD! THIS IS A
BUDGET AND ANALYSIS
REPORT FOR THE MARKET-
ING DEPT. OF A FORTUNE
500 COMPANY. MUST OF
KILLED THE POOR BASTARD
TO LOSE THIS.

In This Part . . .

*A*lmost all of the programs in this book use data files to store or retrieve information. In Part VII you examine the tools and techniques of data file programming. Like other programming languages, QBasic provides two sets of statements for creating and reading files. One set is devoted to text files, which are also known as sequential-access files because programs normally read them from beginning to end. Another set of statements allows you to work with random-access files, which contain fixed-length records that can be read or revised in any order.

To help you explore these important topics, this part presents a diverse collection of programs. A second version of the International Sales program (first presented in Part VI) demonstrates the versatility of text file programming. Then a Restaurant Reviews program allows you to read records from the restaurant database you created back in Chapter 8. Finally, a self-contained database management program gives you a simple way to keep track of telephone numbers; this program is ideal for use on the notebook computer you tote along on business trips.

Chapter 18

Text, Files, and Videotapes

. . . .

In This Chapter

▶ Planning your work with text files

▶ Opening text files for writing or reading

▶ Using the WRITE # statement

▶ Using the PRINT # statement

▶ Anticipating the possibility of a missing file

▶ Using the INPUT # and LINE INPUT # statements

▶ Testing for the end of the file with EOF

. . . .

Data file programming is one of the most important skills you can add to your QBasic repertoire. By creating files on disk, your programs can keep permanent records of the information they generate. In addition, different QBasic programs can exchange data through the medium of disk files. In fact, you've seen several examples of programs that do exactly this:

✔ The Travel Expense Log program (EXPLOG.BAS, Chapter 5) saves expense records in a text file on disk. Then the Travel Expense Table program (EXPTABLE.BAS, Chapter 6) reads this file and generates an expense report.

✔ The Restaurant Database program (RESTINPT.BAS, Chapter 8) stores your personal restaurant reviews in a database file on disk. The Show Restaurants program (SHOWREST.BAS, Chapter 9) retrieves restaurant descriptions from this database for any city that you request.

✔ The Transportation Planner program (TRANPLAN.BAS, Chapter 11) gives you the opportunity to save travel information in a file on disk. The Transportation List program (TRANLIST.BAS, Chapter 12) reads this file and prints your travel plans on paper.

✔ The Business Meetings program (MEETINGS.BAS, Chapter 13) creates a database for your personal notes about the meetings you conduct during business trips. The Meetings List program (MEETLIST.BAS, Chapter 14) prints the information from this file on paper.

The pattern of each pair of programs is the same. One program conducts an input dialog to collect data interactively from the keyboard. After receiving each record of data, the program saves the information to a file on disk. Then a second program opens the file, reads its information, and generates a report or supplies data that you request.

These programs illustrate two kinds of files you can create in QBasic:

- A text file consists exclusively of ASCII characters. You can therefore read the information yourself if you open the file in a text editor. A text file is arranged for *sequential access*; a QBasic program generally reads the data in a text file from beginning to end.

- A random-access file contains records in a fixed-length format. Numeric and string data items in a random-access file are stored in special formats that give each item a predictable length. Thanks to this structure, a QBasic program can go directly to any record in the file without having to read other records first.

Text files and random-access files require different programming techniques and different QBasic statements for reading and writing data. In this chapter you learn how to work with text files, and in Chapter 19 you turn to the topic of random-access file programming. In Chapter 20 you combine both sets of skills as you learn techniques for managing a database in QBasic.

You can use a text file to store data items in an order and a structure that a QBasic program can read conveniently. Alternatively, a text file might contain a table of text and numbers, ready to be printed on paper or incorporated in a larger document for *people* to read. To illustrate both of these file formats, this chapter presents a second version of the International Sales program.

The first version of the program (INTRSALE.BAS, Chapter 17) conducts an input dialog for annual sales data and immediately prints a report from the information you enter. Because the program saves information only in the computer's memory, the sales data is lost when the program ends; the printed report is the only output. By contrast, the second version (INTRSAL2.BAS) saves the raw data to disk in a text file. It then generates a summary report of the sales data, which is saved to disk in a separate text file. The program gives you the option of printing the report right away or simply saving it for use in another document.

As you go through a sample run of the program, you see how files like these enhance your access to the data generated by a program.

Follow the Money

The new version of the International Sales program conducts the same input dialog as the original version. The program begins by asking you for the dollar units you will use when entering the sales data. You can enter a unit such as thousands or millions, or you can simply press Enter to indicate that your input will be in dollars:

```
What dollar units?
e.g., thousands, millions
(Press Enter for dollars.)
->
```

After this initial input, the program begins prompting you for individual years of sales data in geographical categories. You can enter as many years of data as you want. For example, here are four years of data entries, from 1990 to 1993:

```
Year? 1990
American sales? 12866
European sales? 9335
    Asian sales? 10673
    Other sales? 7593

Another year? Y

Year? 1991
American sales? 15790
European sales? 13118
    Asian sales? 14789
    Other sales? 9772

Another year? Y

Year? 1992
American sales? 17855
European sales? 16093
    Asian sales? 15863
    Other sales? 13121

Another year? Y

Year? 1993
American sales? 20760
European sales? 19814
    Asian sales? 18534
    Other sales? 15032

Another year? N
```

As this part of the input dialog proceeds, the program saves each year's data in a text file named ISALES.TXT, which is stored in the root directory of your hard disk. Here is what this file looks like by the end of the dialog:

```
"1990",12866,9335,10673,7593
"1991",15790,13118,14789,9772
"1992",17855,16093,15863,13121
"1993",20760,19814,18534,15032
```

Each year's data is stored on a line by itself. The year itself is a string entry, enclosed in quotation marks. The data items on each line are separated by commas.

When the input dialog is complete, the program opens the ISALES.TXT data file, reads the data line by line, and creates a second file, named ISALES.REP, to store the sales report that the program generates. The format of this second file is the same as the sales summary printed by the first version of the program. For example, Figure 18-1 is the report from this chapter's sample data.

```
                         International Sales Summary
                                (in dollars)

       Year      American    European      Asian       Other       Total
       ----      --------    --------      -----       -----       -----
       1990       $12,866      $9,335    $10,673      $7,593     $40,467
       1991       $15,790     $13,118    $14,789      $9,772     $53,469
       1992       $17,855     $16,093    $15,863     $13,121     $62,932
       1993       $20,760     $19,814    $18,534     $15,032     $74,140

       TOTALS     $67,271     $58,360    $59,859     $45,518    $231,008
```

Figure 18-1:
A sales
table, as
saved on
disk.

As you can see, the ISALES.TXT and ISALES.REP files represent two very different ways of recording the data. The first file simply stores the raw data in a way that's convenient for QBasic to read. The second file presents a formatted table for people to read. Because this table is saved in a disk file, you can easily insert it in a word processed document such as a memo, a business letter, or a sales report. Alternatively, you can send it directly to the printer. In fact, the program's final action is to ask you whether you want to print this report right away:

```
Print the sales report?
```

If you type Y, the program sends the report to the printer; if N, the program ends with no further output. In any event, both text files remain available on disk for you to use in other contexts. If you run the program again, the new sales figures you enter are appended to the end of the existing ISALES.TXT file, and the previous information is retained. Then the program creates a new ISALES.REP file containing a summary report from the entire current data set.

Now take a first look at the program listing, which illustrates a variety of text file programming techniques.

Code It

Here is the listing of the International Sales program, Version 2:

```
' International Sales Program, Version 2 (INTRSAL2.BAS)
' Accepts international sales figures by
' region, saves them to disk, and creates reports.

DECLARE SUB GetAnnualSales ()
DECLARE SUB GetUnits ()
DECLARE SUB PrintSalesSummary ()
DECLARE SUB SaveSalesSummary ()
DECLARE FUNCTION YesNo! (prompt$)

' The units string is global.
DIM SHARED units AS STRING

' Conduct the input dialog.
CLS
GetUnits

' Open the text file to save the input data.
OPEN "\ISALES.TXT" FOR APPEND AS #1
DO
  GetAnnualSales
LOOP UNTIL NOT YesNo("Another year? ")
CLOSE #1

' Create the sales summary report.
SaveSalesSummary

' Offer a printed copy of the sales report.
IF YesNo("Print the sales report? ") THEN PrintSalesSummary

END  ' INTRSAL2.BAS


SUB GetAnnualSales

  ' Conduct the input dialog
  ' for one annual sales record.

  INPUT "Year"; Year$
  INPUT "American sales"; American
  INPUT "European sales"; European
  INPUT "   Asian sales"; Asian
  INPUT "   Other sales"; Other

  ' Write each year's data to the ISALES.TXT file.
  WRITE #1, Year$, American, European, Asian, Other

END SUB  ' GetAnnualSales
```

(continued)

```
SUB GetUnits

  ' Ask the user to indicate
  ' the dollar units for the data.

  PRINT "What dollar units?"
  PRINT "e.g., thousands, millions"
  PRINT "(Press Enter for dollars.)"
  INPUT " -> ", units

  IF LTRIM$(units) = "" THEN
    units = "(in dollars)"
  ELSE
    units = "(in " + units + " of dollars)"
  END IF
  CLS

END SUB   ' GetUnits



SUB PrintSalesSummary

  ' Print the sales report, which
  ' is saved on disk as \ISALES.REP.

  OPEN "\ISALES.REP" FOR INPUT AS #1

  ' Read each line of the report file
  ' and send it to the printer.
  DO WHILE NOT EOF(1)
    LINE INPUT #1, text$
    LPRINT text$
  LOOP

  CLOSE #1

END SUB   ' PrintSalesSummary



SUB SaveSalesSummary

  ' Save the sales report to ISALES.REP.

  ' Open the data file, ISALES.TXT, for reading
  ' and the report file, ISALES.REP, for output.
  OPEN "\ISALES.TXT" FOR INPUT AS #1
  OPEN "\ISALES.REP" FOR OUTPUT AS #2

  ' The title.
  PRINT #2, TAB(27); "International Sales Summary"
  t% = (80 - LEN(units)) / 2
  PRINT #2, TAB(t%); units
  PRINT #2,

  ' The column headings.
  PRINT #2, " Year"; TAB(15); "American"; "      European";
  PRINT #2, "        Asian"; "         Other";
  PRINT #2, "         Total"
```

```
      PRINT #2, " ----"; TAB(15); "---------"; "        --------";
      PRINT #2, "          -----"; "          -----";
      PRINT #2, "          -----"

      ' The sales data.
      template$ = "    $$#,######"
      amerTot = 0
      euroTot = 0
      asiaTot = 0
      otherTot = 0
      grandTot = 0

      ' Read the data file from beginning to end.
      DO WHILE NOT EOF(1)

         ' Get a line of data from ISALES.TXT.
         INPUT #1, Year$, American, European, Asian, Other

         ' Create a line of the report in ISALES.REP.
         PRINT #2, " "; Year$; TAB(10);
         PRINT #2, USING template$; American;
         PRINT #2, USING template$; European;
         PRINT #2, USING template$; Asian;
         PRINT #2, USING template$; Other;
         tot = American + European + Asian + Other
         PRINT #2, USING template$; tot

         ' Calculate the grand totals.
         amerTot = amerTot + American
         euroTot = euroTot + European
         asiaTot = asiaTot + Asian
         otherTot = otherTot + Other
         grandTot = grandTot + tot
      LOOP

      ' The total sales for all regions.
      PRINT #2,
      PRINT #2, "TOTALS"; TAB(10);
      PRINT #2, USING template$; amerTot;
      PRINT #2, USING template$; euroTot;
      PRINT #2, USING template$; asiaTot;
      PRINT #2, USING template$; otherTot;
      PRINT #2, USING template$; grandTot

      ' Close both files.
      CLOSE #1
      CLOSE #2

  END SUB   ' SaveSalesSummary



  FUNCTION YesNo (prompt$)

     ' Get a yes-or-no response.

     PRINT
     PRINT prompt$;
```

(continued)

```
' Wait for Y or N from the keyboard.
DO
   ans$ = UCASE$(INKEY$)
LOOP UNTIL LEN(ans$) = 1 AND INSTR("YN", ans$)
PRINT ans$
PRINT

' Return a value of true or false.
YesNo = (ans$ = "Y")

END FUNCTION   ' YesNo
```

The program contains five procedures, some of them similar to those in the original version. The GetUnits procedure displays the first input prompt, asking you to identify the dollar units in which you plan to enter the sales data. The GetAnnualSales procedure conducts the input dialog for the actual sales data, and stores each year's data in the ISALES.TXT file. The YesNo function is called at the end of each year's input to give you the option of continuing or stopping the dialog. The SaveSalesSummary procedure generates the sales report and creates the ISALES.REP file. Finally, the PrintSalesSummary procedure reads the ISALES.REP file and sends each line of text to the printer if you request a copy of the report.

These procedures contain interesting examples of QBasic's text file tools, including OPEN, WRITE #, PRINT #, and INPUT #. The first statement you need to master is OPEN.

Open Sesame

You use the QBasic OPEN statement to open a file for any of three purposes:

- ✔ To create a new file
- ✔ To append information to an existing file
- ✔ To read data from a file

For text files, the OPEN statement typically appears in the following format:

```
OPEN fileName FOR mode AS #fileNum
```

This statement supplies three essential items of information:

- ✔ The name of the file on disk, *fileName*. The name is always expressed as a string value in the OPEN statement — a literal string enclosed in quotation marks, a string variable, or a string expression. The string may include the file's directory path.

✔ The file *mode* — that is, the kind of operation you intend to perform on the file. For text files, the most common modes are identified by the QBasic keywords OUTPUT, APPEND, and INPUT.

✔ The file number, *fileNum*, an integer from 1 to 255 that identifies the open file in subsequent input or output statements.

For output to a text file, the OPEN command can create a new file or open an existing file. This important distinction is represented by the keywords OUTPUT and APPEND:

✔ The OUTPUT mode creates a new file and prepares to write data to the file. If a file by the same name already exists on disk, the OPEN statement overwrites that file in the OUTPUT mode. In other words, the previous file will be deleted and its data lost.

✔ The APPEND mode opens an existing file and prepares to add new data to the end of the file. Any data already in the file is safely retained. If the named file does not exist yet, the APPEND mode is the same as the OUTPUT mode; the OPEN statement creates a new file and prepares to write data to it.

Your choice between these operations depends on the design of the program you're creating. For example, this chapter's version of the International Sales program opens the ISALES.REP file in the OUTPUT mode, as you can see in the SaveSalesSummary procedure:

```
OPEN "\ISALES.REP" FOR OUTPUT AS #2
```

Each run of the program creates a new sales report, overwriting any previous ISALES.REP file. The new report is based on the entire data set currently stored in the ISALES.TXT file. (To save a report from a previous run, copy or rename the file before running the program again.) ▤

By contrast, the program's main module opens the ISALES.TXT file in the APPEND mode:

```
OPEN "\ISALES.TXT" FOR APPEND AS #1
```

This statement makes the assumption that you want to append additional years of sales data to the file each time you run the program. (If you want to start over again with a new set of sales data, you should either rename the ISALES.TXT file — saving it on disk under the new name you supply — or delete the file from your disk. Then the next run of the program will create a new version of the file.)

Notice the use of the backslash character in the string that supplies the name of the file: `"\ISALES.TXT"`.

The backslash represents the root directory of the current disk, which is where the program creates the file. If you want to specify a disk as part of the file's path, you can do so at the beginning of the string. For example: `"C:\ISALES.TXT"`. ■

After a file is open in the OUTPUT or the APPEND mode, your program can use either the WRITE # statement or the PRINT # statement to begin sending data to the open file. WRITE # is ideal for storing raw data in a format that a QBasic program can easily read back. By contrast, the PRINT # statement and its companion PRINT # USING give you the ability to save data in formats that *people* can read easily. As you'll see in the upcoming sections of this chapter, these commands all use the # notation to identify by number the file to which they are sending data.

The WRITE # stuff

WRITE # sends a line of data items to an open file. This statement automatically supplies important *delimiter* characters to separate data items in the file:

- ✔ A string is enclosed in quotation marks in the file.
- ✔ Data items on each line are separated by commas.
- ✔ Each line of data ends with a carriage-return and line-feed sequence (ASCII characters 13 and 10, respectively).

As you'll learn shortly, QBasic's INPUT # statement uses these special characters to distinguish between one data item and the next as it reads information from a text file.

In the International Sales program, the GetAnnualSales procedure contains a good example of the WRITE # statement. Before calling the procedure, the main program opens the ISALES.TXT file in the APPEND mode, as file #1:

```
OPEN "\ISALES.TXT" FOR APPEND AS #1
```

Then a DO loop makes repeated calls to GetAnnualSales until the user indicates that the input is complete. Each time the procedure is called, it conducts the input dialog for one year's international sales:

```
INPUT "Year"; Year$
INPUT "American sales"; American
INPUT "European sales"; European
INPUT "   Asian sales"; Asian
INPUT "   Other sales"; Other
```

Notice that the input is stored in five variables — one string and five single-precision numeric variables. After receiving the sales data for a given year, the program sends the data to the open ISALES.TXT file:

```
WRITE #1, Year$, American, European, Asian, Other
```

The output file is identified in the WRITE # statement by the notation #1. This is the file number assigned to the open file in the previous OPEN statement. As you've seen, each successive WRITE # statement sends a new line of comma-delimited data to the file:

```
"1990",12866,9335,10673,7593
"1991",15790,13118,14789,9772
"1992",17855,16093,15863,13121
"1993",20760,19814,18534,15032
```

Each line consists of one string data item followed by four numeric items.

All the text that's fit to PRINT #

The PRINT # and PRINT # USING statements produce the same kind of output as PRINT and PRINT USING. The only difference is the destination. As you know, the PRINT and PRINT USING statements display text on the screen; PRINT # and PRINT # USING send output to an open text file, identified by the # notation.

Except for the # clause, the syntax of these output statements is familiar. Each PRINT # statement sends one or more text items to the designated file. The SaveSalesSummary procedure contains a long sequence of examples. The procedure begins by opening the ISALES.REP file in the OUTPUT mode as file #2:

```
OPEN "\ISALES.REP" FOR OUTPUT AS #2
```

 As this procedure illustrates, QBasic allows multiple files to be open at once. The procedure opens ISALES.TXT as file #1, and prepares to read data from the file as it creates each line of the sales report in ISALES.REP. ▣

After the file is open, a series of PRINT # statements sends the title and column headings to the file:

```
PRINT #2, TAB(27); "International Sales Summary"
t% = (80 - LEN(units)) / 2
PRINT #2, TAB(t%); units
PRINT #2,

PRINT #2, " Year"; TAB(15); "American"; "     European";
PRINT #2, "        Asian"; "        Other";
PRINT #2, "        Total"
```

Notice that the PRINT # statement uses the same syntactical elements as PRINT. For example, the TAB function indicates a horizontal position where an output item will be placed. Multiple data items are separated by semicolons in the statement. Normally, each PRINT # statement results in a new line of text in the file, but a semicolon at the end of the statement suppresses the usual carriage-return and line-feed sequence so that additional output can be sent to the same line.

The PRINT # USING statement uses a special format string to control the appearance of data sent to a file. For example, the SaveSalesSummary procedure sets up a format string for numeric data in a string variable named `template$`:

```
template$ = "    $$#,######"
```

Subsequent PRINT # USING statements employ this string to format the numeric data in the sales report as follows:

```
PRINT #2, USING template$; American;
PRINT #2, USING template$; European;
PRINT #2, USING template$; Asian;
PRINT #2, USING template$; Other;
tot = American + European + Asian + Other
PRINT #2, USING template$; tot
```

As you've seen, these statements produce a column-oriented report of annual sales data and totals (see fig. 18-1).

The contrast between the ISALES.TXT and ISALES.REP files clearly illustrates the difference between the QBasic WRITE # and PRINT # statements. Both statements play important roles in data file programming, but each statement has a very specific use.

Open before Reading

To read a text file, you open it in the INPUT mode, using the following syntax:

```
OPEN fileName FOR INPUT AS #fileNum
```

For example, the SaveSalesSummary procedure opens ISALES.TXT to read the raw data from the file and generate a sales report:

```
OPEN "\ISALES.TXT" FOR INPUT AS #1
```

Using the INPUT mode presupposes that the file exists on disk. If the file is missing, the OPEN statement causes a run-time error known as the `File not found` error. In the International Sales program, this error is unlikely because the program creates both files before trying to open them in the INPUT mode. But in other applications, the error can occur whenever a file is unexpectedly missing. In the next section, you learn how to avoid an interruption in your program when a file is not found.

Setting a trap for "File not found"

If QBasic cannot find the disk file named in an OPEN *fileName* FOR INPUT statement, the program run is interrupted by default, and the following error message appears on the screen:

```
File not found
```

This error commonly occurs when a program asks the user to supply a file name interactively from the keyboard. If the user misspells the file name or otherwise supplies a name that doesn't exist on disk, the File not found error takes place and the program run is interrupted.

You can prevent the interruption by creating a special structure known as an *error trap*. An error trap puts QBasic on alert for a potential run-time error. If an error occurs that would normally interrupt the program, the error trap instead directs control of the program to a special block of code — an *error routine* — designed to handle the error more gracefully.

You create an error trap by placing an ON ERROR GOTO statement before the code where you're anticipating a possible run-time error. ON ERROR GOTO refers by name to an error routine located in your program's main module. The routine is identified by a *label*, a name that marks a location in the listing. A label always ends in a colon, which distinguishes it from other kinds of names that you write in a QBasic program.

An example of the ON ERROR GOTO statement — and a corresponding error routine — appears in the Currency Exchange program (CUREXCH.BAS, Chapter 1). You may recall that this program performs currency exchange calculations based on daily exchange rates stored in a text file named EXCHANGE.TXT. A function named CountCountries% makes the first attempt to open this file, as follows:

```
ON ERROR GOTO NoDateFile
   OPEN DateFileName$ FOR INPUT AS #1
ON ERROR GOTO 0
```

The name of the file is stored in the string variable DateFileName$ (so named because the exchange rates in the file apply to a particular date). The OPEN statement tries to open the file for reading. If the open operation is not successful — that is, if QBasic cannot find the file in the specified directory — the ON ERROR GOTO statement redirects control of the program to the routine labeled

NoDateFile. On the other hand, if the program finds the file, the ON ERROR GOTO 0 statement *disables* the error trap after the file is opened. Notice that the error trap is defined for only one statement in the program.

At the bottom of the program's main module, you can see the following short block of code:

```
NoDateFile:
  CLS
  PRINT "Can't find "; DateFileName$; "."
  END
```

This routine simply clears the screen and informs the user that the exchange rate file doesn't exist where it's supposed to be on disk. Specifically, the program displays the following message on the screen:

```
Can't find C:\EXCHANGE.TXT.
```

After this brief explanation, the error routine terminates the program performance.

After a program has successfully opened a file for input, the INPUT # statement can be used to read individual data items from the file. You learn about this statement next.

Know your source

Except for the source of the data, INPUT # is similar to the INPUT statement, which reads information from the keyboard. INPUT # identifies the number of the open file from which it will read data, and provides a list of variables that will receive the input data, as follows:

```
INPUT #fileNum, varName1, varName2, varName3, ...
```

For example, here is the INPUT # statement in the International Sales program that reads each line of data from the ISALES.TXT file:

```
INPUT #1, Year$, American, European, Asian, Other
```

As you can see, the statement reads five data items from the file — a string representing the year and four numeric values representing the annual sales by region. The program then goes on to generate a line of the sales report from the data stored in these variables.

When the INPUT # statement reads data from a text file, it recognizes a comma as a delimiter between one data item and the next. In addition, it reads a value enclosed in quotation marks as a string — even if the string contains commas or other punctuation characters that would normally serve as delimiters between data items. The WRITE # statement is therefore the perfect counterpart to INPUT #. WRITE # organizes data in a file in just the way that INPUT # expects to find it.

To use the INPUT # statement successfully, you have to know how the data is organized in the open text file. The data types of the variables listed in the INPUT # statement must correspond to the types of data stored in the file. In addition, the INPUT # statement should not attempt to read more data than actually exists in the file; doing so causes a run-time error. ▪

Line-by-line

Another way to get information from a text file is to read entire lines at once, with the LINE INPUT # statement. LINE INPUT # recognizes only the end-of-line markers (ASCII 13 and 10) as delimiters in the text. The statement therefore reads a line of text and stores it in a string variable:

```
LINE INPUT #fileNum, stringVarName$
```

LINE INPUT # is perfect for reading text files that contain unpredictable combinations of text and numbers. In this sense, LINE INPUT # is often a good way to read a file that has been created with PRINT # and PRINT USING # statements.

For example, the PrintSalesSummary procedure in the International Sales program uses LINE INPUT # in the process of sending the contents of the ISALES.REP file to the printer. The procedure begins by opening the file for input:

```
OPEN "\ISALES.REP" FOR INPUT AS #1
```

Then a DO WHILE loop reads each line from the file and uses the LPRINT command to send the line to the printer:

```
DO WHILE NOT EOF(1)
  LINE INPUT #1, text$
  LPRINT text$
LOOP
```

The condition of this DO WHILE loop uses a special built-in QBasic function named EOF (for *end of file*). The argument of EOF is the number of an open file. As the program reads the file, EOF returns a value of false as long as there is still more data to be read. But when the program reaches the end of the file, EOF returns a value of true. The condition NOT EOF(1) therefore allows the looping to continue until the program reads the last line of the file.

Say Goodnight, Gracie

When your program is finished with a file, you can use the CLOSE statement to close the file. The syntax is simple:

```
CLOSE #fileNum
```

For example, here is how the SaveSalesSummary procedure closes the two files that it works with:

```
CLOSE #1
CLOSE #2
```

These statements also release the file numbers so they can be used for opening a different file.

Alternatively, you can use the CLOSE statement without a file number:

```
CLOSE
```

This statement closes all open files. Likewise, the END statement that terminates a program performance closes any files that remain open.

Chapter 19

Working with Random-Access Files

A random-access file contains individual records of information. Each record is a collection of data items organized in a consistent format. The most important feature of this file type is access; after opening a file, a program can go directly to any record and read the information it contains. Data access is efficient and reliable.

The best way to create a random-access file in QBasic is to begin with a user-defined record structure. As you learned in Chapter 16, the TYPE statement defines the name of a structure and provides a list of individual field names and their data types. In a subsequent DIM statement, you declare a record variable belonging to the user-defined type. This variable becomes the perfect medium for writing records to — or reading records from — a random-access file. Each write operation stores an entire record, with all its fields of data, in the file. Likewise, each read operation retrieves a complete record from the file and gives your program access to the data in the record.

A program refers to records in a random-access file by number, from 1 up to the current number of records. The record number indicates a record's position in the file. Keeping track of the numbers for specific records is one of the challenging problems in a file-management program. Programmers devise a variety of ways to solve this problem. In some applications, the record number itself has special significance to the user; for example, it may be a part number or an invoice number. In this special case, the user's request for a particular record number may correspond precisely to the record's position in the file.

But more typically, the user needs to request records by some item of information other than the record number. For example, suppose you've created a random-access file to store names and addresses. Your programming goal is to give the user access to any address in the file; the user provides the name of a person to look up in the file, and your program retrieves the address. To achieve this goal, your program has to maintain an *index* of all the names in the file and their corresponding record numbers. If the user requests the address for Mary Doe, your program looks up *Doe, Mary* in the index, finds the record number, and then reads the correct record from the file.

In this chapter, you learn to use QBasic's tools for random-access file programming, and you begin exploring techniques for managing random-access files. A project presented previously in this book — the Restaurant Database program (RESTINPT.BAS, Chapter 8) — serves as an example of a program that *creates* a random-access file. This program helps you develop a personal database of your own restaurant reviews. In each record, you provide your impressions of a restaurant you've visited during a business trip, and you rate the restaurant's quality and price. The program uses the QBasic PUT # statement to store each record in a random-access file named RESTLIST.DB.

To illustrate the process of *reading* records from a file, this chapter then presents a new project named the Restaurant Reviews program. This program begins by opening the RESTLIST.DB file. Using the QBasic GET # statement to read individual records from the file, the program prepares an alphabetized index of the restaurants described in the file. Through this index, the program provides easy access to any record in the database.

Together, these two Restaurant programs give you a solid introduction to the QBasic tools available for random-access files.

It Takes Two

Each time you run the Restaurant Database program, it prepares to add one or more new records to the end of the RESTLIST.DB file. The program conducts a short input dialog for each new record. You begin by supplying the name of the city where the restaurant is located and the name of the restaurant itself. Then you enter a number from 1 to 4 for each of two ratings: quality and price. On the screen, the program translates your ratings into strings of symbols — stars for the quality rating, and dollar signs for the price rating. Finally, you can enter a full line of text describing your general impressions of the restaurant. Here's an example of a new record entry:

```
International Restaurant Database
------------- ---------- --------

Record # 26

City? New York
Name? Cafe Firenze
Quality (1 to 4)? ***
Prices (1 to 4)?  $$
Comments? Unpretentious Italian food; don't skip dessert.

Save this record? Y
Another record? Y
```

Notice that the program tells you the number of the new record (26 in this
example). When you complete the input dialog, the program asks you to
confirm your entry before saving the new record to disk. Finally, you can
continue entering new records, or you can quit the program.

This chapter's new program, named Restaurant Reviews (RESTREVU.BAS),
opens the RESTLIST.DB file and prepares to read the information it contains.
The program begins by offering to print an index of the restaurants currently
stored in the file:

```
Print the restaurant index? Y
```

If you respond by typing Y, the program prints a list of all the restaurants,
organized by city. Here's an example:

```
          Banjul   1. City Cafe

        Chartres   2. Cafe du Monde
                   3. Restaurant de la Poste

          Dakar    4. Cafe Casamancais
                   5. Restaurant Senegalais
                   6. Restaurant de la Place

     Los Angeles   7. Chez Edith
                   8. Sara's Cafe

        New York   9. Andrew's at the Park
                  10. Cafe Firenze
                  11. Kabul Cafe

Northeast Harbor  12. Harbor Hotel

           Paris  13. Cafe Americain
                  14. Cafe du Nord
                  15. Chez Sophie

   San Francisco  16. Bamian Restaurant
```

```
                    17. Cambodian Cafe
                    18. Donnie's Place
                    19. Rudy's

       Santa Fe     20. Cactus Cafe
                    21. Desert View Restaurant

      St. Louis     22. Jack's Place
                    23. River View Cafe

     Strasbourg     24. Cafe de l'Ile
                    25. Restaurant de l'Alsace
                    26. Taverne de la Place
```

This index is your guide to locating any restaurant currently described in the database. To prepare the index, the program alphabetizes the list in two ways: first by city and then by restaurant names in each city. The numbers printed in the index are for your convenience in choosing a restaurant. The program subsequently invites you to enter the number of any restaurant in the index (from 1 to 26 in this example) to view the corresponding record from the database:

```
Which restaurant review do you want to read?
Enter a number from 1 to 26 -->
```

When you enter a number, the program reads the record you've requested from the database and displays its information on the screen:

```
Which restaurant review do you want to read?
Enter a number from 1 to 26 --> 14

Paris
-----
Cafe du Nord              ****    $$$
   --> Quiet atmosphere, excellent food; good for meetings.


Another Restaurant?
```

By pressing Y in response to the `Another Restaurant?` prompt, you can retrieve another record; the program clears the screen and then repeats the dialog. When you're ready to stop the program, press N in response to the `Another Restaurant?` prompt.

From your point of view as the user, the restaurant records are conveniently arranged by city. But this order doesn't match the way the records are stored in the file. For example, here are the record numbers in this particular database file:

```
    1.  Dakar              Restaurant Senegalais
    2.  Paris              Cafe du Nord
    3.  Strasbourg         Cafe de l'Ile
    4.  New York           Andrew's at the Park
    5.  San Francisco      Donnie's Place
    6.  Los Angeles        Sara's Cafe
    7.  San Francisco      Rudy's
```

```
 8.  Paris              Cafe Americain
 9.  Chartres           Cafe du Monde
10.  Dakar              Cafe Casamancais
11.  Dakar              Restaurant de la Place
12.  Santa Fe           Cactus Cafe
13.  Santa Fe           Desert View Restaurant
14.  Strasbourg         Restaurant de l'Alsace
15.  St. Louis          River View Cafe
16.  San Francisco      Cambodian Cafe
17.  New York           Kabul Cafe
18.  Chartres           Restaurant de la Poste
19.  Banjul             City Cafe
20.  Northeast Harbor   Harbor Hotel
21.  St. Louis          Jack's Place
22.  Paris              Chez Sophie
23.  San Francisco      Bamian Restaurant
24.  Los Angeles        Chez Edith
25.  Strasbourg         Taverne de la Place
26.  New York           Cafe Firenze
```

This original order is chronological, in a sense; it's the order in which the records were entered. One of the program's important jobs is to keep track of the actual record numbers, which indicate the position of each record in the file. At the same time, the program provides the user with a more convenient numbering system, based on the alphabetical order of the index list. As you'll see when you inspect the code, the program uses an array of records to represent the index in memory and to manage these two numbering systems.

The Reviews Are In

Here is the listing of the Restaurant Reviews program:

```
' Restaurant Reviews (RESTREVU.BAS)
' Prints an index of the restaurant reviews
' in the RESTLIST.DB database, and lets the
' user choose which restaurants to read about.

DECLARE SUB GetChoice ()
DECLARE SUB MakeIndex ()
DECLARE SUB PrintList ()
DECLARE SUB ShowRecord (Rest AS ANY)
DECLARE FUNCTION YesNo! (prompt$)

' Define the record type.
TYPE RestaurantType
   City AS STRING * 20
   RName AS STRING * 25
   Rating AS STRING * 1
   Prices AS STRING * 1
   Comments AS STRING * 65
END TYPE
```

(continued)

```
' Define the record type for
' the index array.
TYPE RestIndexType
  City AS STRING * 20
  RName AS STRING * 25
  RPos AS INTEGER
END TYPE

' Declare the global Restaurant variable.
DIM SHARED Restaurant AS RestaurantType

' The numRecs variable represents the
' number of records in the database.
DIM SHARED numRecs AS INTEGER

' Open the database file and begin the input dialog.
OPEN "\RESTLIST.DB" FOR RANDOM AS #1 LEN = LEN(Restaurant)

' Declare the RestIndex array and then
' create the restaurant index.
numRecs = LOF(1) / LEN(Restaurant)
DIM SHARED RestIndex(numRecs) AS RestIndexType

CLS
IF numRecs = 0 THEN
  PRINT "Run the RESTINPT.BAS program to"
  PRINT "create the restaurant database."
ELSE

  MakeIndex

  ' Conduct the dialog.
  IF YesNo("Print the restaurant index? ") THEN PrintList
  DO
    GetChoice
  LOOP UNTIL NOT YesNo("Another Restaurant? ")

END IF

END   ' RESTREVU.BAS



SUB GetChoice

  ' Elicit the user's restaurant choice,
  ' read the corresponding review from the
  ' database, and show the information on
  ' the screen.

  CLS
  PRINT "Which restaurant review do you want to read?"
  PRINT "Enter a number from 1 to"; numRecs;
  INPUT "--> ", choice%
  PRINT

  ' If choice% is in the correct range, read the
  ' record from the database. The RPos field in the
  ' RestIndex array represents the record number.
```

```
    IF choice% > 0 AND choice% <= numRecs THEN
      GET #1, RestIndex(choice%).RPos, Restaurant
      ShowRecord Restaurant
    END IF

END SUB  ' Getchoice


SUB MakeIndex

  ' Create an index of all the restaurants
  ' in the RestIndex array.

  FOR i% = 1 TO numRecs
    GET #1, i%, Restaurant
    RestIndex(i%).City = Restaurant.City
    RestIndex(i%).RName = Restaurant.RName
    RestIndex(i%).RPos = i%
  NEXT i%

  ' Sort the index by cities
  ' and restaurant names.

  FOR i% = 1 TO numRecs - 1
    FOR j% = i% TO numRecs
      iKey$ = RestIndex(i%).City + RestIndex(i%).RName
      jKey$ = RestIndex(j%).City + RestIndex(j%).RName
      IF iKey$ > jKey$ THEN
        SWAP RestIndex(i%), RestIndex(j%)
      END IF
    NEXT j%
  NEXT i%

END SUB  ' MakeIndex


SUB PrintList

  ' Print the list of restaurants,
  ' organized by city locations.

  DIM cityField AS STRING * 20
  CLS
  prevCity$ = ""
  FOR i% = 1 TO numRecs

    ' Display the city only when the City
    ' field contains a new value.
    IF RestIndex(i%).City <> prevCity$ THEN
      LPRINT
      RSET cityField = RTRIM$(RestIndex(i%).City)
      LPRINT cityField;
    END IF
    prevCity$ = RestIndex(i%).City
    LPRINT TAB(22); USING "###. "; i%;
    LPRINT RestIndex(i%).RName
  NEXT i%

END SUB  ' PrintList
```

(continued)

```
SUB ShowRecord (Rest AS RestaurantType)

  ' Display the fields of a restaurant.

  PRINT Rest.City
  PRINT STRING$(LEN(RTRIM$(Rest.City)), "-")
  PRINT Rest.RName;

  ' Display **** or $$$$ symbols for
  ' Rating and Prices fields.
  PRINT STRING$(VAL(Rest.Rating), "*");
  PRINT SPACE$(8 - VAL(Rest.Rating));
  PRINT STRING$(VAL(Rest.Prices), "$")

  ' Display comments on a new line.
  PRINT "   --> "; Rest.Comments
  PRINT

END SUB   ' ShowRecord



FUNCTION YesNo (prompt$)

  ' Get a yes or no response.

  PRINT
  PRINT prompt$;

  ' Wait for a Y or an N from the keyboard.
  DO
    ans$ = UCASE$(INKEY$)
  LOOP UNTIL LEN(ans$) = 1 AND INSTR("YN", ans$)
  PRINT ans$
  PRINT

  ' Return a value of true or false.
  YesNo = (ans$ = "Y")

END FUNCTION   ' YesNo
```

The program's main module defines two important data structures. The RestaurantType structure represents the format in which records are stored in the database. The RestIndexType is designed as a structure for the restaurant index that the program maintains in the computer's memory. You examine both of these structures later in this chapter.

In addition, the program contains five procedures. Two of them, MakeIndex and PrintList, are devoted to creating, sorting, and printing the restaurant index. The GetChoice procedure prompts the user for a restaurant number from the index, and the ShowRecord procedure displays the selected record on the screen. Finally, the YesNo function accepts the user's response to the Another Restaurant? prompt.

Your main focus in this chapter is on the procedures that read records from the database and create the index — GetChoice and MakeIndex. But first, a look back at the Restaurant Database program shows you how the RESTLIST.DB file is created in the first place.

Designing a Random-Access File

QBasic supplies a variety of tools for working with random-access files. Three of the most important are

 ✔ OPEN, to open a file in the RANDOM mode

 ✔ PUT #, to write a record to the file

 ✔ GET #, to read a record from the file

In addition, you use TYPE and DIM to prepare data structures for the file. Here are the typical programming steps you follow to create and work with random-access files in QBasic:

1. Write a TYPE statement to define the structure of the records you intend to store in the file.

2. Write a DIM statement to declare a record variable for storing information on its way to or from the file.

3. Use the OPEN statement to open the file in the RANDOM mode. In this mode, a file is available for both writing and reading information.

4. Use the PUT # statement to write individual records to the file.

5. Use the GET # statement to read individual records from the file.

The Restaurant Database and Restaurant Reviews programs both begin their work by defining the structure that represents individual restaurant records in the database:

```
TYPE RestaurantType
   City AS STRING * 20
   RName AS STRING * 25
   Rating AS STRING * 1
   Prices AS STRING * 1
   Comments AS STRING * 65
END TYPE
```

The structure has five fields, which are all fixed-length strings. The City field represents the location of a given restaurant, and RName is the name of the restaurant. Rating and Prices are the quality and price ratings assigned to the restaurant, respectively. The Comments field represents the additional line of general information about the restaurant. After defining this structure, both programs declare a record variable belonging to the user-defined type:

```
DIM SHARED Restaurant AS RestaurantType
```

When a program reads a record from the database file or prepares to write a record to the file, the following names represent the five fields of the record:

```
Restaurant.City
Restaurant.RName
Restaurant.Rating
Restaurant.Prices
Restaurant.Comments
```

Both programs use the Restaurant variable in OPEN, PUT #, and GET # statements.

Mode of operation

As you learned in Chapter 18, a program opens a text file in the OUTPUT mode to write information to the file, and in the INPUT mode to read information from the file. By contrast, an open random-access file is available for both reading and writing. The QBasic keyword that represents this file mode is RANDOM.

The OPEN statement for a random-access file normally contains a LEN clause that indicates the length of records in the file. Keep in mind that access to information in the file is based on the fact that all records have a consistent length. Thanks to this fixed length, QBasic can easily determine where a given record begins and ends. Accordingly, the LEN clause tells QBasic the length of the records in the file. Here is the general syntax for opening a random-access file:

```
OPEN fileName FOR RANDOM AS #fileNum LEN = recordLength
```

As usual, *fileName* is the name and path of the file on disk, and *fileNum* is an integer that identifies the file in subsequent input and output statements. In the LEN clause, *recordLength* is the length, in bytes, of a record in the file.

How do you supply a value for the record length? Well, one way would be to calculate the lengths of all the fields in the record structure you plan to use for the file, find the sum of these lengths, and supply this literal numeric value in the LEN clause. For example:

```
LEN = 112
```

But fortunately, QBasic supplies a simple tool that does these calculations for you — the LEN function. You've seen how LEN works for string values; given a string argument, LEN returns the number of characters in the string. Now you learn that LEN can take any type of variable as its argument, including a record variable. LEN returns the total length of all the fields in the record. Consequently, you can write the LEN clause as follows:

```
LEN = LEN(recordVariable)
```

Don't be confused by the double appearance of LEN in this clause. The first LEN is the keyword for the clause itself; the second refers to QBasic's built-in function that supplies the length of a variable.

For example, here is how the Restaurant programs open the RESTLIST.DB database as a random-access file:

```
OPEN "\RESTLIST.DB" FOR RANDOM AS #1 LEN = LEN(Restaurant)
```

The record variable Restaurant has been declared in a previous DIM statement, and its structure has been defined in a TYPE statement. The expression LEN(Restaurant) therefore tells QBasic the length of records in the RESTLIST.DB file. After this statement, QBasic is ready to write records to the file or read records from the file.

After opening a random-access file, an application typically needs to find out the number of records currently stored in the file. QBasic's built-in LOF (length of file) function returns the total length, in bytes, of any open file. LOF takes one argument — the file number assigned to the file in the corresponding OPEN statement. If you divide the length of the file by the length of a single record in the file, the result is the number of records. For example, here is how the Restaurant Reviews program calculates the current number of records in the database:

An old way to define the record structure

In older versions of BASIC, the TYPE statement didn't exist; you couldn't define record structures or declare record variables for use with random-access files. These versions of BASIC provided a clumsy technique for defining the structure of a random-access file. After opening a file, you had to use the FIELD # statement to declare special field variables for use with the file. For example, the restaurant database might have been defined as follows:

```
OPEN "\RESTLIST.DB" FOR RANDOM AS #1 LEN = 112

FIELD #1, 20 AS City$, 25 AS RName$
FIELD #1, 1 AS Rating$, 1 AS Prices$
FIELD #1, 65 AS Comments$
```

You should never have to resort to this old technique; but you may occasionally run across it in programs written for previous versions of BASIC. Note that the FIELD # statement and its associated tools are supported by QBasic, so you can still run programs that use this approach.

```
numRecs = LOF(1) / LEN(Restaurant)
```

Notice the use of the expression `LEN(Restaurant)` to find the length of a single record.

After a random-access file is opened, a program uses PUT # to write records to the file and GET # to read records from the file.

PUTting it to a file

The PUT # statement sends a complete data record to a particular position in an open random-access file. Here is the usual syntax for this statement:

```
PUT #fileNum, recordNum, recordVariable
```

In this format, *fileNum* is the integer that identifies the open file; this is the same number assigned to the file in the corresponding OPEN statement. The next value, *recordNum*, is an integer specifying the position where the record will be stored in the file. Finally, *recordVariable* is the variable containing the record that PUT # writes to the file. Before the PUT # statement, your program assigns values to the fields of *recordVariable*.

Of the three items you supply in the PUT # statement, *recordNum* is probably the trickiest. Depending on the value of *recordNum*, PUT # does one of two things:

- ✔ If *recordNum* is a value from 1 up to the current number of records in the file, PUT # *overwrites* an existing record in the file. For example, suppose a file contains 10 records, and you supply a value of 5 as the *recordNum*. Your PUT # statement writes a new record to position 5 in the file.

- ✔ If *recordNum* is equal to 1 greater than the current number of records in the file, PUT # *appends* a new record to the file. For example, in a file containing 10 records, you supply a *recordNum* value of 11 to append a new record. As a result of this PUT # statement, the length of your file increases by one record.

The Restaurant Database program (RESTINPT.BAS) allows you to append new records to the end of the RESTLIST.DB file during each run. Consequently, one of the program's initial actions is to determine the number of the first new record that will be added to the file. This operation is performed by a call to the GetRecordNum% function. The function uses the QBasic LOF and LEN functions to calculate the new record number:

```
GetRecordNum% = LOF(1) / LEN(Restaurant) + 1
```

In other words, the next new record number should be 1 greater than the current number of records in the file.

In the DoInput procedure, this value is assigned to the variable `recordNum`. The procedure conducts an input dialog to elicit values for the five fields of a new record:

```
LINE INPUT "City? "; Restaurant.City
LINE INPUT "Name? "; Restaurant.RName
Restaurant.Rating = GetRating$("Quality (1 to 4)? ", "*")
Restaurant.Prices = GetRating$("Prices (1 to 4)?  ", "$")
LINE INPUT "Comments? "; Restaurant.Comments
```

Then the following PUT # statement appends the new record to the end of the file:

```
PUT #1, recordNum, Restaurant
```

Anticipating the possibility of another new record after this record, the program then increases the value of `recordNum` by 1:

```
recordNum = recordNum + 1
```

In this way, each PUT # statement adds a new record to the file. Careful management of the `recordNum` variable prevents the possibility of overwriting any of the existing records in the database.

 QBasic allows you to omit the *recordNum* argument in the PUT # statement, as follows:

```
PUT #fileNum, , recordVariable
```

If you write the statement in this way, each succeeding PUT # automatically writes a record to the *next* position in the file. This can be a convenient way to store an initial set of records in a new file. But if your program opens an existing file that contains records, QBasic initially sets the current record number at 1. If you don't specify a new starting record number, a series of PUT # statements can therefore overwrite the existing records. To avoid loss of data, you should always make sure you know where PUT # will be writing data in your file. ∎

Get that record!

GET # reads a complete data record from a particular position in an open random-access file. Here is the syntax:

```
GET #fileNum, recordNum, recordVariable
```

Again, *fileNum* is the integer that identifies the open file, and *recordNum* is the position from which the record will be read. In this case, *recordVariable* receives the record from the file. After GET #, your program refers to the individual fields of *recordVariable* to gain access to the information that's been read from the file.

Because the first task in the Restaurant Reviews program (RESTREVU.BAS) is to create an index for the restaurant database file, the program uses a FOR loop to read through the file from beginning to end:

```
FOR i% = 1 TO numRecs
  GET #1, i%, Restaurant
  ' ...
NEXT i%
```

The program has assigned the current length of the file (that is, the number of records) to the global variable numRecs. During the iterations of this FOR loop, the counter variable i% represents record numbers from 1 to the last record in the file. The GET # statement reads each record in turn. After each GET #, the fields of the newly accessed record are represented by Restaurant.City, Restaurant.RName, and so on.

Just as in PUT #, *recordNum* is optional in the GET # statement:

```
GET #fileNum, , recordVariable
```

If you write the statement this way, each succeeding GET # reads the *next* record in the file. In a program that doesn't need to know the number of records in the file, you can therefore use a DO loop to read the records from beginning to end. For example, if the record variable Restaurant is declared appropriately, the following code displays the City and RName fields from all the records in the RESTLIST.DB file:

```
OPEN "\RESTLIST.DB" FOR RANDOM AS #1 LEN = LEN(Restaurant)

DO WHILE NOT EOF(1)
  GET #1, , Restaurant
  PRINT Restaurant.City; "  "; Restaurant.RName
LOOP
```

In this loop, the GET # statement doesn't specify a record number. QBasic automatically increments the record number after each GET #. When the loop reaches the end of the file — that is, when EOF(1) returns a value of true — the program stops reading records. ■

Creating order from chaos

The order in which records are entered into a database is often random. For example, suppose you're developing an address database. You're unlikely to enter all the addresses in alphabetical order by people's names. Instead, you'll probably enter an address into the database when you happen to think of someone you want to include, or when you run across the scrap of paper on which you'd jotted down an important address some weeks ago.

TIP

SEEK # and you shall find

In some applications, you may want to begin by specifying a starting point in your database for subsequent PUT # or GET # operations. QBasic's SEEK # statement allows you to do this. SEEK # sets the position for a particular open file:

```
SEEK #fileNum, recordNum
```

After SEEK #, you can use the PUT # statement to write a record to the *recordNum* position in the database:

```
PUT #fileNum, , recordVariable
```

Alternatively, use a GET # statement to read a record from the SEEK # position:

```
GET #fileNum, , recordVariable
```

An example of the SEEK # statement appears in the Show Restaurants program (SHOWREST.BAS, Chapter 9). In response to the user's request for restaurants in a particular city, the program begins by resetting the file position to the first record in the database:

```
SEEK #1, 1
```

The program then searches from the beginning to the end of the database for records that match the user's city choice.

Conversely, the following SEEK # statement sets the current record number to the position immediately *after* the final record in the database:

```
SEEK #1, LOF(1) / LEN(Restaurant) + 1
```

There's nothing unusual about randomly ordered entries in a database. But when you get ready to use the information, you want it to be presented in a planned order. For example, you may want to print your addresses in alphabetical order by people's names, in numeric order by zip codes, or in some other order that meets a particular requirement.

Fortunately, your computer is very good at rearranging records in a specified order. As you know, this task is called *sorting*. One practical way to present database records in a sorted order is to create an index for the database and then to sort the index rather than the database itself. This technique allows you to leave a potentially large database file in its original order, and focus on sorting the smaller data set represented by the index.

For example, in the case of an address database, you might create an index consisting of all the names in the database and their corresponding record numbers. Your program can easily sort the index in alphabetical order by names, and can then produce a sorted list of addresses by retrieving each record from the database in the order represented by the index.

The Restaurant Reviews program illustrates another use of an index for accessing records from a database. The program creates an index consisting of the City and RName fields from each record, along with the corresponding record numbers. The index is stored in memory as an array of records — a smaller array than the one that would have been needed to store the entire database in memory. After alphabetizing the index, the program presents the list of restaurants to the user in printed form. When the user makes a selection from this list, the program uses the corresponding record number to retrieve the entire restaurant record from the database.

In greater detail, here are the steps the program follows to create and manage this index:

1. A TYPE statement in the program's main module declares a special structure for the elements of the index array. The structure contains three fields: the City and RName fields from the restaurant records, plus a field named RPos to record the record number of each restaurant:

```
TYPE RestIndexType
   City AS STRING * 20
   RName AS STRING * 25
   RPos AS INTEGER
END TYPE
```

2. After opening the database and calculating the number of records currently stored in the database, the program declares a dynamic array of RestIndexType records to represent the index:

```
OPEN "\RESTLIST.DB" FOR RANDOM AS #1 LEN = LEN(Restaurant)
numRecs = LOF(1) / LEN(Restaurant)
DIM SHARED RestIndex(numRecs) AS RestIndexType
```

As you can see, the index contains one element for each record in the array.

3. The program next makes a call to the MakeIndex procedure, which begins by reading the City and RName fields from each record in the database and saving the record numbers in the RPos field of the index array:

```
FOR i% = 1 TO numRecs
   GET #1, i%, Restaurant
   RestIndex(i%).City = Restaurant.City
   RestIndex(i%).RName = Restaurant.RName
   RestIndex(i%).RPos = i%
NEXT i%
```

4. The MakeIndex procedure then sorts the index first by the City field and then by the RName field. This is accomplished by combining these two fields into a single key for each record, and swapping the positions of any two records that are out of order:

```
FOR i% = 1 TO numRecs - 1
  FOR j% = i% TO numRecs
    iKey$ = RestIndex(i%).City + RestIndex(i%).RName
    jKey$ = RestIndex(j%).City + RestIndex(j%).RName
    IF iKey$ > jKey$ THEN
      SWAP RestIndex(i%), RestIndex(j%)
    END IF
  NEXT j%
NEXT i%
```

If the user requests, the program sends a copy of this sorted index to the printer.

5. Finally, the GetChoice procedure invites the user to select a restaurant from this index by number. The user's selection is stored in the integer variable `choice%`. If this value is in the range of numbers representing the current records in the database, the procedure uses a GET # statement to read the requested record from the database:

```
GET #1, RestIndex(choice%).RPos, Restaurant
```

Keep in mind that `choice%` represents the user's selection from the index. The corresponding record number is provided by the `RestIndex(choice%).RPos` expression. In other words, the `RPos` field in the index array represents the database position from which the program reads the record. Once this record is available, the program calls the ShowRecord procedure to display the restaurant information on the screen:

```
ShowRecord Restaurant
```

As this process continues, the program allows the user to view any number of records from the database.

The Restaurant Reviews program is worth examining carefully; its indexing technique is an important one for use in database management programs. Chapter 20 presents another database program that demonstrates other aspects of this technique.

Chapter 20

Managing a Database

● ●

● ●

A program in charge of a database typically gives you simple ways to perform several important operations on individual records. Probably the two most basic operations are appending and retrieving records. You want be able to add new records at any point during your work with the database, and you want the program to find and display records that you request.

You've seen combinations of programs that provide these kinds of services. For example, the Restaurant Database program (RESTINPT.BAS, Chapter 8) allows you to add records to a database of personal restaurant reviews. Two companion programs give you access to the information in the database: The Show Restaurants program (SHOWREST.BAS, Chapter 9) displays lists of restaurants for a given city, and the Restaurant Review program (RESTREVU.BAS, Chapter 19) gives you access to individual restaurant reviews from a printed index.

In this chapter, you turn to a program that offers several database operations in a single menu. This new example is called the Telephone Database program (PHONE.BAS); the database it manages is a simple collection of names and phone numbers. The records in the database have fields for a person's name (first and last), along with three phone numbers: work phone, home phone, and fax number.

You can use this convenient program on business trips, when your primary tool for communication with the outside world is the ubiquitous telephone, and your notebook computer is never far from view. The program gives you a quick way to look up people's phone numbers. You find a record simply by typing a person's name. You can also add new phone records to your database at any time.

But there's more. Telephone numbers have an unpleasant way of changing frequently; accordingly, the program allows you to revise any record when necessary. Finally, you may occasionally want to produce a printed directory of all the telephone numbers in your database. The program offers this capability as well.

Simplicity is always the key to an effective database management program. People want fast and easy ways to find information so they can get on with their work. Paradoxically — from your point of view as a programmer — simplicity can be extremely difficult to provide. The Telephone Database program is very easy to use, but it is also the longest and most detailed project in this book. To provide a convenient set of basic database operations, the program contains nearly 250 lines of code. Although this appears to be a simple database tool — allowing you to add, retrieve, revise, and print phone records — the program has many detailed tasks to perform in the background.

Before examining the code behind the program's major operations, begin by taking a look at how the program runs.

Your Electronic Phone Book

The program displays a menu of options on the screen, along with a prompt that tells you how to select an option:

```
Telephone and Fax Numbers
- - - - - - - - - - - - - - - - - - - - - - - - -
    A)dd names
    F)ind names
    C)hange a record
    P)rint a directory

    Q)uit

Press A, F, C, P, or Q -->
```

This menu returns to the screen after each database operation you complete. Some options let you work with multiple records before returning to the menu. For example, when you choose the A)dd names option, you can add any number of new records to the database in sequence. Likewise, the F)ind names option lets you retrieve and examine records for any number of names in a row. By contrast, the C)hange a record option assumes you need to revise only one record at a time.

When you choose the P)rint a directory option, the program sends an alphabetized phone directory to your printer and then returns the menu to the screen. The last option, Q)uit, ends the program.

Your initial task is to begin entering records into the database. You press A at the main menu to choose the A)dd names option. The program begins the input dialog for a new record. You enter the first and last name of the person whose phone numbers you want to save in the database. Then you type as many as three numbers for this record, as in the following (fictitious) example:

```
Enter a new record:

First name? Jamie
 Last name? Haines

Phone numbers:
Work? 011-33-5-44-11-55
Home? 011-33-5-19-24-11
 Fax? 011-33-5-16-83-12


Save this record? Y


Another?
```

The phone number fields are long enough to accommodate area codes, extensions, and international telephone numbers with unseemly quantities of digits. If you have no number to enter for a particular field, you simply press Enter without any typing; you can fill in a missing number later by choosing the C)hange a record option. When you complete the five fields, the program gives you a chance to review your entry and decide whether to save it in the database. Press Y in response to the Save this record? prompt to append the new record to your database. Then press Y again in response to Another? if you want to continue entering new records. The main menu returns to the screen when you press N.

The program requires entries for the both the first and last name to save a new record in the database. If you attempt to enter a record in which one of these fields is missing, the program rejects your entry:

```
Enter a new record:

First name?
 Last name? Smith

You must enter a first name and a last name.

Another?
```

The first and last names are the keys by which the program organizes and retrieves information from the database; for consistency and reliability, the program therefore needs both entries. Likewise, the program prevents you from entering the same record twice. If you type the name of a person who is already in the database, the A)dd names option simply displays the existing record. For example:

```
Enter a new record:

First name? Melissa
 Last name? Kawasaki

This name is already on file:

Melissa Kawasaki
Work: (702) 555-1872
Home: (702) 555-1891
Fax:  (702) 555-1287


Another?
```

If two people have the same name, use a middle initial to distinguish between the two names in the database.

Once your database contains a collection of records, you can begin using the program to look up phone numbers. To do so, you choose the F)ind names menu option, and then enter the first and last name of the person you want to look up. The program immediately displays the complete record on the screen:

```
First name? Danielle
 Last name? Hahn

Danielle Hahn
Work: (805) 555-1821
Home: (805) 555-1612
Fax:  (805) 555-1367


Another?
```

If you misspell a name — or otherwise enter a name that's not in the database — the program displays an appropriate error message:

```
First name? Billy
 Last name? Wilson

Can't find that name.


Another?
```

When you need to revise a phone number, choose the C)hange a record option. Again the program prompts you for the first and last name of the person whose record you need to revise. Then the program looks up the record, displays it on the screen, and allows you to change any or all of the three phone numbers in the record:

```
First name? Abdou
 Last name? N'Diaye

Abdou N'Diaye
Work: 011-221-5-98-34-34
Home: 011-221-5-87-89-13
Fax:  011-221-5-16-71-32

Press Enter to keep an existing number:

New work number? 011-221-5-98-34-34
New home number? 011-221-5-87-89-13
New  fax number? 011-221-5-16-71-55


Save changes? Y
```

To keep a given phone number the way it is, you simply press Enter in response to the appropriate New prompt; the program automatically redisplays the current number. When you get to the field you want to change, type the new number and press Enter. At the end, the program gives you a chance to review your revision and decide whether to save the change in the database. Press Y in response to the Save changes? prompt to complete the revision, or press N to abandon the changes and keep the record in its original form.

Finally, the P)rint a directory option prints a complete list of all the names and phone numbers in your database. Conveniently, the records are printed in six-line intervals appropriate for use on gummed labels you can purchase for your printer. For example, here is the directory for a database containing about a dozen records:

```
BARTH, Helene
Work: (809) 555-7863
Home: (809) 555-2131
Fax:  (809) 555-1238


CONTI, Kati
Work: (213) 555-5187
Home: (213) 555-7113
Fax:  (213) 555-6691


DENEAU, Keith
Work: (212) 555-9344
Home: (212) 555-6711
Fax:  (212) 555-1287


HAHN, Danielle
Work: (805) 555-1821
Home: (805) 555-1612
Fax:  (805) 555-1367
```

(continued)

```
HAINES, Jamie
Work: 011-33-5-44-11-55
Home: 011-33-5-19-24-11
Fax:  011-33-5-16-83-12


HIRAKAWA, Shirley
Work: (314) 555-2397
Home: (314) 555-4512
Fax:  (314) 555-5671


KAWASAKI, Melissa
Work: (702) 555-1872
Home: (702) 555-1891
Fax:  (702) 555-1287


MACDONNELL, Thomas
Work: (605) 555-8961
Home: (605) 555-2138
Fax:  (605) 555-1334


N'DIAYE, Abdou
Work: 011-221-5-98-34-34
Home: 011-221-5-87-89-13
Fax:  011-221-5-16-71-55


REISS, Allan
Work: (510) 555-7261
Home: (415) 555-6187
Fax:  (415) 555-3367


SAMPLE, Brian
Work: (615) 555-1832
Home: (615) 555-1871
Fax:  (615) 555-7861


THAMES, Alisa
Work: (812) 555-1236
Home: (812) 555-8459
Fax:  (812) 555-1129


VIOLIN, Jacques
Work: 011-33-1-12-23-12
Home: 011-33-1-53-12-34
Fax:  011-33-1-53-22-19


ZELLER, Neil
Work: (615) 555-1241
Home: (615) 555-8711
Fax:  (615) 555-1769
```

If you select the P)rint a Directory option at a moment when your printer
is not on — or is otherwise unavailable — the program displays the following
error message:

```
Your printer is not responding.
Press the spacebar to continue.
```

The message disappears when you press the spacebar, but the program's menu
remains on the screen for other selections.

You'll find that the Telephone Database program continues to work effectively
and efficiently as your phone database expands. Whether you have a few dozen
or a few hundred records in the database, the database operations work the same.

Now it's time to take off your user's hat and don your programmer's hat to
begin looking at the code.

Code It

You've been warned about the program's length. Here's the complete listing:

```
' Telephone Database Program (PHONE.BAS)
' Creates and maintains a database of
' telephone and fax numbers.

DECLARE SUB AddRecord ()
DECLARE SUB ChangeRecord (rec%)
DECLARE SUB CreateIndex ()
DECLARE SUB FindRecord (found%)
DECLARE SUB Pause ()
DECLARE SUB PrintDirectory ()
DECLARE SUB ShowMenu (isDone AS INTEGER)
DECLARE SUB ShowPhoneRec ()
DECLARE FUNCTION MakeName$ (f$, l$)
DECLARE FUNCTION Search% (findText$)
DECLARE FUNCTION YesNo! (prompt$)

' Boolean constants.
CONST False = 0
CONST True = NOT False

' The structure for phone records.
TYPE PhoneType
   FirstName AS STRING * 20
   LastName AS STRING * 20
   WorkPhone AS STRING * 25
   HomePhone AS STRING * 25
   FaxNumber AS STRING * 25
END TYPE
```

(continued)

```
' Global variable declarations.
DIM SHARED PrinterOK AS INTEGER   ' Is printer on?
DIM SHARED Phones AS PhoneType    ' The Phones record.
DIM SHARED numPhones AS INTEGER   ' The number of records.

' Open the database file...
OPEN "\PHONES.DB" FOR RANDOM AS #1 LEN = LEN(Phones)

' ...and compute the number of records.
numPhones = LOF(1) / LEN(Phones)

' The structure for the index array.
TYPE IndexType
  FullName AS STRING * 41
  RecNum AS INTEGER
END TYPE

' Declare the Index array and create the index.
DIM SHARED Index(numPhones) AS IndexType
CreateIndex

' Display the recurring menu and
' respond to the user's selections.
DO
  ShowMenu done%
LOOP UNTIL done%

END   ' PHONE.BAS


' Error routine to handle a
' nonresponsive printer.
NoPrinter:
  PrinterOK = False
  PRINT
  PRINT "Your printer is not responding."
  Pause
RESUME NEXT



SUB AddRecord

  ' Conduct a dialog for a new record.

  CLS
  PRINT "Enter a new record:"
  PRINT
  INPUT "First name"; Phones.FirstName
  INPUT " Last name"; Phones.LastName

  ' Don't allow blank name fields.
  blankFirst% = (RTRIM$(Phones.FirstName) = "")
  blankLast% = (RTRIM$(Phones.LastName) = "")
  IF blankFirst% OR blankLast% THEN
    PRINT
    PRINT "You must enter a first name and a last name."
```

```
' Continue the dialog if
' the user supplies both names.
ELSE

   ' Search for this name in the database.
   temp$ = MakeName$(Phones.FirstName, Phones.LastName)
   isFound% = Search%(temp$)

   ' If the name doesn't already
   ' exist, accept a new record.
   IF isFound% = 0 THEN
      PRINT
      PRINT "Phone numbers:"
      INPUT "Work"; Phones.WorkPhone
      INPUT "Home"; Phones.HomePhone
      INPUT " Fax"; Phones.FaxNumber
      PRINT

      ' Ask the user to confirm the new record.
      IF YesNo("Save this record? ") THEN
         numPhones = numPhones + 1
         PUT #1, numPhones, Phones
         REDIM Index(numPhones) AS IndexType
         CreateIndex
      END IF

   ' If the name is already in the database,
   ' display the record on the screen.
   ' Don't continue the input dialog.
   ELSE
      PRINT
      PRINT "This name is already on file:"
      recInFile% = Index(isFound%).RecNum
      GET #1, recInFile%, Phones
      ShowPhoneRec
   END IF
END IF

END SUB   ' AddRecord



SUB ChangeRecord (rec%)

  ' Conduct a dialog for revising an existing
  ' phone record in the database.

  ' Allow the user to retain existing fields.
  PRINT "Press Enter to keep an existing number:"
  PRINT

  ' Revise the work phone number.
  INPUT ; "New work number"; work$
  IF RTRIM$(work$) = "" THEN
    PRINT Phones.WorkPhone
  ELSE
    PRINT
    Phones.WorkPhone = work$
  END IF
```

(continued)

```
    ' Revise the home phone number.
    INPUT ; "New home number"; home$
    IF RTRIM$(home$) = "" THEN
      PRINT Phones.HomePhone
    ELSE
      PRINT
      Phones.HomePhone = home$
    END IF

    ' Revise the fax number.
    INPUT ; "New  fax number"; fax$
    IF RTRIM$(fax$) = "" THEN
      PRINT Phones.FaxNumber
    ELSE
      PRINT
      Phones.FaxNumber = fax$
    END IF

    ' Ask the user to confirm the changes.
    PRINT
    IF YesNo("Save changes? ") THEN
      PUT #1, rec%, Phones
    END IF

END SUB   ' ChangeRecord



SUB CreateIndex

  ' Create the index for the phone database.

  ' Read each element of the index array.
  FOR i% = 1 TO numPhones
    GET #1, i%, Phones
    temp$ = MakeName$(Phones.FirstName, Phones.LastName)
    Index(i%).FullName = temp$
    Index(i%).RecNum = i%
  NEXT i%

  ' Sort the index array by the FullName field.
  FOR i% = 1 TO numPhones - 1
    FOR j% = i% + 1 TO numPhones
      IF Index(i%).FullName > Index(j%).FullName THEN
        SWAP Index(i%), Index(j%)
      END IF
    NEXT j%
  NEXT i%

END SUB   ' CreateIndex



SUB FindRecord (found%)

  ' Conduct a dialog to find a phone
  ' record that the user wants to view.
```

```
CLS
INPUT "First name"; first$
INPUT " Last name"; Last$

' Search for the record in the index.
searchName$ = MakeName$(first$, Last$)
rec% = Search%(searchName$)

' If the record was found,
' read it from the database...
IF rec% > 0 THEN
  inFileRec% = Index(rec%).RecNum
  GET #1, inFileRec%, Phones

  ' ... and show it on the screen.
  ShowPhoneRec

' If the record was not found,
' display an appropriate message.
ELSE
  PRINT
  PRINT "Can't find that name."
  PRINT
END IF

' Return the actual record number
' (not the index array subscript)
' to the calling procedure.
found% = inFileRec%

END SUB  ' FindRecord



FUNCTION MakeName$ (f$, l$)

  ' Concatenate the first and last name fields
  ' into a standard uppercase and trimmed format.

  MakeName$ = UCASE$(RTRIM$(l$) + " " + RTRIM$(f$))

END FUNCTION  ' MakeName$



SUB Pause

  ' Pause until the user responds.

  PRINT "Press the spacebar to continue.";
  DO
    sp$ = INKEY$
  LOOP UNTIL sp$ = " "

END SUB  ' Pause
```

(continued)

```
SUB PrintDirectory

  ' Print a complete directory of all
  ' the phone records in the database.

  ' First check to see if the printer
  ' is on. (If not, the NoPrinter error
  ' routine takes over.)
  PrinterOK = True
  ON ERROR GOTO NoPrinter
    LPRINT
  ON ERROR GOTO 0

  ' If the printer is on, read each
  ' record from the database file
  ' in the sorted Index order...
  IF PrinterOK THEN
    FOR i% = 1 TO numPhones
      GET #1, Index(i%).RecNum, Phones

      ' ... and send the record
      '     to the printer.
      LPRINT UCASE$(RTRIM$(Phones.LastName)); ", ";
      LPRINT Phones.FirstName
      LPRINT "Work: "; Phones.WorkPhone
      LPRINT "Home: "; Phones.HomePhone
      LPRINT "Fax:  "; Phones.FaxNumber
      LPRINT
      LPRINT
    NEXT i%
  END IF

END SUB   ' PrintDirectory



FUNCTION Search% (findText$)

  ' Perform a binary search to look
  ' for a name in the Index array.

  ' Initialize position markers.
  pos1% = 1
  pos2% = numPhones
  posX% = 0

  ' Search for the target string.
  DO WHILE pos1% <= pos2% AND posX% = 0
    midPos% = (pos1% + pos2%) \ 2
    midStr$ = RTRIM$(Index(midPos%).FullName)
    IF findText$ = midStr$ THEN
      posX% = midPos%
    ELSEIF findText$ > midStr$ THEN
      pos1% = midPos% + 1
    ELSE
      pos2% = midPos% - 1
    END IF
  LOOP
```

```
  ' Return the Index subscript where the
  ' name is located, or zero if the name
  ' was not found.
  Search% = posX%

END FUNCTION   ' Search%


SUB ShowMenu (isDone AS INTEGER)

  ' Show the program's menu on
  ' the screen and respond to the
  ' user's choices.

  CLS
  title$ = "Telephone and Fax Numbers"
  PRINT title$
  PRINT STRING$(LEN(title$), "-")
  PRINT TAB(5); "A)dd names"
  PRINT TAB(5); "F)ind names"
  PRINT TAB(5); "C)hange a record"
  PRINT TAB(5); "P)rint a directory"
  PRINT
  PRINT TAB(5); "Q)uit"
  PRINT
  PRINT "Press A, F, C, P, or Q --> ";

  ' Ignore any irrelevant keystrokes.
  DO
    choice$ = UCASE$(INKEY$)
    oneChar% = (LEN(choice$) = 1)
    inChars% = (INSTR("AFCQP", choices$) <> 0)
  LOOP UNTIL oneChar% AND inChars%
  PRINT choice$

  ' Make the appropriate procedure calls.
  isDone% = False
  SELECT CASE choice$
    CASE "A"
      DO
        AddRecord
      LOOP UNTIL NOT YesNo("Another? ")
    CASE "F"
      DO
        FindRecord (x%)
      LOOP UNTIL NOT YesNo("Another? ")
    CASE "C"
      FindRecord isFound%
      IF isFound% <> 0 THEN
        ChangeRecord isFound%
      ELSE
        Pause
      END IF
    CASE "P"
      PrintDirectory
    CASE "Q"
      isDone% = True
  END SELECT

END SUB   ' ShowMenu
```

(continued)

```
SUB ShowPhoneRec

  ' Display a phone record
  ' on the screen.

  PRINT
  PRINT RTRIM$(Phones.FirstName); " ";
  PRINT Phones.LastName
  PRINT "Work: "; Phones.WorkPhone
  PRINT "Home: "; Phones.HomePhone
  PRINT "Fax:  "; Phones.FaxNumber
  PRINT

END SUB   ' ShowPhoneRec


FUNCTION YesNo (prompt$)

  ' Get a yes or no response.

  PRINT
  PRINT prompt$;

  ' Wait for Y or N from the keyboard.
  DO
    ans$ = UCASE$(INKEY$)
  LOOP UNTIL LEN(ans$) = 1 AND INSTR("YN", ans$)
  PRINT ans$
  PRINT

  ' Return a value of true or false.
  YesNo = (ans$ = "Y")

END FUNCTION   ' YesNo
```

The program contains eleven procedures: eight SUB procedures and three functions. The ShowMenu procedure displays the recurring menu on the screen and accepts the user's selections from the keyboard. Depending on the selection, the program then calls one of four procedures to carry out a particular database operation: AddRecord, FindRecord, ChangeRecord, or PrintDirectory. The remaining procedures perform related tasks. In particular, the CreateIndex procedure creates and alphabetizes the index that the program uses to locate specific records in the database, and the Search% function searches through the index to find the record number for a requested name.

Before examining these procedures, take a look at the program's major data structures.

Everyone Needs a Little Structure

The program's main module defines two structures. One represents records in the database itself, and the other is for the index that the program creates to locate records in the database. The PhoneType structure defines the five database fields — two for the first and last name, and three for the phone numbers — as follows:

```
TYPE PhoneType
   FirstName AS STRING * 20
   LastName AS STRING * 20
   WorkPhone AS STRING * 25
   HomePhone AS STRING * 25
   FaxNumber AS STRING * 25
END TYPE
```

The program then declares one variable, Phones, belonging to this data type, and also an integer variable, numPhones, to keep track of the number of records stored in the database at any time. Both of these are global variables:

```
DIM SHARED Phones AS PhoneType
DIM SHARED numPhones AS INTEGER
```

With these variables declared, the program is ready to open the database file and calculate the current record count. These tasks are accomplished with the OPEN statement and the LOF and LEN functions (QBasic tools you learned about in Chapter 19):

```
OPEN "\PHONES.DB" FOR RANDOM AS #1 LEN = LEN(Phones)
numPhones = LOF(1) / LEN(Phones)
```

Next, the program defines a structure named IndexType:

```
TYPE IndexType
   FullName AS STRING * 41
   RecNum AS INTEGER
END TYPE
```

Each element of the index contains two fields:

- ✔ FullName is a concatenation of the last name and first name, uniquely identifying a given record in the database.
- ✔ RecNum is the corresponding record number in the database.

The Index array contains one element for each record in the database:

```
DIM SHARED Index(numPhones) AS IndexType
```

After declaring this array, the program calls the CreateIndex procedure to develop the index. A FOR loop at the beginning of the procedure reads each record in turn from the database, assigns a combination of the FirstName and

LastName fields to Index(i%).FullName, and stores the record number in Index(i%).RecNum:

```
FOR i% = 1 TO numPhones
  GET #1, i%, Phones
  temp$ = MakeName$(Phones.FirstName, Phones.LastName)
  Index(i%).FullName = temp$
  Index(i%).RecNum = i%
NEXT i%
```

The program's MakeName$ function combines the two name fields in a way that becomes the program's standard format for this field. The function places the last name first, trims the trailing spaces from both fields, and converts the whole string to capital letters:

```
MakeName$ = UCASE$(RTRIM$(l$) + " " + RTRIM$(f$))
```

For example, John Doe becomes DOE JOHN. The CreateIndex procedure then sorts the Index array in alphabetical order by the FullName field, so that the program can use the index as an effective tool for finding records in the database.

After the call to CreateIndex, the main program is ready to begin the action. A DO loop makes repeated calls to the ShowMenu procedure to display the menu on the screen:

```
DO
  ShowMenu done%
LOOP UNTIL done%
```

Each call to the ShowMenu procedure allows the user to select a particular database operation. Depending on the user's menu choice, ShowMenu calls one of the main database management procedures: AddRecord, FindRecord, ChangeRecord, or PrintDirectory. When the user selects the Q)uit option, ShowMenu returns a value of true in the variable done%, and the program ends.

In the upcoming sections of this chapter, you examine each of the program's major operations in turn.

Updating Your Record Collection

The AddRecord procedure begins by eliciting string values for the FirstName and LastName fields of the Phones record:

```
INPUT "First name"; Phones.FirstName
INPUT " Last name"; Phones.LastName
```

Before continuing the input dialog, the procedure has to make sure that neither of these fields is blank:

```
blankFirst% = (RTRIM$(Phones.FirstName) = "")
blankLast% = (RTRIM$(Phones.LastName) = "")
IF blankFirst% OR blankLast% THEN
   PRINT
   PRINT "You must enter a first name and a last name."
```

If there is a blank field, the program displays an appropriate message and terminates the dialog for the current record. The user can start over with a new record. But if a complete name has been received, the next task is to search for the name in the current database:

```
ELSE
   temp$ = MakeName$(Phones.FirstName, Phones.LastName)
   isFound% = Search%(temp$)
```

As you've seen, the MakeName$ function combines the first and last names in a standard string format. The Search% function then compares this string with entries in the `FullName` field of the `Index` array. If the new name entry is already in the database, Search% returns its subscript in the index; otherwise, Search% returns a value of zero.

The Search% function uses an efficient algorithm known as the *binary search*. This algorithm works by repeatedly dividing parts of the data in half and focusing the search on the correct half until the target data item is located. A binary search requires a sorted list or a data table sorted by a key field. The procedure makes comparisons between the target data item and selected items in the sorted list or field. The procedure is designed to complete its task quickly by making as few comparisons as possible. ▪

As long as the new name entry is not already in the database, AddRecord continues the input dialog for the remaining three fields of the `Phones` record, and then asks the user to confirm the new entry:

```
IF isFound% = 0 THEN
   PRINT
   PRINT "Phone numbers:"
   INPUT "Work"; Phones.WorkPhone
   INPUT "Home"; Phones.HomePhone
   INPUT " Fax"; Phones.FaxNumber
   PRINT

   IF YesNo("Save this record? ") THEN
```

When the user confirms the new record entry, the procedure has four important tasks:

1. Increase by 1 the integer variable `numPhones` — the current record count.

2. Write the new record to the database, using a PUT # statement.

3. Redimension the dynamic `Index` array to accommodate the new record count.

4. Rebuild the index.

These tasks are completed in four economical lines of code:

```
numPhones = numPhones + 1
PUT #1, numPhones, Phones
REDIM Index(numPhones) AS IndexType
CreateIndex
```

Notice that the CreateIndex procedure — which creates the original index — is also responsible for updating the index after each new record entry.

Conversely, if the Search% function finds that the new name entry is already in the database, the AddRecord procedure provides an explanatory message, reads the existing record from the database, and displays it on the screen, as follows:

```
PRINT "This name is already on file:"
recInFile% = Index(isFound%).RecNum
GET #1, recInFile%, Phones
ShowPhoneRec
```

The Search% function returns the record's subscript in the index array, which the program stores in the variable isFound%. The Index(isFound%).RecNum expression therefore represents the record's position in the database. After the GET # statement reads the record, a call to the ShowPhoneRec procedure displays the record on the screen.

In summary, the AddRecord procedure has a lot more to do than simply appending records to the database. Each new entry has to be validated in two ways: the record must include a complete name (FirstName and LastName), and the name must be new to the database. And finally, when a record *is* accepted for inclusion in the database, the procedure has to update the index so that subsequent operations can be performed successfully. All in all, AddRecord is one of the most complicated procedures in the program. FindRecord is a lot easier.

I Know It's Here Somewhere

FindRecord begins by eliciting the name that the user wants to search for in the database. Then a call to the MakeName$ function converts the name to the program's standard search format, and the Search% function looks for the name in the index:

```
INPUT "First name"; first$
INPUT " Last name"; Last$

searchName$ = MakeName$(first$, Last$)
rec% = Search%(searchName$)
```

If Search% returns a value greater than zero — indicating that the record has been found — FindRecord reads the requested record from the file and displays it on the screen:

```
IF rec% > 0 THEN
    inFileRec% = Index(rec%).RecNum
    GET #1, inFileRec%, Phones

    ShowPhoneRec
```

Otherwise, if the record is not in the database, the procedure displays an appropriate message:

```
ELSE
    PRINT
    PRINT "Can't find that name."
    PRINT
END IF
```

The procedure assigns the record number to its argument variable found%:

```
found% = inFileRec%
```

This value is passed back to the procedure that calls FindRecord. The program makes important use of this value when the user chooses the C)hange a record option.

Record Changer

The ShowMenu procedure makes two procedure calls when the user wants to revise a record:

```
FindRecord isFound%
IF isFound% <> 0 THEN
    ChangeRecord isFound%
```

The FindRecord procedure gets the user's record request and then searches for the record. If the record exists, FindRecord displays it and supplies the corresponding record number as the argument value. In the ShowMenu procedure, the record number is represented by isFound%. If this value is not zero — that is, if FindRecord found the record — ShowMenu calls the ChangeRecord procedure. This reuse of the FindRecord procedure vastly simplifies the process of revising a record.

ChangeRecord gives the user an opportunity to revise the three phone numbers, and then writes the revised record to the correct position in the database. To let the user keep the current value in any of the phone number fields, ChangeRecord uses a special feature of the INPUT statement — a feature you may remember reading about in Chapter 5. A semicolon immediately after the INPUT keyword instructs QBasic to keep the cursor on the input line after the user presses Enter to complete the entry. For example, here is how the ChangeRecord procedure elicits the first of the three phone number fields:

```
INPUT ; "New work number"; work$
```

If the user presses Enter without typing a revised phone number entry, the procedure simply displays the current value of the number field on the input line:

```
IF RTRIM$(work$) = "" THEN
   PRINT Phones.WorkPhone
```

In this case, there is no change in the value of the Phones.WorkPhone field. But if the user enters a new value, the procedure stores the new entry in the field:

```
ELSE
   PRINT
   Phones.WorkPhone = work$
END IF
```

This same pattern of statements is repeated for each of the three number fields. Then, if the user confirms, the ChangeRecord procedure uses the PUT # statement to write the revised record to its original position in the database:

```
IF YesNo("Save changes? ") THEN
   PUT #1, rec%, Phones
END IF
```

Notice that rec% represents the record number, as originally supplied by the FindRecord procedure.

The last of the four database operations is represented by the P)rint a directory option in the program's recurring menu.

It's Not a Paperless World Just Yet

The PrintDirectory procedure uses a simple FOR loop to print each record of the database. The loop uses the sorted Index array to read records from the database in alphabetical order; then the LPRINT statement sends each field of a given record to the printer, as follows:

```
FOR i% = 1 TO numPhones
   GET #1, Index(i%).RecNum, Phones
```

```
LPRINT UCASE$(RTRIM$(Phones.LastName)); ", ";
LPRINT Phones.FirstName
LPRINT "Work: "; Phones.WorkPhone
LPRINT "Home: "; Phones.HomePhone
LPRINT "Fax:  "; Phones.FaxNumber
```

The only possible snag in this operation occurs if the printer isn't available for output. To help prevent an interruption in the program if this error occurs, the procedure sets up an error trap and uses a single LPRINT statement to test the printer:

```
ON ERROR GOTO NoPrinter
    LPRINT
ON ERROR GOTO 0
```

If the printer isn't on, this mechanism sends control of the program to the routine identified by the NoPrinter label, at the end of the main module:

```
NoPrinter:
  PrinterOK = False
  PRINT
  PRINT "Your printer is not responding."
  Pause
RESUME NEXT
```

Notice that this routine sets the value of the variable PrinterOK to false. Back in the PrintDirectory procedure, the output operation is performed only if PrinterOK is true — that is, if the error routine has *not* been performed.

The Essential Role of the Index

As you've seen, each operation in this program uses the database index in its own way. As you look back over the program's code, you might want to review these important features:

- ✔ The AddRecord procedure first uses the index to make sure that a new name entry is not in the database yet. If the name is found, the procedure uses the index in the process of reading the record from the database and displaying it on the screen. Then, after appending a new record to the database, AddRecord is responsible for rebuilding the index.

- ✔ The FindRecord procedure looks up the record number for an existing record in the index.

- ✔ Likewise, the ChangeRecord procedure uses the index to find a record and to write a revision back to the correct position in the database.

- ✔ The PrintDirectory procedure uses the entire index, from beginning to end, to produce an alphabetized directory.

Clearly the Index array is an essential tool in the process of managing this database.

Part VIII

Photo Opportunities: Graphics in QBasic

The 5th Wave
By Rich Tennant

"These kidnappers are clever, Lieutenant. Look at this ransom note, the use of 4-color graphics to highlight the victim's photograph. And the fonts! They must be creating their own—must be over 35 typefaces here...."

In This Part . . .

*P*art VIII takes up a topic that QBasic programmers love to hate: graphics. True, QBasic gives you a variety of versatile statements for creating impressive graphics on the display screen. But, all in all, these statements are about as easy to understand as the instruction sheets for federal income taxes. (Well, on second thought, maybe nothing in QBasic is ever quite *that* difficult.)

The three chapters in Part VIII present programs that display sales graphs on the screen. Chapter 21 discusses a special category of ASCII characters you can use to create text graphics; Chapters 22 and 23 introduce selected topics in high-resolution graphics. The programs in these chapters are among the most challenging in this book, but you may find their output exceptionally satisfying.

Chapter 21

Displaying Text Graphics

● ●

In This Chapter

▶ Planning a text graphics program

▶ Using the CHR$ and STRING$ functions

▶ Using the LOCATE statement

▶ Creating a chart with ASCII characters

● ●

*I*n this chapter, you learn to use a special set of ASCII characters to display "text graphics" on the screen. As you know, ASCII (American Standard Code for Information Interchange) is a table that assigns integer values to the set of characters available on your computer. The first half of the code is the standard part. It assigns integers from 0 to 127 to the most commonly used characters: letters, digits, punctuation marks, and control characters that represent basic operations such as a line feed or a carriage return. When a program stores a string of characters in the computer's memory, they're recorded as ASCII integers.

The second half of the code, from 128 to 255, is less standard. For personal computers that run DOS, this half of the code provides a variety of special characters — such as foreign language alphabets and mathematical and technical symbols — and a set of four dozen graphics characters for producing boxes, graphs, and other pictorial displays on the text screen. As shown in Figure 21-1, these graphics characters are assigned ASCII values from 176 to 223.

176 ▓	184 ╖	192 ╚	200 ╚	208 ╨	216 ╪
177 ▒	185 ╣	193 ╧	201 ╔	209 ╤	217 ╛
178 █	186 ║	194 ╥	202 ╩	210 ╥	218 ┌
179 │	187 ╗	195 ├	203 ╦	211 ╙	219 █
180 ┤	188 ╝	196 ─	204 ╠	212 ╘	220 ▄
181 ╡	189 ╜	197 ┼	205 ═	213 ╒	221 ▌
182 ╢	190 ╛	198 ╞	206 ╬	214 ╓	222 ▐
183 ╖	191 ╗	199 ╟	207 ╧	215 ╫	223 ▀

Figure 21-1:
The ASCII
graphics
characters.

By juxtaposing strings of these characters in carefully planned patterns, you can create attractive and informative screen images. The QBasic tools for using these characters are simple. Two built-in functions that you're already familiar with — CHR$ and STRING$ — give you access to the characters themselves, and QBasic's LOCATE statement enables you to place these characters at precise locations on the screen.

To illustrate these tools, this chapter presents a project called the Sales Graph program (SGRAPHA.BAS). The program reads a file of sales data from disk and transforms the numeric data into a stacked column chart on the screen. The sales figures are provided by the International Sales program (INTRSAL2.BAS, Chapter 18), which creates a text file called ISALES.TXT to store sales data entered from the keyboard. The Sales Graph program reads ISALES.TXT, displays the file's data as a table at the top of the screen, and then uses the remainder of the text screen for a column chart depicting the numeric data.

A Picture Is Worth a Thousand Words

Before you run the program, make sure the ISALES.TXT file is available in the root directory of your hard disk. You create this file by running INTRSAL2.BAS. If you run the Sales Graph program before creating the sales file, the following message appears on the screen:

```
Can't find \ISALES.TXT.
Run the INTRSAL2.BAS program
to generate the sales data.
```

The ISALES.TXT file contains one line of text for each year's sales data that you enter from the keyboard. For example, here is the sample file presented in Chapter 18:

```
"1990",12866,9335,10673,7593
"1991",15790,13118,14789,9772
"1992",17855,16093,15863,13121
"1993",20760,19814,18534,15032
```

As you might recall, the four figures for each year represent annual sales amounts in four geographical categories: American, European, Asian, and Other. Each time you run the International Sales program, you append new lines of sales data to the existing file.

The Sales Graph program can work with as many as five years of sales data. If your ISALES.TXT file contains more than five years of information, the program reads only the first five lines. The program conducts no input dialog. When you run the program, it simply reads the sales file and immediately produces a combination of numeric, text, and graphic output on the screen. For example, Figure 21-2 shows the output for the sample data.

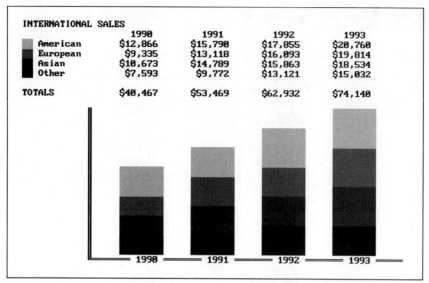

Figure 21-2:
The
International
Sales graph.

Notice the elements of the output. The data table appears at the top of the screen. The program transposes the row-column orientation of the data; the years are in the columns of the table, and the four geographical categories are in the rows. The last row of the table shows the total sales for each year.

At the far left side of the table, just before the region names, the program displays a column of graphic patterns that serve as a key to the chart. Each pattern represents one of the four regions. The columns in the chart are made up of stacks of rectangular patterns, where each rectangle represents the sales level for one region in a given year. By stacking four regional sales rectangles for a given year, the chart gives you a quick way to compare the total sales for the four-year period. Finally, to provide a frame for the chart area, the program displays vertical and horizontal axes in a double-line pattern.

Looking back at Figure 21-1, you can easily find the ASCII graphics characters that the program uses to build this chart. The four characters that make up the column stacks are numbered 176, 177, 178, and 219. The horizontal axis is created with ASCII character 205, and the vertical axis is 186. The corner character connecting the two axes is ASCII character 200. The program's task is to arrange these seven characters in patterns on the screen to create the chart you see.

To erase the program's output from the screen — and terminate the program run — press the Spacebar on your keyboard. You can experiment with additional runs of the program by creating new or revised sales files.

Code It

Here is the listing of the Sales Graph program:

```
' Sales Graph program, ASCII version (SGRAPHA.BAS)
' Displays an ASCII graph of the international
' sales data stored in the ISALES.TXT file.

DECLARE SUB Pause ()
DECLARE SUB ShowGraph ()
DECLARE SUB ShowData ()
DECLARE SUB ReadRegionNames ()
DECLARE SUB ReadSalesFile ()
DECLARE FUNCTION CountYears% ()

' Global constants
CONST MaxYears = 5   ' The maximum years in the graph.
CONST Regions = 4    ' The number of sales regions.
CONST T = 13         ' The tab setting in screen output.

' The global variable recCount represents
' the number of lines of data in ISALES.TXT.
DIM SHARED recCount AS INTEGER

' Count the lines, but don't allow
' a greater number than MaxYears.
recCount = CountYears%
IF recCount > MaxYears THEN recCount = MaxYears

' Global arrays for the data and the graph.
DIM SHARED RegionNames(Regions) AS STRING
DIM SHARED RegionSymbols(Regions) AS STRING
DIM SHARED Years(recCount) AS STRING
DIM SHARED Sales(recCount, Regions) AS DOUBLE
DIM SHARED Totals(recCount) AS DOUBLE

ReadRegionNames   ' Read the DATA lines.
ReadSalesFile     ' Read the ISALES.TXT file.
ShowData          ' Display the sales data.
ShowGraph         ' Display the sales graph.

END   ' SGRAPHA.BAS

' DATA lines contain the names of the four
' regions and the ASCII graphics characters
' that will represent them in the graph.
DATA American, 176, European, 177
DATA Asian, 178, Other, 219


' Error routine.
' Displays a message if the
' data file is missing.
NoDataFile:
CLS
PRINT "Can't find \ISALES.TXT."
```

```
PRINT "Run the INTRSAL2.BAS program"
PRINT "to generate the sales data."
END

FUNCTION CountYears%

  ' Count the number of lines in the
  ' ISALES.TXT file.

  lCount% = 0

  ' Set up an error trap to
  ' take over in the event of
  ' a missing file.
  ON ERROR GOTO NoDataFile
    OPEN "\ISALES.TXT" FOR INPUT AS #1
  ON ERROR GOTO 0

  DO WHILE NOT EOF(1)
    LINE INPUT #1, s$

    ' lCount% is the line count.
    lCount% = lCount% + 1
  LOOP
  CLOSE #1

  CountYears% = lCount%

END FUNCTION   ' CountYears%

SUB Pause

  ' Hold the output on the
  ' screen until the user
  ' presses the spacebar.

  DO
    i$ = INKEY$
  LOOP UNTIL i$ = " "
  CLS

END SUB   ' Pause

SUB ReadRegionNames

  ' Read the four region names and the
  ' ASCII characters that will represent
  ' them in the graph--all are stored in the
  ' DATA lines in the program's main module.

  FOR i% = 1 TO Regions
    READ RegionNames(i%)
    READ symbol%
    RegionSymbols(i%) = STRING$(8, symbol%)
  NEXT i%

END SUB   ' ReadRegionNames
```

(continued)

```
SUB ReadSalesFile

  ' Read the ISALES.TXT file into
  ' the Sales array.

  OPEN "\ISALES.TXT" FOR INPUT AS #1
  FOR i% = 1 TO recCount

    ' Read the years.
    INPUT #1, Years(i%)
    Totals(i%) = 0
    FOR j% = 1 TO Regions

      ' Read the sales data.
      INPUT #1, Sales(i%, j%)
      Totals(i%) = Totals(i%) + Sales(i%, j%)
    NEXT j%
  NEXT i%

  CLOSE #1

END SUB  ' ReadSalesFile

SUB ShowData

  ' Display the data table at
  ' the top of the screen.

  ' The PRINT USING template.
  template$ = "    $$#,#######"

  CLS
  PRINT "INTERNATIONAL SALES"

  ' Display the row of years.
  FOR i% = 1 TO recCount
    PRINT TAB(T * i% + 8); Years(i%);
  NEXT i%
  PRINT

  ' Display the sales data.
  FOR i% = 1 TO Regions

    ' Create a key for the graph.
    PRINT LEFT$(RegionSymbols(i%), 2); " ";
    PRINT RegionNames(i%); TAB(T);
    FOR j% = 1 TO recCount
      PRINT USING template$; Sales(j%, i%);
    NEXT j%
    PRINT
  NEXT i%

  ' Display the row of totals.
  PRINT
  PRINT "TOTALS"; TAB(T);
  FOR i% = 1 TO recCount
    PRINT USING template$; Totals(i%);
  NEXT i%

END SUB  ' ShowData
```

```
SUB ShowGraph

  ' Create a graph of ASCII characters
  ' for the sales data.

  ' VertField is the number of text
  ' rows available for the graph.
  CONST VertField = 16

  ' Find the largest annual total sales.
  maxTotal = 0
  FOR i% = 1 TO recCount
    IF Totals(i%) > maxTotal THEN
      maxTotal = Totals(i%)
    END IF
  NEXT i%

  ' Calculate the conversion factor
  ' for drawing column graphs within
  ' the available vertical space.
  convFactor = VertField / maxTotal

  ' Create the columns of the graph.
  FOR i% = 1 TO recCount
    col% = i% * T + 6
    row% = 24

    ' Create the "stacks" of each column.
    FOR j% = Regions TO 1 STEP -1
      height% = Sales(i%, j%) * convFactor

      ' Determine the height of each stack.
      FOR k% = 1 TO height%
        LOCATE row%, col%
        PRINT RegionSymbols(j%);
        row% = row% - 1
      NEXT k%
    NEXT j%
  NEXT i%

  ' Draw the horizontal axis.
  LOCATE 25, T
  PRINT STRING$(60, 205);

  ' Display labels for the columns.
  FOR i% = 1 TO recCount
    LOCATE 25, T * i% + 8
    PRINT " "; Years(i%); " ";
  NEXT i%

  ' Draw the vertical axis.
  FOR i% = 10 TO 24
    LOCATE i%, T
    PRINT CHR$(186);
  NEXT i%

  ' Display the "origin" of the graph.
  LOCATE 25, T
  PRINT CHR$(200);
```

(continued)

```
' Keep the graph on the screen
' until the user presses the spacebar.
Pause

END SUB  ' ShowGraph
```

The program contains six procedures: one FUNCTION and five SUBs. The CountYears% function counts the number of years of data in the ISALES.TXT file and stores the value in the global variable `recCount`. ReadSalesFile then reads the sales data, and ReadRegionNames reads the region names from DATA lines located at the end of the main module. The program stores the data in a group of one- and two-dimensional arrays:

- ✔ The `Years` array stores the years as strings, such as `"1989"` and `"1990"`.
- ✔ The `Sales` array contains the sales data in a two-dimensional arrangement.
- ✔ The `Totals` array stores the total sales for each year, which the program calculates as it reads the file.
- ✔ The `RegionNames` array contains strings representing the four sales regions.
- ✔ The `RegionSymbols` array contains the ASCII characters used to represent the regions in the column chart.

Once these arrays contain information, the ShowData procedure displays the sales table on the screen, and the ShowGraph procedure builds the chart. The Pause procedure waits for you to press the Spacebar before clearing the screen and terminating the program.

In the sections ahead, you look primarily at the ShowGraph procedure and the ReadRegionNames procedure. These procedures illustrate the use of the CHR$ and STRING$ functions and demonstrate the LOCATE statement in the process of displaying ASCII graphics on the screen.

Painting with CHR$ and STRING$

CHR$ and STRING$ give you two ways to gain access to the graphics characters in the upper ranges of the ASCII code. As you learned in Chapter 10, CHR$ takes a single integer argument — a code number from 0 to 255 — and returns the corresponding character. For example, the following statement displays the character corresponding to ASCII code 200:

```
PRINT CHR$(200);
```

In the ShowGraph procedure, this is the statement that displays the corner character connecting the vertical and horizontal axes of the graph.

The STRING$ function accepts an ASCII code number as its second argument. The first argument is an integer specifying the length of the string that the function will return. For example, this statement displays a string consisting of ASCII character 205, the horizontal double-line character:

```
PRINT STRING$(60, 205);
```

The string, which is 60 characters long, forms the horizontal axis that the Sales Graph program displays below the column chart.

Before displaying these characters, your program has to select the screen locations where they should appear. The LOCATE statement is the tool for this job.

Location, Location, Location

The LOCATE statement positions the cursor at a specific character position on the screen so that a subsequent PRINT statement can display information at the selected position. LOCATE expresses a screen position as a pair of numeric coordinates in the form *row, column*. Here is the statement's basic syntax:

```
LOCATE row, column
```

The standard text screen is 25 rows high by 80 characters wide. The *row* coordinate is therefore a value from 1 to 25, and the *column* coordinate ranges from 1 to 80. For example, the following statements display an exclamation point at the approximate center of the text screen:

```
CLS
LOCATE 13, 40
PRINT "!"
```

If other information is already displayed at the position specified by a LOCATE statement, the subsequent PRINT statement overwrites the existing text.

In a grid of 25 lines by 80 columns — 2000 character positions — the use of the LOCATE statement requires careful planning. But the statement is a very important tool for use with ASCII graphics. The default behavior of the PRINT statement is sequential — that is, each new PRINT statement normally displays its output just after that of the previous PRINT statement. LOCATE gives you much greater control over the way information is displayed on the screen.

The ShowGraph procedure illustrates the power of the LOCATE statement.

TIP

Tricking QBasic into giving you more space

Although the standard text screen is a grid of characters 25 rows long by 80 columns wide, you can use the QBasic WIDTH statement to change these dimensions. The syntax of this statement is as follows:

```
WIDTH columns, rows
```

where *columns* is always a value of 40 or 80, but *rows* may be 25, 30, 43, 50, or 60. (The use of these *rows* settings depends on the capabilities of your display hardware and on the screen mode you select.) When you change the dimensions of the screen, the shape and size of characters on the screen adjust accordingly.

It's Time to Make the Columns

After the Sales Graph program displays the data table at the top of the screen — and reserves one line of text at the bottom of the screen for the horizontal axis — there are 16 rows remaining for the full height of the tallest column in the chart. The trickiest problem in the ShowGraph procedure is finding the correct proportion for each column within these 16 rows. The heights of the columns and their patterned stacks must be in correct proportion to the sales figures — or at least, the proportions should be as accurate as is possible within the resolution defined by the text screen. The ShowGraph procedure calculates these proportions during the process of creating the chart.

The procedure begins by defining a constant named VertField to represent the maximum vertical space of 16 rows:

```
CONST VertField = 16
```

Because this space is available for only the tallest column in the chart, the procedure's next task is to determine which year of sales has the largest total. The annual totals are stored in the Totals array. To find the largest value, the program loops through this array and compares each value with the current value of maxTotal:

```
maxTotal = 0
FOR i% = 1 TO recCount
  IF Totals(i%) > maxTotal THEN
    maxTotal = Totals(i%)
  END IF
NEXT i%
```

Next the ShowGraph procedure calculates a conversion factor for finding the correct proportion of each element in the chart. This factor is equal to the number of rows of vertical space, divided by the largest total annual sales figure:

```
convFactor = VertField / maxTotal
```

To find the row height that will correctly represent any individual sales figure in the Sales array, the program simply multiplies the value by convFactor:

```
height% = Sales(i%, j%) * convFactor
```

Once convFactor is calculated, the program is ready to begin creating the columns of the chart. The job is accomplished in a sequence of three FOR loops, one nested within another. The number of columns is represented by the variable recCount. The outermost loop determines the starting screen positions for each column of the chart:

```
FOR i% = 1 TO recCount
  col% = i% * T + 6
  row% = 24
```

The horizontal position moves progressively from the left to the right side of the screen as i% increases from 1 to recCount. But the starting row% position is always 24, the bottom row of the chart area. A middle loop goes backward through each region in a given year's sales data and calculates height%, the number of rows that will be used to build the stack for a given region:

```
FOR j% = Regions TO 1 STEP -1
  height% = Sales(i%, j%) * convFactor
```

Finally, the innermost loop uses LOCATE and PRINT to display a string of ASCII characters for each row:

```
FOR k% = 1 TO height%
  LOCATE row%, col%
  PRINT RegionSymbols(j%);
  row% = row% - 1
NEXT k%
```

After displaying a string of characters, the program decreases the value of row% by 1 to determine the position of the next row up.

The RegionSymbols array contains a string of ASCII characters to represent each region in the chart. The ReadRegionNames procedure assigns values to this array while it fills the RegionNames array with the names of the geographic regions. The regions and their corresponding ASCII code values are read from the DATA lines at the bottom of the main module:

```
DATA American, 176, European, 177
DATA Asian, 178, Other, 219
```

Notice that each region is represented by a distinct ASCII graphics character. The following FOR loop reads the information from these DATA lines:

```
FOR i% = 1 TO Regions
  READ RegionNames(i%)
  READ symbol%
  RegionSymbols(i%) = STRING$(8, symbol%)
NEXT i%
```

As you can see, the program uses the STRING$ function to produce a string of 8 characters for each element of the RegionSymbols array. This determines the width of each column in the chart.

The ShowData procedure uses this same array to produce the key of graphic symbols shown at the left side of the data table:

```
PRINT LEFT$(RegionSymbols(i%), 2); " ";
PRINT RegionNames(i%); TAB(T);
```

In this case, a width of two ASCII characters is sufficient to display the shaded pattern that represents each region in the graph.

The ASCII charting technique requires some considerable attention to detail, but the results are attractive and useful. The ASCII sales chart gives you a clear picture of the relative strength of sales over the four-year period. In Chapter 22, you can compare this chart — and the corresponding programming techniques — with a program that produces a chart in high-resolution graphics.

Chapter 22
Drawing Graphics on the Screen

● ●

In This Chapter

▶ Planning a graphics program

▶ Understanding the SCREEN statement

▶ Choosing colors

▶ Using the VIEW and WINDOW statements

▶ Drawing lines and rectangles on the screen

▶ Creating a column chart with the LINE statement

● ●

*U*p to this point in your work with QBasic, you've used the screen to display text, numbers, and special characters available in the ASCII character set. In this chapter, you begin exploring the QBasic tools for graphics programming.

To create graphics, you first switch your system to a graphics screen *mode*. The QBasic SCREEN statement provides access to all the modes that are available for your particular display hardware. There are a dozen screen modes in all, each identified by number and characterized by a variety of features, including the following:

▸ *The graphics resolution.* Resolution is expressed in terms of a rectangular grid of pixels. A *pixel* is an individual point of color you can control on the screen. Different modes supply different dimensions of horizontal and vertical pixel positions. For example, this chapter's program uses screen mode 9, which has a resolution of 640 horizontal pixel positions by 350 vertical pixel positions.

▸ *The number of colors available in the mode.* The number ranges from just a few colors to many thousands.

▸ *The number of rows and columns of text you can display in the mode.* In some modes you can choose different text arrangements, using the WIDTH command you learned about in Chapter 21.

> ✔ *The display hardware required for using the mode.* A display system consists of an adapter board inside your computer and the screen that's attached to it. Standard systems are identified by their initials, such as CGA (Color Graphics Adapter), EGA (Enhanced Graphics Adapter), and VGA (Video Graphics Array) — names you've become familiar with if you've bought a computer over the last several years.

Once you select a graphics screen mode, you can use a variety of QBasic commands to draw shapes in color at specific locations on the screen. For example, the PSET statement illuminates a single pixel of color, the LINE statement draws a line or a box, and the CIRCLE statement produces a circle, an ellipse, an arc, or a wedge.

As an exercise with graphics programming, this chapter presents a second version of the Sales Graph program, which was introduced in Chapter 21. Recall that the first version of the program (SGRAPHA.BAS) uses ASCII graphics characters to display a stacked column chart depicting international sales. This chapter's version (SGRAPHG.BAS) uses a selection of QBasic's graphics tools to create a similar chart on a graphics screen.

Begin now by taking a look at the program's output.

Fine-Tuning the Chart

Like the first version, the second version of the Sales Graph program gets its data from the ISALES.TXT file, stored in the root directory of your hard disk. If this file doesn't exist yet, you can create it by running the second version of the International Sales program (INTRSAL2.BAS, Chapter 18). This new version of the Sales Graph program uses a graphics screen mode designed for EGA or VGA displays. If you try to run the program on an incompatible system, the following message appears on the screen:

```
This program requires
an EGA or a VGA display.
```

The chart in the upcoming example is produced from the same data used to illustrate the ASCII version of the program. The ISALES.TXT file contains four years of sales data, from 1990 to 1993. Each line of data represents sales in four international regions:

```
"1990",12866,9335,10673,7593
"1991",15790,13118,14789,9772
"1992",17855,16093,15863,13121
"1993",20760,19814,18534,15032
```

After reading the ISALES.TXT file, the program switches your system to the graphics mode, displays the sales data as a table at the top of the screen, and then builds the column chart.

Figure 22-1 shows the program's screen output in black and white. When you run the program on a system with a color monitor, the four chart stacks are displayed in color. Corresponding colors appear in the key to the chart, located to the left of the data table. Producing this display is the program's only action. When you're finished looking at the chart, press the Spacebar to end the run.

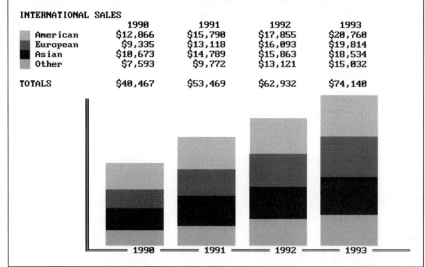

Figure 22-1:
The
International
Sales chart
in a
graphics
screen
mode.

Comparing this chart carefully with the output of the ASCII version (fig. 21-2), you can see that the graphics program depicts the data more precisely. Thanks to the high resolution of the graphics screen mode, the proportions of stacks and columns accurately reflect the values in the sales table.

Code It

Here is the listing of the graphics mode version of the Sales Graph program:

```
' Sales Graph program, graphics mode version (SGRAPHG.BAS)
' Displays a high-resolution graph of the international
' sales data stored in the ISALES.TXT file.

DECLARE SUB Pause ()
DECLARE SUB ShowGraph ()
DECLARE SUB ShowData ()
```

(continued)

```
DECLARE SUB ReadRegionNames ()
DECLARE SUB ReadSalesFile ()
DECLARE FUNCTION CountYears% ()

' Global constants
CONST MaxYears = 5   ' The maximum years in the graph.
CONST Regions = 4    ' The number of sales regions.
CONST T = 13         ' The tab setting for text output.

' The global variable recCount represents
' the number of lines of data in ISALES.TXT.
DIM SHARED recCount AS INTEGER

' Count the lines, but don't allow
' a greater number than MaxYears.
recCount = CountYears%
IF recCount > MaxYears THEN recCount = MaxYears

' Global arrays for the data and the graph.
DIM SHARED RegionNames(Regions) AS STRING
DIM SHARED Years(recCount) AS STRING
DIM SHARED Sales(recCount, Regions) AS DOUBLE
DIM SHARED Totals(recCount) AS DOUBLE

' Select the graphics mode.
ON ERROR GOTO ModeProblem
   SCREEN 9
ON ERROR GOTO 0

ReadRegionNames   ' Read the DATA lines.
ReadSalesFile     ' Read the ISALES.TXT file.
ShowData          ' Display the sales data.
ShowGraph         ' Display the graph in SCREEN 9.

' Return to the text mode.
SCREEN 0

END   ' SGRAPHG.BAS

' The names of the four regions.
DATA American, European, Asian, Other




' Error routine.
' Displays a message if the
' data file is missing.
NoDataFile:
CLS
PRINT "Can't find \ISALES.TXT."
PRINT "Run the INTRSAL2.BAS program"
PRINT "to generate the sales data."
END



' Displays a message if the
' necessary display hardware is
' not available.
ModeProblem:
```

```
CLS
PRINT "This program requires "
PRINT "an EGA or a VGA display."
END


FUNCTION CountYears%

  ' Count the number of lines in the
  ' ISALES.TXT file.

  lCount% = 0

  ' Set up an error trap to
  ' take over in the event of
  ' a missing file.
  ON ERROR GOTO NoDataFile
    OPEN "\ISALES.TXT" FOR INPUT AS #1
  ON ERROR GOTO 0

  DO WHILE NOT EOF(1)
    LINE INPUT #1, s$

    ' lCount% is the line count.
    lCount% = lCount% + 1
  LOOP
  CLOSE #1

  CountYears% = lCount%

END FUNCTION   ' CountYears%


SUB Pause

  ' Hold the output on the
  ' screen until the user
  ' presses the spacebar.

  DO
    i$ = INKEY$
  LOOP UNTIL i$ = " "
  CLS

END SUB   ' Pause


SUB ReadRegionNames

  ' Read the four region names stored in the
  ' DATA lines in the program's main module.

  FOR i% = 1 TO Regions
    READ RegionNames(i%)
  NEXT i%

END SUB   ' ReadRegionNames
```

(continued)

```
SUB ReadSalesFile

  ' Read the ISALES.TXT file into
  ' the Sales array.

  OPEN "\ISALES.TXT" FOR INPUT AS #1
  FOR i% = 1 TO recCount

    ' Read the years.
    INPUT #1, Years(i%)
    Totals(i%) = 0
    FOR j% = 1 TO Regions

      ' Read the sales data.
      INPUT #1, Sales(i%, j%)
      Totals(i%) = Totals(i%) + Sales(i%, j%)
    NEXT j%
  NEXT i%

  CLOSE #1

END SUB  ' ReadSalesFile



SUB ShowData

  ' Display the data table at
  ' the top of the screen.

  ' The PRINT USING template.
  template$ = "    $$#,######"

  CLS
  PRINT "INTERNATIONAL SALES"

  ' Display the row of years.
  FOR i% = 1 TO recCount
    PRINT TAB(T * i% + 8); Years(i%);
  NEXT i%
  PRINT

  ' Display the sales data.
  FOR i% = 1 TO Regions
    PRINT "  "; RegionNames(i%); TAB(T);
    FOR j% = 1 TO recCount
      PRINT USING template$; Sales(j%, i%);
    NEXT j%
    PRINT
  NEXT i%

  ' Create a key for the graph.
  VIEW (0, 28)-(15, 83)
  WINDOW (0, 5)-(1, 1)
  FOR y% = 1 TO 4
    LINE (0, y%)-STEP(1, 1), 13 - y%, BF
  NEXT y%

  ' Display the row of totals.
  PRINT
```

```
      PRINT "TOTALS"; TAB(T);
      FOR i% = 1 TO recCount
        PRINT USING template$; Totals(i%);
      NEXT i%

END SUB  ' ShowData



SUB ShowGraph

  ' Draw a high-resolution column graph.

  ' VertField is the height, in pixels,
  ' of the chart area.
  CONST VertField = 216

  ' Define the viewport and its coordinates.
  VIEW (104, 119)-(639, 335)
  WINDOW (0, 216)-(535, 0)

  ' Find the largest annual total sales.
  maxTotal = 0
  FOR i% = 1 TO recCount
    IF Totals(i%) > maxTotal THEN
      maxTotal = Totals(i%)
    END IF
  NEXT i%

  ' Calculate the conversion factor
  ' for drawing column graphs within
  ' the available vertical space.
  convFactor = VertField / maxTotal

  ' Create the columns of the graph
  x% = 24   ' The initial x-coordinate.
  FOR i% = 1 TO recCount
    y% = 0  ' The initial y-coordinate.
    ' Create the stacks of each column.
    FOR j% = Regions TO 1 STEP -1
      height% = Sales(i%, j%) * convFactor
      LINE (x%, y%)-STEP(84, height%), j% + 8, BF
      y% = y% + height%  ' The y-coordinate increment.
    NEXT j%
    x% = x% + 105   ' The x-coordinate increment.
  NEXT i%

  ' Draw the horizontal axis.
  LOCATE 25, T
  PRINT STRING$(60, 205);

  ' Display labels for the columns.
  FOR i% = 1 TO recCount
    LOCATE 25, T * i% + 8
    PRINT " "; Years(i%); " ";
  NEXT i%
```

(continued)

```
' Draw the vertical axis.
FOR i% = 10 TO 24
  LOCATE i%, T
  PRINT CHR$(186);
NEXT i%

' Display the "origin" of the graph.
LOCATE 25, T
PRINT CHR$(200);

' Keep the graph on the screen
' until the user presses the spacebar.
Pause

END SUB  ' ShowGraph
```

Except for the ShowGraph procedure, which displays the sales chart on the screen, this program is similar to the first version. The main module declares a group of global arrays to store the sales data. After switching to a graphics screen mode, the program calls the ReadRegionNames and ReadSalesFile procedures to read the data, and the ShowData and ShowGraph procedures to produce the screen output.

The first task ahead of you is to learn the characteristics of the screen modes available for your display hardware.

What's Your Mode?

Since the first IBM PC, there have been three generations of standard display systems in common use for personal computers: CGA, EGA, and VGA. Along with these, a variety of brand-name systems have appeared, featuring their own special characteristics and requirements. Due partly to this complicated history of products, the SCREEN statement offers a bewildering variety of modes for you to choose from. If your computer has one of the latest VGA systems, you can use almost any mode. But if you have an older system, you have to choose from a smaller set of modes that are compatible with your system.

The modes available in QBasic are numbered from 0 to 13. In its simplest form, the SCREEN statement selects and activates one of these modes:

```
SCREEN mode
```

For example, the Sales Graph program selects screen mode 9 for its output:

```
SCREEN 9
```

The default screen mode is the text screen, which you've been using all along; its number is zero. The last statement in the Sales Graph program switches your system back to the text mode:

```
SCREEN 0
```

Here's a summary of the screen modes available in QBasic:

- ✔ Screen 0 displays only text, in a grid of rows and columns specified by the WIDTH statement.

- ✔ Screens 1 and 2 are available for almost any standard graphic system, including the oldest CGA displays. Screen 1 has a resolution of 320 horizontal pixel positions by 200 vertical pixel positions, and screen 2 provides 640 by 200 pixel positions.

- ✔ Screens 3 and 4 are designed for specific brands of systems, including Hercules, Olivetti, and AT&T.

- ✔ Screen modes 5 and 6 are unused.

- ✔ Screens 7, 8, 9, and 10 offer a variety of resolutions and color selections for EGA and VGA systems. Screens 7 and 8 have the same resolutions as 1 and 2, respectively. Screens 9 and 10 provide superior resolutions of 640 by 350.

- ✔ Screens 11, 12, and 13 are available only for VGA and compatible systems. Screens 11 and 12 have resolutions of 640 by 480, and 13 provides 320 by 200. These three modes have the largest selections of colors.

For complete information about the features of each mode, look up the Screen Modes topic in QBasic's online help system. Follow these steps to view this topic in the Help window:

1. Type SCREEN in the QBasic editor. (Alternatively, if you are working in a program that uses this statement, move the cursor to the SCREEN keyword.)

2. Press F1 to open the Help window. The SCREEN Statement topic appears. Near the beginning of the topic, you'll see a bracketed cross-reference to the Screen Mode topic.

3. Move the mouse pointer to the Screen Mode cross-reference, and click the right mouse button. The resulting Screen Mode topic contains a complete list of the modes available for all display systems. ■

The horizontal and vertical position of individual pixels in a graphics screen mode are identified by a pair of integers known as *coordinates*. You learn how to use this notation next.

It's all relative — or is it?

Coordinates appear in the following form:

```
(x, y)
```

where *x* is the horizontal location and *y* is the vertical location of a pixel on the graphics screen. By default, the upper-left corner pixel in any graphics mode has the coordinates (0, 0). The first coordinate increases for pixels located across the screen to the right, and the second coordinate increases for pixels located down the screen. For example, here are the four corner pixel coordinates in screen 9, which has a resolution of 640 by 350 pixels:

(0, 0)	Upper-left corner
(639, 0)	Upper-right corner
(0, 349)	Lower-left corner
(639, 349)	Lower-right corner

Coordinates in this form appear in many QBasic graphics statements. One of the simplest examples is the PSET statement, which illuminates a single pixel at a specified screen location:

```
PSET (x, y)
```

For example, the PSET statement in the following sequence draws a single point at the approximate center of the SCREEN 9 graphics mode:

```
SCREEN 9
PSET (320, 175)
```

Here's an interesting experiment with the PSET statement; this program draws individual points at random locations in the SCREEN 9 graphics mode:

```
SCREEN 9
DO
   x% = RND * 639
   y% = RND * 349

   PSET (x%, y%)

   s$ = INKEY$
LOOP UNTIL s$ = " "
```

Each iteration of the DO loop uses the QBasic RND function to produce a random set of (x%, y%) coordinates. The subsequent PSET statement illuminates the pixel at that random location. As the program runs, more and more points are drawn on the screen. To stop the program, press the Spacebar.

The notation (320, 175) is known as an *absolute coordinate* because it refers to a fixed location on the graphics screen. QBasic also allows you to write relative coordinates, using the keyword STEP:

```
STEP(x, y)
```

A *relative coordinate* refers to a point located at a specified horizontal and vertical distance from the *last point referenced* on the screen. For example, consider this sequence of statements:

```
SCREEN 9
PSET (320, 175)
PSET STEP(10, 10)
```

The first PSET statement illuminates the pixel at (320, 175), and the second illuminates another point that is 10 pixel locations to the right and 10 down. The STEP coordinates can also be negative. In the default coordinate system, a negative *x* value results in a horizontal coordinate located to the left of the last point referenced; likewise, a negative *y* value results in a vertical coordinate located above the last point referenced. For example, these statements draw one point at the center of the screen and another located above and to the left of the center:

```
SCREEN 9
PSET (320, 175)
PSET STEP(-10, -10)
```

Here's a program that further illustrates the use of relative coordinates. It draws a random squiggle on the graphics screen by illuminating randomly selected pixels relative to the last point referenced:

```
SCREEN 9

DO
    x% = -1 + INT(RND * 3)
    y% = -1 + INT(RND * 3)
    c% = INT(RND * 16)

    IF POINT(0) >= 638 THEN x% = x% - 1
    IF POINT(0) <= 1 THEN x% = x% + 1
    IF POINT(1) >= 348 THEN y% = y% - 1
    IF POINT(1) <= 1 THEN y% = y% + 1

    PSET STEP(x%, y%), c%

    s$ = INKEY$
LOOP UNTIL s$ = " "
```

The DO loop assigns random values of -1, 0, or 1 to the variables x% and y%. A sequence of IF statements keep the drawing inside the dimensions of the screen. (The QBasic POINT function gives the current coordinates of the graphic "cursor." POINT(0) gives the horizontal coordinate, and POINT(1) gives the vertical coordinate.) The subsequent PSET STEP statement illuminates a pixel adjacent to the last point referenced. The program continues its random squiggling until you press the Spacebar.

In PSET and other graphics statements, you can select a color for the point or shape you display on the screen. In the next section you learn how.

Hooray for the red, white, and blue!

Color is a complicated subject in QBasic, for two reasons. First, each screen mode has its own set of available colors, so you may have to adjust the way you use color depending on the mode you select. Second, the QBasic graphics statements refer to colors in two ways — as actual color values or as attributes. Here's the distinction between these two terms:

- ✔ A *color value* is an integer that represents a specific color. The range of available color values varies widely from mode to mode.

- ✔ An *attribute* is an integer to which you can assign a selected color for use in a particular context. (You use the QBasic PALETTE statement to make these assignments.) The number of attributes available in a particular screen mode determines the number of different colors you can display on the screen at one time. The color value you assign to an attribute determines the actual color that appears on the screen.

You can simplify your work by using the default color assignments for particular attributes. As long as you're content to use the default colors, the distinction between color value and attribute becomes unimportant. Several of the screen modes available for a VGA system have 16 attributes, with the following default assignments:

0	Black
1	Blue
2	Green
3	Cyan
4	Red
5	Magenta
6	Brown
7	White
8	Gray
9	Light blue

10	Light green
11	Light cyan
12	Light red
13	Light magenta
14	Yellow
15	High-intensity white

You can use these 16 integers to represent colors in particular graphics statements. To draw a point on the screen in a selected color, you write the PSET statement as follows:

```
PSET (x, y), color
```

where *color* is an attribute number. For example, using the default attribute assignments, the following sequence displays a blue dot in the center of the mode 9 graphics screen:

```
SCREEN 9
PSET (320, 175), 1
```

To experiment with colors, try running this variation on a programming exercise presented previously in this chapter:

```
SCREEN 9
DO
  x% = RND * 639
  y% = RND * 349
  c% = RND * 16

  PSET (x%, y%), c%

  s$ = INKEY$
LOOP UNTIL s$ = " "
```

The program displays points at random locations and in randomly selected colors. It continues filling the screen until you press the Spacebar.

This chapter's version of the Sales Graph program shows you more about colors. But before you return to this program, you need to explore the topic of screen coordinates a little further. As you've seen, the coordinate systems of all graphics modes begin by default at the upper-left corner of the screen, with the address (0, 0). In some applications, this default may prove inconvenient. You might prefer to work with a system that begins at the lower-left corner of the screen, at the center of the screen, or at some other location of your choice. The QBasic VIEW and WINDOW statements allow you to create a coordinate system that suits your purposes in a particular application.

A program with a window and a view

You use the VIEW statement to define a *viewport*, which is a rectangular screen area in which you plan to draw graphics. The WINDOW statement redefines the coordinate system for the current viewport. You often use VIEW and WINDOW together. In each statement, you specify two coordinate pairs as follows:

```
VIEW (x1, y1)-(x2, y2)
WINDOW (x3, y3)-(x4, y4)
```

The coordinates in the VIEW statement represent the upper-left and lower-right corners of the viewport. The coordinates in the subsequent WINDOW statement define a new addressing system within the viewport; *(x3, y3)* becomes the upper-left corner of the viewport, and *(x4, y4)* becomes the lower-right corner.

The only rationale for using these statements is to simplify your work in a graphics program. For example, suppose you want to draw a graph in a rectangular area at the upper-left corner in SCREEN mode 9. For your graph, you need an area that is 201 pixels wide by 201 pixels high. For convenience, you want to reorganize the coordinate system within this area so that the center of the viewport has the address (0, 0). Here is how you can accomplish this:

```
SCREEN 9
VIEW (0, 0)-(200, 200)
WINDOW (-100, 100)-(100, -100)
```

After these statements, the center address of the viewport is (0, 0) and the four corners have these coordinates:

(-100, 100)	Upper-left corner
(100, 100)	Upper-right corner
(-100, -100)	Lower-left corner
(100, -100)	Lower-right corner

The Sales Graph program contains two practical examples of viewports and custom coordinate systems. The first is in the key to the chart, which the program displays in a thin vertical area just to the left of the data table:

```
VIEW (0, 28)-(15, 83)
WINDOW (0, 5)-(1, 1)
```

And the second is in the chart itself, which is displayed in the lower half of the screen:

```
VIEW (104, 119)-(639, 335)
WINDOW (0, 216)-(535, 0)
```

The program uses the QBasic LINE statement to draw rectangles within each of these viewports.

Drawing a Straight Line

If you can't even draw a straight line, this section will help you. One form of the LINE statement draws a straight line, in a selected color, from one point to another on a graphics screen:

```
LINE (x1, y1)-(x2, y2), color
```

In this syntax, *(x1, y1)* is the starting point of the line, *(x2, y2)* is the ending point, and *color* is the attribute selection. For example, the following sequence draws a diagonal blue line from the upper-left corner to the lower-right corner of the mode 9 screen:

```
SCREEN 9
LINE (0, 0)-(639, 349), 1
```

You can express the starting and ending points in the LINE statement as absolute or relative coordinates. For example, this statement uses the STEP clause to determine the ending point of a line that begins in the center of the screen:

```
SCREEN 9
LINE (320, 175)-STEP(50, 50), 1
```

In this case, QBasic adds the STEP coordinates to the absolute coordinates of the starting point — resulting in a line that ends at (370, 225).

You can use the LINE statement also to draw rectangles on the screen. For this purpose, the LINE statement has an additional parameter — the letter B (for box) — as follows:

```
LINE (x1, y1)-(x2, y2), color, B
```

For example, this statement draws a blue box around the perimeter of the mode 9 screen:

```
LINE (0, 0)-(639, 349), 1, B
```

To *fill* the box with the specified color, add the letter F just after the B. For example, this statement draws a solid blue rectangle that is 50 pixels wide by 50 pixels high:

```
LINE (320, 175)-STEP(50, 50), 1, BF
```

This form of the LINE statement is a convenient way to build column charts, as illustrated in the Sales Graph program.

Creating Colossal Columns

The ShowGraph procedure creates the chart. Because the top eight lines of the screen are taken up by the sales data, the procedure begins by designating the lower two-thirds of the screen as the viewport for the chart area:

```
VIEW (104, 119)-(639, 335)
WINDOW (0, 216)-(535, 0)
```

In the custom coordinate system defined by the WINDOW statement, the lower-left corner of the viewport has the address (0, 0). The procedure defines the name VertField as a constant representing the height, in pixels, of the chart area:

```
CONST VertField = 216
```

Given this height, the next task is to find the largest annual sales amount and calculate a conversion factor for determining the correct proportion of each element in the chart:

```
FOR i% = 1 TO recCount
  IF Totals(i%) > maxTotal THEN
    maxTotal = Totals(i%)
  END IF
NEXT i%

convFactor = VertField / maxTotal
```

To find the correct height for any stack in the chart, the program can simply multiply this convFactor by the sales amount that the stack will represent. The calculation takes place in a pair of FOR loops. The outer loop completes each column, and the inner loop draws each stack of a given column. The variable x% represents the left coordinate of a given column, and y% represents the starting vertical coordinate of each stack. The program builds each column from the bottom up:

```
x% = 24
FOR i% = 1 TO recCount
  y% = 0
  FOR j% = Regions TO 1 STEP -1
    height% = Sales(i%, j%) * convFactor
```

Given the values of x%, y%, and height%, the following LINE statement draws each stack in the chart:

```
LINE (x%, y%)-STEP(84, height%), j% + 8, BF
```

The lower-left corner of each stack is (x%, y%). The upper-right corner is determined by the relative coordinates STEP(84, height%). The color attributes (calculated by the expression j% + 8) range from 9 to 12; as you've learned, the default color values of these attributes are light blue, light green, light cyan, and light red. Finally, the BF parameter specifies that each stack will be drawn as a solid rectangle of color.

After drawing a given stack, the procedure increases the value of y% by height%, so that the next stack will be drawn immediately above the current one:

```
y% = y% + height%
```

Likewise, the program increases the value of x% for each new column:

```
x% = x% + 105
```

You can find additional examples of the VIEW, WINDOW, and LINE statements in the ShowData procedure, which creates a key to the chart to the left of the data table. The key consists of a vertical column of solid squares; each square shows the color that represents a particular sales region:

```
VIEW (0, 28)-(15, 83)
WINDOW (0, 5)-(1, 1)
FOR y% = 1 TO 4
  LINE (0, y%)-STEP(1, 1), 13 - y%, BF
NEXT y%
```

Chapter 23 presents yet another version of the Sales Graph program; this time, it creates a pie chart depicting the data. As this next program demonstrates, the VIEW and WINDOW statements prove very useful in procedures that draw circles on the screen.

Chapter 23

The Shape of
Things to Come

• •

In This Chapter

▶ Planning a pie chart application

▶ Understanding the CIRCLE statement

▶ Understanding the PAINT statement

▶ Creating a pie chart

• •

*I*n the previous chapter, you learned how to use several important graphics statements: SCREEN activates a graphics mode; VIEW and WINDOW define a viewport and establish a convenient coordinate system for the viewport; PSET draws points on a graphics screen; and LINE draws lines and rectangles on the screen.

QBasic has numerous other tools designed to help you exploit the features of your graphic display system. In this chapter, you look at two more of them: the CIRCLE statement, for displaying circles, arcs, and wedges on the screen; and the PAINT statement, for filling shapes with color. Together, CIRCLE and PAINT are ideal for creating pie charts on the screen.

To illustrate the CIRCLE and PAINT statements, this chapter presents the third in a series of charting exercises. This one is called the Sales Pie Chart program (SGRAPHP.BAS). Like the graphics programs in Chapters 21 and 22, this new program presents charts for international sales data organized by regions. But unlike its predecessors, the Sales Pie Chart program creates multiple charts for a given data set — specifically, one chart for each year of data.

You begin your work in this chapter by examining the program's output, and then you take a close look at the procedure that displays the charts.

Running the π Chart

The program produces its output in graphics mode 9, available for EGA and VGA systems. When you run the program, it reads the sales data from the ISALES.TXT file you've created with the International Sales program (INTRSAL2.BAS, Chapter 18). As you can see in Figure 23-1, the Sales Pie Chart program displays the data table on the screen and initially draws a pie chart for the first year of data. The chart contains four color wedges, representing the four sales regions: blue for American sales, green for European sales, cyan for Asian sales, and red for other sales. The entire pie represents total sales for the year, and each wedge shows the portion represented by a given region.

To view the chart for the next year, press the Spacebar. The program immediately redraws the chart to represent the next column of data in the table. Continue pressing the Spacebar to cycle through the entire data set. When the final year's chart appears on the screen, another press of the Spacebar ends the program.

The program listing is familiar, except for the new version of the ShowGraph procedure.

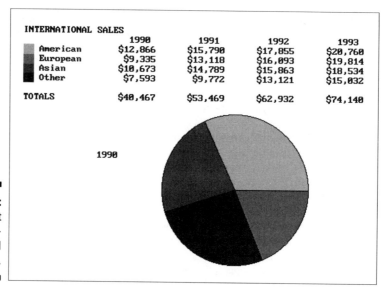

Figure 23-1:
A pie chart
for inter-
national
sales.

INTERNATIONAL SALES

	1990	1991	1992	1993
American	$12,866	$15,790	$17,855	$20,760
European	$9,335	$13,118	$16,093	$19,814
Asian	$10,673	$14,789	$15,863	$18,534
Other	$7,593	$9,772	$13,121	$15,032
TOTALS	$40,467	$53,469	$62,932	$74,140

1990

Code It

Here's the complete listing of the Sales Pie Chart program:

```
' Sales Pie Chart program (SGRAPHP.BAS)
' Displays a pie chart for individual years of
' the international sales data stored in the
' ISALES.TXT file.

DECLARE SUB Pause ()
DECLARE SUB ShowGraph ()
DECLARE SUB ShowData ()
DECLARE SUB ReadRegionNames ()
DECLARE SUB ReadSalesFile ()
DECLARE FUNCTION CountYears% ()

' Global constants
CONST MaxYears = 5   ' The maximum years in the graph.
CONST Regions = 4    ' The number of sales regions.
CONST T = 13         ' The tab setting for text output.

' The global variable recCount represents
' the number of lines of data in ISALES.TXT.
DIM SHARED recCount AS INTEGER

' Count the lines, but don't allow
' a greater number than MaxYears.
recCount = CountYears%
IF recCount > MaxYears THEN recCount = MaxYears

' Global arrays for the data and the graph.
DIM SHARED RegionNames(Regions) AS STRING
DIM SHARED Years(recCount) AS STRING
DIM SHARED Sales(recCount, Regions) AS DOUBLE
DIM SHARED Totals(recCount) AS DOUBLE

' Select the graphics mode.
ON ERROR GOTO ModeProblem
   SCREEN 9
ON ERROR GOTO 0

ReadRegionNames   ' Read the DATA lines.
ReadSalesFile     ' Read the ISALES.TXT file.
ShowData          ' Display the sales data.
ShowGraph         ' Display the pie charts.

' Return to the text mode.
SCREEN 0

END   ' SGRAPHP.BAS
```

(continued)

```
' The names of the four regions.
DATA American, European, Asian, Other

' Error routines.
' Displays a message if the
' data file is missing.
NoDataFile:
CLS
PRINT "Can't find \ISALES.TXT."
PRINT "Run the INTRSAL2.BAS program"
PRINT "to generate the sales data."
END

' Displays a message if the
' necessary display hardware is
' not available.
ModeProblem:
CLS
PRINT "This program requires "
PRINT "an EGA or a VGA display."
END


FUNCTION CountYears%

    ' Count the number of lines in the
    ' ISALES.TXT file.

    lCount% = 0

    ' Set up an error trap to
    ' take over in the event of
    ' a missing file.
    ON ERROR GOTO NoDataFile
        OPEN "\ISALES.TXT" FOR INPUT AS #1
    ON ERROR GOTO 0

    DO WHILE NOT EOF(1)
        LINE INPUT #1, s$

        ' lCount% is the line count.
        lCount% = lCount% + 1
    LOOP
    CLOSE #1

    CountYears% = lCount%

END FUNCTION   ' CountYears%


SUB Pause

    ' Hold the output on the
    ' screen until the user
    ' presses the spacebar.
```

```
    DO
      i$ = INKEY$
    LOOP UNTIL i$ = " "
    CLS

END SUB   ' Pause



SUB ReadRegionNames

  ' Read the four region names stored in the
  ' DATA lines in the program's main module.

  FOR i% = 1 TO Regions
    READ RegionNames(i%)
  NEXT i%

END SUB   ' ReadRegionNames



SUB ReadSalesFile

  ' Read the ISALES.TXT file into
  ' the Sales array.

  OPEN "\ISALES.TXT" FOR INPUT AS #1
  FOR i% = 1 TO recCount

    ' Read the years.
    INPUT #1, Years(i%)
    Totals(i%) = 0
    FOR j% = 1 TO Regions

      ' Read the sales data.
      INPUT #1, Sales(i%, j%)
      Totals(i%) = Totals(i%) + Sales(i%, j%)
    NEXT j%
  NEXT i%

  CLOSE #1

END SUB   ' ReadSalesFile



SUB ShowData

  ' Display the data table at
  ' the top of the screen.

  ' The PRINT USING template.
  template$ = "    $$#,######"

  CLS
  PRINT "INTERNATIONAL SALES"
```

(continued)

```
' Display the row of years.
FOR i% = 1 TO recCount
  PRINT TAB(T * i% + 8); Years(i%);
NEXT i%
PRINT

' Display the sales data.
FOR i% = 1 TO Regions
  PRINT "   "; RegionNames(i%); TAB(T);
  FOR j% = 1 TO recCount
    PRINT USING template$; Sales(j%, i%);
  NEXT j%
  PRINT
NEXT i%

' Create a key for the graph.
VIEW (0, 28)-(15, 83)
WINDOW (0, 5)-(1, 1)
FOR y% = 1 TO 4
  LINE (0, y%)-STEP(1, 1), 13 - y%, BF
NEXT y%

' Display the row of totals.
PRINT
PRINT "TOTALS"; TAB(T);
FOR i% = 1 TO recCount
  PRINT USING template$; Totals(i%);
NEXT i%

END SUB   ' ShowData



SUB ShowGraph

  ' Draw pie charts for each
  ' year of data.

  DIM totSales AS DOUBLE
  pi = 4 * ATN(1)

  ' Define the viewport and its coordinates.
  VIEW (160, 126)-(479, 349)
  WINDOW (-1, 1)-(1, -1)

  ' Draw a separate chart for each year.
  FOR i% = 1 TO recCount

    ' Compute the total sales
    ' for the current year.
    totSales = 0
    FOR j% = 1 TO Regions
      totSales = totSales + Sales(i%, j%)
    NEXT j%

    ' Display the year as a title.
    LOCATE 14, 15
    PRINT Years(i%)
```

```
      ' The starting angle is a
      ' small nonzero number.
      a1 = .0001

      ' Draw the wedges of the chart.
      FOR j% = 1 TO Regions

         ' Calculate the ending angle of the wedge,
         ' based on the ratio of sales to total sales.
         a2 = a1 + (2 * pi) * (Sales(i%, j%) / totSales)

         ' Draw the wedge and fill it with color.
         CIRCLE (0, 0), .9, 15, -a1, -a2 + .0001, .77
         x = COS((a1 + a2) / 2) * .5
         y = SIN((a1 + a2) / 2) * .5
         PAINT (x, y), j% + 8, 15

         ' The next starting angle is
         ' the current ending angle.
         a1 = a2
      NEXT j%
      Pause
      CLS
   NEXT i%

END SUB  ' ShowGraph
```

Like the other two graphics programs, the Sales Pie Chart program stores the sales data in a two-dimensional array named Sales. After the data is read from the ISALES.TXT file by the ReadRegionNames procedure, the ShowData procedure organizes the information in table form on the screen. Then the ShowGraph procedure begins to display the individual pie charts for each year of data.

In the upcoming sections, you focus on the syntax and usage of the CIRCLE and PAINT statements, and then you learn how the program creates the pie charts.

Running Circles around Your Code

In its simplest form, the CIRCLE statement draws the circumference of a circle on a graphics screen:

```
CIRCLE (x, y), radius, color
```

In this syntax, *(x, y)* represents the center of the circle, *radius* is the length in pixels from the circle's center to the circumference, and *color* is an attribute number. For example, the following sequence draws a blue circle of radius 150 on the mode 9 graphics screen:

```
SCREEN 9
CIRCLE (320, 175), 150, 1
```

A convenient way to draw a circle is to use the VIEW and WINDOW statements to set up an approximately square viewport in which the center point has the coordinates (0, 0). You can then use (0, 0) as the center of the circle, and half the width of the viewport as the radius, as in this sequence:

```
SCREEN 9
VIEW (95, 0)-(544, 349)
WINDOW (-1, 1)-(1, -1)
CIRCLE (0, 0), 1, 1
```

You can use the CIRCLE statement also to draw arcs and wedges on the screen. An *arc* is a segment of the circumference of a circle. A *wedge* is an enclosed area consisting of an arc and two radius lines serving as the sides of the wedge. Both of these shapes are defined by beginning and ending angles within the full 360-degree sweep of the circle.

Not coming full circle

Here is the syntax for creating an arc:

```
CIRCLE (x, y), radius, color, angle1, angle2
```

where *angle1* is the circle's angle at the beginning of the arc, and *angle2* is the angle at the end of the arc.

Angles in the CIRCLE statement are always expressed in radians rather than degrees. As you may recall from high school math, a full circle of 360 degrees is equal to a radian measurement of 2π. QBasic doesn't have a function that supplies the value of π, but you can calculate the value using the following assignment statement:

```
pi = 4 * ATN(1)
```

If you want to know why this statement successfully calculates π, here's an explanation: The trigonometric tangent (TAN) of a 45-degree angle is 1. The radian equivalent of 45 degrees is $\pi/4$. It follows that the arctangent (ATN) of 1 is $\pi/4$. Multiplying the arctangent of 1 by 4 therefore supplies the value of π. ■

An angle of 0 in a circle is represented by the radius line that extends horizontally to the right from the center of the circle. Angles from 0 to 2π are measured counterclockwise around the circle. Knowing this, you can draw an arc at any position around the circumference of a circle, by specifying a beginning angle and an ending angle. For example, the following sequence displays an arc that makes up the first quarter of a circumference — that is, the upper-right portion of the circle.

```
pi = 4 * ATN(1)

SCREEN 9
VIEW (95, 0)-(544, 349)
WINDOW (-1, 1)-(1, -1)

CIRCLE (0, 0), 1, 1, 0, pi / 2
```

Notice the starting and ending angles of the arc; it extends from an angle of 0 to π/2 radians.

Here's a more elaborate exercise with arcs. The following program displays a full circle, consisting of 15 arcs of different colors:

```
pi = 4 * ATN(1)

SCREEN 9
VIEW (95, 0)-(544, 349)
WINDOW (-1, 1)-(1, -1)

a1 = 0
FOR i% = 1 TO 15
   a2 = 2 * pi * (i% / 15)
   CIRCLE (0, 0), .8, i%, a1, a2
   a1 = a2
NEXT i%
```

The arcs are created in a FOR loop, and the angles are represented by the variables a1 and a2. The first arc is drawn at angles 0 to 2π/15. After each arc is drawn, the loop assigns the value of a2 to a1. In other words, the beginning angle of the *next* arc will be the same as the ending angle of the current arc. Try running this program on your computer, and examine the FOR loop and its result carefully.

The syntax for drawing a wedge is almost the same as that for an arc, as you learn next.

A piece of pie

To instruct QBasic to draw a wedge instead of an arc, you supply the starting and ending angles as negative numbers:

```
CIRCLE (x, y), radius, color, -angle1, -angle2
```

For example, the following sequence draws a quarter-circle wedge:

```
pi = 4 * ATN(1)

SCREEN 9
VIEW (95, 0)-(544, 349)
WINDOW (-1, 1)-(1, -1)

CIRCLE (0, 0), 1, 1, -.0001, -pi / 2
```

Notice that the first angle in this wedge is a small negative number (-.0001) rather than zero. The CIRCLE statement has a quirk: Using 0 or 2π as one of the angles of a wedge produces unexpected results. You should generally use a number that is slightly offset from 0 or from -2π. (You may have to experiment with these angle values to produce the wedges you want.)

The following exercise produces a design of 15 concentric wedges in different outline colors:

```
pi = 4 * ATN(1)

SCREEN 9
VIEW (95, 0)-(544, 349)
WINDOW (-1, 1)-(1, -1)

a1 = .0001
FOR i% = 1 TO 15
  a2 = 2 * pi * (i% / 15)
  CIRCLE (0, 0), .8, i%, -a1, -a2 + .0001
  a1 = a2
NEXT i%
```

You can once again see how the program calculates the angles of each wedge, a1 and a2. The first value of a1 is a small nonzero number. The value of a2 is always calculated as a portion of 2π. After drawing each wedge, the loop assigns the old value of a2 to a1 so that the next wedge will begin where the current one has ended.

The CIRCLE command has another flaw. Unlike the LINE command, CIRCLE has no automatic way to produce shapes that are filled with color. If you want to create solid color wedges, you need to use another QBasic tool, the PAINT statement.

Coloring in the Lines

PAINT fills an enclosed area with a selected color. Here is the syntax of this statement:

```
PAINT (x, y), color, borderColor
```

The coordinates *(x, y)* identify any point inside the area that you want to color; *color* is a numeric attribute representing the color that will be used to fill the area; and *borderColor* is the color of the shape that encloses the area.

The area must be completely enclosed for a successful PAINT operation. If there is a hole in the border, PAINT leaks out onto the rest of the screen. ▪

When you use PAINT, you have to be careful to find a point (x, y) that is inside the enclosed area. In some cases this is an easy task. For example, the following passage uses CIRCLE to draw a white circumference, and then uses PAINT to fill the circle with the color blue:

```
SCREEN 9
VIEW (95, 0)-(544, 349)
WINDOW (-1, 1)-(1, -1)

CIRCLE (0, 0), .8, 15
PAINT (0, 0), 1, 15
```

To identify the interior of the circle, this PAINT statement simply uses the coordinates of the center.

But in other instances, finding a point inside a shape can be considerably more difficult. For example, the following program draws 15 concentric wedges and then uses PAINT to fill each one with color:

```
pi = 4 * ATN(1)

SCREEN 9
VIEW (95, 0)-(544, 349)
WINDOW (-1, 1)-(1, -1)

a1 = .0001
FOR i% = 1 TO 15
  a2 = 2 * pi * (i% / 15)
  CIRCLE (0, 0), .8, 15, -a1, -a2

  fx = .4 * COS((a1 + a2) / 2)
  fy = .4 * SIN((a1 + a2) / 2)
  PAINT (fx, fy), i%, 15

  a1 = a2
NEXT i%
```

The variables `fx` and `fy` represent the coordinates of a point inside each wedge. To calculate these values, the program requires two elaborate formulas using the trigonometric functions COS and SIN. These formulas calculate the addresses of points around the circumference of an inner circle. Each point is located halfway between the two sides of a wedge. The Sales Pie Chart program uses this same technique, as you learn in the final section of this chapter.

Creating a Pie Chart

To simplify the work of creating the charts, the ShowGraph procedure begins by defining a viewport and a coordinate system, as follows:

```
VIEW (160, 126)-(479, 349)
WINDOW (-1, 1)-(1, -1)
```

Then the program uses a sequence of FOR loops to draw the pie charts. The outer loop selects each year of sales data in turn, and a first inner loop calculates the total sales, totSales, for a given year:

```
FOR i% = 1 TO recCount
  totSales = 0
  FOR j% = 1 TO Regions
    totSales = totSales + Sales(i%, j%)
  NEXT j%
```

Then a second inner loop draws each wedge of the current chart. The angles of each wedge are represented by a1 and a2. As you've seen in other programs, the initial value of a1 is a small number close to zero:

```
a1 = .0001
FOR j% = 1 TO Regions
  a2 = a1 + (2 * pi) * (Sales(i%, j%) / totSales)
```

The procedure calculates the value of a2 as a fraction of the full sweep of the circle. In this case, the portion of the wedge is calculated as the current sales amount, Sales(i%, j%), divided by the total sales for the year, totSales. This calculated value is added to the current value of a1 to produce an ending angle for the wedge.

Given these two angles, the procedure draws each wedge as follows:

```
CIRCLE (0, 0), .9, 15, -a1, -a2 + .0001, .77
```

Because the procedure has set up a convenient viewport, the center of the circle is simply (0, 0), and the radius is .9, slightly less than half the width of the viewport. Each wedge is drawn in bright white, represented by the attribute number 15. For simplicity, the program adds a value of .0001 to each value of a2, even though only the last value really needs to be adjusted.

What is the last parameter in this CIRCLE statement, represented here as .77? This optional parameter is known as the *aspect* of the circle. It controls the ratio of the circle's vertical diameter to the horizontal diameter. In some programs, *aspect* is used to display ellipses on the screen — in effect, circles that are stretched horizontally or vertically. But in this program, the *aspect* value of .77 simply corrects the slightly skewed proportions of the viewport in which the circle is drawn. Without the *aspect* parameter, the pie chart appears a little flat rather than nicely circular. ▪

The next task is to fill a given wedge with color. This is accomplished by using COS and SIN to calculate the coordinates of a point inside the wedge — as in the formulas you saw previously in this chapter — and using the PAINT statement to fill the wedge with color:

```
x = COS((a1 + a2) / 2) * .5
y = SIN((a1 + a2) / 2) * .5
PAINT (x, y), j% + 8, 15
```

The border color is 15, bright white. The fill color is calculated as j% + 8, and therefore changes for each wedge of the chart.

Finally, to prepare for the next wedge, the procedure assigns the current value of a2 to a1. When the current chart is complete, a call to the Pause procedure waits for the user to press the Spacebar before the program draws the next pie chart:

```
    a1 = a2
  NEXT j%
  Pause
  CLS
NEXT i%
```

Together, CIRCLE and PAINT do a nice job of creating the pie chart. True, the procedure would be easier if the CIRCLE statement were designed differently. But this program has also given you a chance to experiment with three QBasic trigonometric functions: ATN in the calculation for π, and COS and SIN in the process of filling each wedge with color.

Part IX
The Part of Tens

"I SAAIID WHAT COMPANY DO YOU REPRESENT?"

In This Part . . .

*H*ere are some *lists of ten* designed to add to your programming pleasure. Chapter 24 is a list of the best (the favorite or most commonly used) menu commands. Chapter 25 offers structured programming tips. (They're called rules, but don't take that too seriously.)

Chapter 24
Ten Best QBasic Menu Commands

• •

In This Chapter

▶ New

▶ Open

▶ Save

▶ Print

▶ Cut, Copy, and Paste

▶ New SUB and New FUNCTION

▶ SUBs

▶ Find and Change

▶ Start

▶ Help Contents

• •

*T*he QBasic programming environment has a trim collection of eight pull-down menus arranged across the top row of the screen. The three dozen commands in these menus are devised to help you develop, save, debug, and run your programs. There's not much fat in these commands; you'll probably use them all at one time or another. But there are ten or so commands you'll need almost every time you write a program; these are summarized in this chapter.

You can use the keyboard or the mouse to choose a command from a QBasic menu. From the keyboard, you press three keys: Alt to activate the menu bar, the first letter of a menu name to pull down the menu, and then the highlighted letter of the command to choose it. With the mouse, you click a menu to pull it down and then click the command you want.

In addition, several commands have keyboard shortcuts for more direct access. As in any other software environment, you quickly learn the shortcuts for the commands and other operations you perform most often. Here's a list of the most useful ones:

F1	Get help
F2	Open the SUBs dialog box to view the list of procedures
F3	Repeat a Find operation
F4	View the output screen
F5	Start or continue the current program (Shift-F5 to restart after an interruption)
F6	Activate the next window

The commands in the Debug menu have their own shortcuts. Turn to Chapter 3 for an introduction to debugging in QBasic.

Starting Anew

The New command (File menu) clears the current code from the View window so you can begin a new program. If you've already saved the current program, it is cleared away immediately. But if you've made any changes without saving them to disk, QBasic displays a message box with the following question:

```
Loaded file is not saved. Save it now?
```

Click Yes to save the program before clearing it, No to abandon any changes you've made, Cancel to back out of the New command, or Help to get more information about these options. Take this step with caution. If you clear a program without saving it, you can't get it back.

Open Sesame

The Open command (File menu) loads an existing QBasic program from disk and displays its listing in the View window. When you choose the Open command, the Open dialog box appears on the screen.

If you know the name of the file you want to open, you can type it directly into the File Name box. If the file is not in the current directory, you can also include a path name for locating the file. Press Enter to open the file.

Alternatively, you can select a directory from the box labeled Dirs/Drives. Press Alt-D to activate the box and then use the arrow keys to highlight the directory you want to switch to. Press Enter to open the directory. When you do so, the Files box displays a list of all the QBasic programs in the new directory. Press Alt-F to activate the File box, use the arrow keys to highlight a file name, and press Enter.

You can also use the mouse to make selections in the Open dialog box. Double-click a directory name to change directories, click a file name to select it, and click OK to open the file.

If an unsaved program is currently displayed in the View menu, QBasic asks you if you want to save it before opening a new program. Click Yes to save the current program or No to abandon the current program without saving it.

What a Save!

You use the File menu's Save and Save As commands to save your current programming project to disk.

The first time you save a new program, the Save dialog box appears on the screen. (You can choose either Save or Save As at this point in your work; both commands display the same dialog box options.) Enter a name for the program file; by default, QBasic supplies a BAS extension. If you want to save the file somewhere other than in the current directory, select the directory name in the Dirs/Drives box. Then press Enter or click OK to save the file.

If you've already saved the current program once, choose Save to update the file on disk whenever you make substantial changes in the code. No dialog box appears on the screen in this case; QBasic simply saves your program to the existing file. As in any other application, the more often you save your work, the less likely you are to lose any of it.

Sometimes you might want to save multiple versions of a program under different file names. To do this, choose the Save As command, enter a new file name, and press Enter. To avoid confusion, be careful to document different versions of a program by writing clear comments at the top of each main module. The comments should explain how and why each version differs from the others.

Start the Presses!

The Print command in the File menu gives you a quick way to print some or all of the code in the current program. When you choose this command, the Print dialog box offers you three options: Selected Text Only, Current Window, and Entire Program. You can print a highlighted selection of code, all the code in the current View window, or the entire program listing. Select an option and press Enter to begin printing.

The catch to printing just a section of code is that you must mark the selection before you choose the Print command. To do so, move the cursor to the beginning of the selection. Then hold down the Shift key and press the arrow keys to highlight the selection you want to print. QBasic displays the selection as dark text against a light background. (To select a portion of your program with the mouse, hold down the left mouse button and drag the mouse from the beginning to the end of the selection.) Then choose the Print command and activate the Selected Text Only option.

You can use the Print command also to print topics from the QBasic online Help window. See Chapter 4 for details.

Cut, Copy, Paste — Then Color

You use the Cut and Paste commands to *move* a selection of code from one place to another in your program. You use Copy and Paste commands to *copy* a selection. These three commands use the QBasic Clipboard as a temporary memory area for cut-and-paste or copy-and-paste operations.

Here's an outline of the steps for moving a block of code in your program:

1. Select the block of code you want to move. From the keyboard, hold down the Shift key and press the arrow keys to make the selection. Alternatively, drag the mouse from the beginning to the end of the code you want to move.

2. Pull down the File menu and choose Cut. The selected text disappears from the listing. QBasic has copied it to the Clipboard.

3. Select the location where you want to move the code. If you are moving the code from one place to another in the current procedure or main module, simply place the cursor at the beginning of the new location. If you want to move the code to a new procedure, press F2 to open the SUBs dialog box, select the procedure to which you want to move the code, and press Enter. Then move the cursor to the new location.

4. Pull down the File menu and choose the Paste command. QBasic copies the code from the Clipboard to the new location you selected.

To copy (rather than move) a block of code, follow the previous steps but choose the Copy command rather than the Cut command in step 2. The selected code remains at its original position. When you complete the steps, duplicate code appears in the new location.

The selection remains in the Clipboard until you replace it with other code by choosing the Cut or Copy command again. You can therefore make multiple copies of the selection by choosing the Paste command more than once.

The Cut, Copy, and Paste commands all have keyboard shortcuts:

Cut	Shift+Del
Copy	Ctrl+Ins
Paste	Shift+Ins

If you have trouble remembering these shortcuts, you're not alone. It may be easier — and it is certainly more reliable — to choose the commands directly from the Edit menu.

Unfortunately, there is no Undo command in QBasic. If you cut a selection of code to the Clipboard and then inadvertently choose the Cut or Copy command again, the previous contents of the Clipboard are lost. This is an easy way to lose valuable code, almost before you realize what has happened. ▪

You can use copy-and-paste operations to copy code from one program to another. Open the program that contains the code you want to copy, select the code, and choose the Copy command. Then open the program to which you want to copy the code, or choose the New command if you want to copy the code to a new programming project. Choose Paste to copy the code. This is a good trick for copying general-purpose procedures from one program to another.

You can also copy sample code from the Help window to the View window. See Chapter 4 for details.

Trying Something New

When you want to create a new procedure in your current programming project, pull down the Edit menu and choose New SUB or New FUNCTION. Both commands display a small dialog box on the screen, asking you to supply the name of the new procedure. When you type the name and press Enter, QBasic creates the first and last lines of the new procedure (SUB and END SUB or FUNCTION and END FUNCTION) and displays the lines in the View window. You can then begin filling in the code.

In the top-down programming style, you typically write calls to a procedure before you write the procedure itself. If you do this, you can use the following shortcut for designating the name of the new procedure. In the statement that calls the procedure, place the cursor next to or within the procedure's name. Then choose the New SUB or New FUNCTION command. The procedure name automatically appears in the Name box of the resulting dialog box. To create the procedure, press Enter.

Alternatively, you can create a procedure by entering a SUB or FUNCTION statement anywhere in your program. QBasic automatically supplies the END SUB or END FUNCTION statement, and displays the new procedure by itself in the View window.

Changing Your View

To help you work on each part of your program independently, the View window displays one procedure (or main module) at a time. As you develop a collection of procedures and functions in a program, you'll want a quick way to switch the view from one procedure to another. The SUBs command in the View menu is the tool for the job.

If you memorize no other shortcut key in QBasic, you should learn the one for the SUBs command: F2. ▨

Press F2 and the SUBs dialog box appears on the screen. The main feature of the box is a list of all the procedure names in the current program. At the top of the list is the program's file name; this represents the main module. Following the main module you see an alphabetized list of all the procedures in the program. Use the arrow keys or the mouse to highlight the procedure you want to view. A short message appears just beneath the list box describing the highlighted procedure. For example:

```
Sort is a SUB in RNDWORDS.BAS
```

or

```
C is a FUNCTION in RNDWORDS.BAS
```

Press Enter to display the highlighted procedure in the View window.

The SUBs dialog box also enables you to delete a procedure from the current program as follows. In the SUBs list, highlight the name of the procedure that you want to delete, and then press Alt-D (or click Delete). QBasic displays a message box with the following question:

```
Delete procedure from module?
```

Press Enter to go through with the deletion, or press Esc to cancel. Be careful when you delete procedures; you can't undo this action. ▨

Sometimes you may want to view two procedures at once so that you can compare their code or easily copy code from one to another. To do so, pull down the View menu and choose the Split command. QBasic divides the View window in two and initially displays a copy of the current procedure in each window. Press F6 to activate the next window, and then press F2 to select a new procedure to be displayed in the current window.

Initially, the split divides the View window into two windows of the same size. To change the sizes, use the mouse to drag the border between them up or down, or press Alt-+ (plus) or Alt--(minus) from the keyboard.

To restore the View window to its unsplit status, choose the Split command from the View menu again.

Quick Change Artist

When you want to find a word in your program or replace a word with a new word, the Find and Change commands help you carry out the operation quickly. In particular, these commands can simplify your work with variables when you want to find all the references to a specific variable or change a variable's name throughout your program.

To find the next occurrence of a variable name or another name, pull down the Search menu and choose Find. In the Find What box, enter the name you want to find. The Find dialog box has two options that can help you narrow the search: Match Upper/Lowercase and Whole Word.

To select the Match Upper/Lowercase option, press Alt-M. This tells QBasic to search for the exact uppercase-lowercase combination that you've entered in the Find What box. To select the Whole Word option, press Alt-W. This tells QBasic to search for instances of the text as a word by itself, not embedded in other text. QBasic displays an X next to the option or options you select.

Press Enter or click OK to begin the search. If the text is found in your listing, QBasic highlights it in the View window. (If necessary, QBasic switches to the procedure that contains the text.) To repeat the same Find operation (that is, to search for the next occurrence), press F3.

To perform a search-and-replace operation, pull down the Search menu and choose Change. In the Change dialog box, enter the text you want to replace in the Find What box. Then enter the replacement text in the Change To box. Optionally, select the Match Upper/Lowercase and Whole Word options.

To change the text on a case-by-case basis, press Alt-V or click Find and Verify. QBasic finds and highlights each occurrence in turn and allows you to make the change or skip to the next occurrence. If you're sure you want to change all the occurrences at once, press Alt-C or click Change All.

On Your Mark . . .

When you're ready to run the current program, pull down the Run menu and choose Start. It doesn't matter what part of the program is currently displayed in the View window; the program always starts with the statements in the main module. QBasic switches to the output screen, where you see the information your program is designed to display.

When the program run is complete, the following message appears at the bottom of the output screen:

```
Press any key to continue
```

Press a key to return to the View window.

If a break occurs in your program due to a run-time error, a breakpoint, or an intentional break (caused when you press Ctrl-Break), you have two choices for resuming the program:

✔ Press F5 to continue the program from where it left off

✔ Press Shift-F5 to start the program again from the beginning

If no break has occurred, you can use F5 as the shortcut for running a program from the beginning of the main module.

What's Inside?

The Contents command opens a Help window with a variety of general and introductory topics about QBasic. The topics include information about the programming environment, instructions about the language itself, lists of keyboard techniques and shortcut keys, and a selection of reference tables.

To select any topic and open a new Help window, double-click any topic. Alternatively, use the Tab key to move the cursor to the target topic or press the first letter of the topic; then press Enter.

To return to the Contents window from any other Help window, select the Contents option at the upper-left corner of the window.

There are many other ways to get help in QBasic. Turn to Chapter 4 for more information.

Chapter 25

Ten Rules of Structured Programming

• •

In This Chapter

▶ Planning the main module

▶ Writing procedures

▶ Using FUNCTION procedures

▶ Avoiding excessive global variables

▶ Sending arguments

▶ Using control structures

▶ Using data structures

▶ Defining named constants

▶ Creating temporary program stubs

▶ Reusing general-purpose procedures

• •

*Q*Basic doesn't force you to organize your work in any particular way. That's why people like it as a first language. It's accessible, unpretentious, informal, and requires no major commitments. It's ideal for quick, small-scale, do-it-yourself programming projects.

But QBasic can also run programs of more significant length and ambition. As you build experience and competence in QBasic programming, you might find yourself involved in more challenging projects — programs that contain hundreds of lines of code rather than dozens. How should you go about organizing your work when you're faced with a long and complex project?

A carefully structured approach is the answer. Behind an informal facade, QBasic has the essential characteristics of a structured programming language. These characteristics include features you've learned about in this book: true procedures and functions, top-down modular code organization, a strong variety of control structures and data structures, global and local variables, argument passing by value or by reference, and named constants.

How do these features relate to the process of developing a significant program? This is the question you consider in this chapter. The ten rules presented here will help you develop long projects efficiently and reliably, which is the main point of structured programming. You don't have to follow these rules for every program you write. But the weightier the project, the more the rules begin to make sense.

Rule #1: Keep the main module short

The main module of a long program typically contains some combination of the following elements:

- ✔ *Comments identifying the program's purpose.* Don't skimp here.

- ✔ *DECLARE statements for the program's SUB and FUNCTION procedures.* QBasic supplies these statements when you save your program to disk. You may want to gather them together at a location below the program's initial comments.

- ✔ *Declarations for variables, arrays, and other data structures that the program uses.* These include DIM statements for variables used only in the main module and DIM SHARED statements for global variables.

- ✔ *CONST definitions for named constants (also known as symbolic constants).* Constants defined in the main module are available everywhere in your program.

- ✔ *Calls to the program's major procedures, that is, the procedures that organize the work of the program.* These major procedures may in turn make calls to other procedures that carry out detailed tasks.

- ✔ *An END statement that marks the end of the main module.*

Together, the declarations and procedure calls in the main module stand as a kind of outline of the program's action and data requirements — without the algorithmic details. Looking at the main module, you should be able to see what the program does and how it's organized, but you should not necessarily be able to see how the program works.

Rule #2: Keep procedures short

The ideal length for a procedure is a page of code or less. If a procedure starts to get longer than a page, you should figure out ways to divide it into several procedures. For example, you might

> ✔ Create new SUB procedures out of subtasks in the procedure.
>
> ✔ Design FUNCTION procedures to take over calculations that the procedure needs to perform.

The shorter a procedure and the more clearly and narrowly you define its task, the easier the procedure is to develop, debug, and maintain.

Rule #3: Create lots of functions

When the purpose of a block of code is to calculate a numeric value or build a string value, consider creating a FUNCTION procedure for the code. Functions don't have to be long or elaborate. The only criterion is that there must be a defined value that the function is responsible for supplying.

Functions are elegant, economical, and adaptable; a function call is legal virtually anywhere you can place a constant value, an expression, or a variable name in a QBasic statement. Furthermore, you can reuse a function after you've written it. Rather than write the same passage of code multiple times to calculate a particular value, a function enables you to produce the value with just a single call.

Rule #4: Declare most variables locally

In the early versions of BASIC, all variables were global. This was one of the reasons why BASIC programs were so difficult to write and why BASIC had such a bad reputation.

In QBasic, you can designate local variables that are available only in the procedures where they are declared. The advantages are clear:

> ✔ Local variables give a procedure independence and portability.
>
> ✔ Local variables make a procedure easier to debug.
>
> ✔ Local variables avoid conflicts between multiple procedures that may use the same variable names.

There are some exceptions. Sometimes you can simplify a program by declaring major data structures globally. In this way you avoid having to pass a structure as an argument many times in your program's procedure calls. For example, an array of records that represents the major table of information in a database management program should probably be declared globally.

Rule #5: Be careful when sending arguments by reference

This rule is a subtle one, but it can cause difficult problems if you're not careful. When you make a call to a SUB or FUNCTION procedure, you send the arguments that the procedure requires. In the call itself, the arguments can take a variety of forms, including values, expressions, or variables. When an argument appears as a variable, you must watch out for the possibility that the procedure itself will make unwanted changes in the value of the variable. This is because QBasic, by default, sends variable arguments *by reference* rather than *by value*.

For example, consider the following call to the procedure named DoSomething, which takes one integer argument:

```
withWhat% = 10
DoSomething withWhat%
```

Here the argument is sent as the integer variable `withWhat%`, which starts out with a value of 10. Suppose the DoSomething procedure receives this argument in the `i%` variable. At some point during the procedure, DoSomething increases the value of `i%` by 1:

```
SUB DoSomething (i%)
  ' ...
  i% = i% + 1
  ' ...
END SUB  ' DoSomething
```

After DoSomething returns control to the procedure that called it, `withWhat%` suddenly has a new value of 11 rather than the original 10. When QBasic sends a variable argument by reference, the caller and the procedure have access to the same memory location for the variable even though they refer to the value by different names — `withWhat%` and `i%` in this example. When DoSomething changes the value of `i%`, the new value is "passed back" to `withWhat%` as a side effect of the procedure.

Occasionally, this side effect is a planned and intentional part of a procedure. Some procedures are *designed* to accept variable arguments whose values they change. But more often the phenomenon is accidental and unexpected. There are two solutions to the problem: one is a Band-Aid, and the other is a cure.

The easy solution is to send a variable by value when you suspect that the procedure you are calling may make unwanted changes in the variable. To send a variable argument by value, you enclose it in parentheses in the call statement. For example:

```
DoSomething (withWhat%)
```

This instructs QBasic to make a copy of the value of withWhat% in memory and to let the DoSomething procedure work with the copy, not the original value. No matter what DoSomething does to the copy, the value of withWhat% remains unchanged.

A much better solution is to write procedures more carefully. If a side effect is not part of the design of a procedure, make sure that no side effect occurs. You can accomplish this in the DoSomething procedure by simply copying the value of i% to a temporary local variable:

```
SUB DoSomething (i%)
  ' ...
  temp% = i%
  temp% = temp% + 1
  ' ...
END SUB  ' DoSomething
```

Then use temp% rather than i% to represent the value received as an argument. The value of i% never changes, and withWhat% in turn is safe from side effects.

For a full discussion of this phenomenon, turn to Chapter 9.

Rule #6: Choose appropriate control structures

Because loops and decisions are vital parts of programming, QBasic provides two major varieties of each. Choosing the right control structure for a given job inevitably helps to reduce complexity, improve readability, and guarantee reliable operations in your program.

You can use either FOR or DO to create a loop. A FOR statement is ideal when the loop goes through a known number of iterations or focuses on a particular sequence of numeric values. A FOR loop provides a control variable that determines the extent of the looping and may also play a central role in the job that the loop performs. For example, a control variable often appears as the index into an array that the loop processes.

DO loops, on the other hand, are perfect when you do not necessarily know how long the repetition will continue, but you can express a condition that will stop the iterations. The looping is controlled by either a WHILE clause or an UNTIL clause in a DO loop. In a WHILE clause, the looping stops when the condition switches from true to false. Conversely, in an UNTIL clause, a switch from false to true terminates the loop. If the WHILE or UNTIL condition is at the bottom of the loop (as part of the final LOOP statement), there will always be at least one iteration. A condition at the top of the loop (in the DO statement) may prevent any iterations if the value of the condition is "wrong" at the outset.

For a complete introduction to DO loops and FOR loops, see Chapters 12 and 13, respectively.

You can express a decision as an IF statement or a SELECT structure. An IF structure — with ELSEIF and ELSE clauses — divides a decision into multiple blocks of code, only one of which will be chosen for each performance of the decision. The choice is based on the value of one or more conditions located on the IF and ELSEIF lines. A complex decision may contain not only multiple ELSEIF sections, but also *nested* decisions in particular blocks of code. See Chapter 11 for examples.

A SELECT decision is the ideal structure for a decision based on the value of a particular expression. A SELECT structure provides a sequence of CASE blocks, each one proposing one or more values for the expression. A CASE block is selected if there is a match between the value of the expression and the proposed values in the CASE statement. SELECT structures are often used to process menu choices.

For a discussion of the SELECT statement, along with a variety of examples, see Chapter 12.

Rule #7: Define appropriate data structures

QBasic enables you to use not only simple variables but also arrays and user-defined types to represent data in a program. An *array* is a list, table, or other multidimensional collection of data values, each belonging to the same numeric or string type. A *user-defined type,* also known as a *record type,* contains a list of fields representing diverse types of data. After you define a record type, you can use it to declare single-record variables or arrays of records.

Most BASIC programmers are comfortable using arrays because this data structure has been available since the earliest versions of the language. The user-defined type, however, is a newer data structure, borrowed from other languages such as Pascal and C. Some programmers neglect this type, even when it is by far the most appropriate way to represent data in a program.

For example, suppose you are writing a program that processes monthly financial data. For each month of the year, you want a way to store the name of the month, the income level for the month, and two categories of expenses. An old way of setting up this data is to create a group of one-dimensional arrays for each field of data:

```
DIM monthName$(12)
DIM grossIncome(12)
DIM expense1(12)
DIM expense2(12)
```

To access a particular month's financial information in this data scheme, you must gather information from each of the four arrays, with references such as

```
monthName$(i%)
grossIncome(i%)
expense1(i%)
expense2(i%)
```

A much simpler way to organize the same data is to define a record type and then declare an array of records:

```
TYPE Financial
  monthName AS STRING * 10
  grossIncome AS SINGLE
  expense1 AS SINGLE
  expense2 AS SINGLE
END TYPE
DIM Monthly(12) AS Financial
```

With this structure, you can refer to all the data for a given month as

```
Monthly(i%)
```

This simple notation enables you to pass an entire record to a procedure as an argument. In addition, if you want to sort the information by one of the fields, you can exchange the positions of two entire records with a single SWAP statement. For example:

```
SWAP Monthly(i%), Monthly(j%)
```

To refer to individual fields of a record, you use the *record.field* notation, as follows:

```
Monthly(i%).monthName
Monthly(i%).grossIncome
Monthly(i%).expense1
Monthly(i%).expense2
```

Watch for situations in which a user-defined record type is the most elegant way to organize a program's data.

Rule #8: Use named constants for unchanging data values

The CONST statement is available in QBasic to define named constants. You can define any number of named constants for use in a program. In addition to the convenience they provide in references to commonly used data items, named constants can significantly improve the readability of your code.

One common use of constants is to define names for the logical values `true` and `false`. This is accomplished in programs in this book as follows:

```
CONST false = 0
CONST true = NOT false
```

These names enable you to set up logical variables for controlling loops and decisions in a program, as in the following passage:

```
DO
  done% = true
  FOR i% = 1 TO items% - dist%
    j% = i% + dist%
    IF info(i%) > info(j%) THEN
      SWAP info(i%), info(j%)
      done% = false
    END IF
  NEXT i%
LOOP UNTIL done%
```

The outer loop in this passage continues until the `done%` variable retains its original value of `true` throughout an entire iteration.

CONST statements in the main module of a program define named constants that are available to all procedures. You can use CONST inside a procedure to create local named constants.

Rule #9: Use stubs to test a program in stages

In the top-down approach to programming, you're likely to write calls to procedures before you write the procedures themselves. Unfortunately, this can prevent you from testing a program in the preliminary stages of its development. If QBasic encounters a procedure call that is not matched by a procedure definition, a `Syntax Error` message appears. You can solve this problem by writing short stubs for procedures that you haven't completed yet.

For example, suppose you've developed a program's main module, which includes calls to procedures named ProcOne, ProcTwo, and ProcThree. You've also written the code for ProcOne, and you'd like to be able to test it before you continue with the rest of the program. But when you try to run the program, QBasic balks at the calls to the unwritten procedures and declines to run any part of the code.

To solve this problem, you can write simple, temporary procedures to hold the places of ProcTwo and ProcThree. For example, the stub for ProcThree might display a message on the screen indicating the unfinished status of the procedure:

```
SUB ProcThree

    PRINT "ProcThree is not available yet."

END SUB
```

After you create stubs for any unwritten procedures, you can run your program at its current level of completion and test the results of procedures that are complete.

Rule #10: Develop a library of general-purpose procedures

Don't reinvent the wheel for each program you write. Keep a list of the general-purpose procedures you create that might prove useful in other programs. Feel free to copy code from one program to another and reuse it either verbatim or with revisions.

Index

• C •

• **F** •

• _U_ •

PROGRAMMING BOOK SERIES

QBasic Programming for Dummies Disk Offer

Tired of typing all that code? The major QBasic programs presented in this book are available on disk. The price of the disk is $15. To order, send your check payable to EMA Software to this address:

EMA Software
QBasic Programming For Dummies Disk
P.O. Box 460458
San Francisco, CA 94146-0458

California residents add appropriate sales tax.

Indicate whether you need a $5^1/_4$ inch or $3^1/_2$ inch floppy disk. If you don't give a preference, you'll receive a $3^1/_2$ inch disk (formatted for 1.44 MB).

Note that the disk does *not* include Microsoft QBasic. QBasic comes with DOS when you install version 5 or later on your computer.

EMA Software is not associated with IDG Books.

IDG BOOKS WORLDWIDE REGISTRATION CARD

RETURN THIS REGISTRATION CARD FOR FREE CATALOG

Title of this book: **QBasic Programming For Dummies**

My overall rating of this book: ❏ Very good [1] ❏ Good [2] ❏ Satisfactory [3] ❏ Fair [4] ❏ Poor [5]

How I first heard about this book:

❏ Found in bookstore; name: [6] _____

❏ Advertisement: [8]

❏ Word of mouth; heard about book from friend, co-worker, etc.: [10]

❏ Book review: [7]

❏ Catalog: [9]

❏ Other: [11]

What I liked most about this book:

_____

_____

What I would change, add, delete, etc., in future editions of this book:

_____

_____

Other comments:

_____

Number of computer books I purchase in a year: ❏ 1 [12] ❏ 2-5 [13] ❏ 6-10 [14] ❏ More than 10 [15]

I would characterize my computer skills as: ❏ Beginner [16] ❏ Intermediate [17] ❏ Advanced [18] ❏ Professional [19]

I use ❏ DOS [20] ❏ Windows [21] ❏ OS/2 [22] ❏ Unix [23] ❏ Macintosh [24] ❏ Other: [25] _____
(please specify)

I would be interested in new books on the following subjects:
(please check all that apply, and use the spaces provided to identify specific software)

❏ Word processing: [26]

❏ Data bases: [28]

❏ File Utilities: [30]

❏ Networking: [32]

❏ Other: [34]

❏ Spreadsheets: [27]

❏ Desktop publishing: [29]

❏ Money management: [31]

❏ Programming languages: [33]

I use a PC at (please check all that apply): ❏ home [35] ❏ work [36] ❏ school [37] ❏ other: [38] _____

The disks I prefer to use are ❏ 5.25 [39] ❏ 3.5 [40] ❏ other: [41] _____

I have a CD ROM: ❏ yes [42] ❏ no [43]

I plan to buy or upgrade computer hardware this year: ❏ yes [44] ❏ no [45]

I plan to buy or upgrade computer software this year: ❏ yes [46] ❏ no [47]

Name: _____ Business title: [48] _____ Type of Business: [49] _____

Address (❏ home [50] ❏ work [51] /Company name: _____)

Street/Suite# _____

City [52] /State [53] /Zipcode [54]: _____ Country [55] _____

❏ **I liked this book!** You may quote me by name in future
IDG Books Worldwide promotional materials.

My daytime phone number is _____

IDG BOOKS

THE WORLD OF
COMPUTER
KNOWLEDGE

❏ YES!

Please keep me informed about IDG's World of Computer Knowledge.
Send me the latest IDG Books catalog.